NEW PLAYS
for the
BLACK THEATRE

Edited by
WOODIE KING, JR.

THIRD WORLD PRESS
CHICAGO, ILLINOIS

NEW PLAYS
for the
BLACK THEATRE

Contents

Introduction

This anthology represents the best of the new breed of Black playwrights. It certainly is not exclusive. Some of the brightest are missing. Why? Because this anthology had a goal. The goal was/is to deliver plays that are easily producible on almost any college campus; plays that small Black theatres will welcome simply because they can produce them. All the plays herein are peopled by not more than five characters. Many are two or three characters.

When we approached Third World Press with the idea of this anthology, the founder and president of the company felt it was/is timely; felt that we should proceed and that the introduction to it should attempt, in some way, to give an overview of the Black Theatre, in this country in particular and in the world in general, over the past twenty-five years. He felt that this anthology should reach out to the students as well as the professors about this important contribution to Black American awareness.

This introduction will focus on the many contributions practitioners of Black theatre made to the American theatre and how these contributions translate to the rest of the world; i.e., the politics and the economics.

Black theatre gives the world a truer picture of what is happening with us on a day to day basis because we very seldom depict the past in our work; we create the present. You can note this in all of the plays in this anthology. Our political situation is a guide for most of the darker people of the world. Africa's cries for freedom are a reverberation of Blacks crying out in the turbulent 60's. The politics of Black theatre is a cry for change and for all that that means, whether we are on a university campus, in a non-profit resident theatre, or on Broadway. The politics of our "being there" causes traumatic repercussions. Witness, if you will, the small budgets universities allot Black studies and Black theatre departments; witness the panels on federal, state, and city funding sources and who and how much funding they think should be given to non-profit Black theatre; witness the scarcity of professional Black plays on or off Broadway.

In the 50's and 60's when we had "isms," (i.e., communism, the radical left, nationalism) we fared a lot better. We must find an "ism" to bind us. Blackness is not enough. In the 50's we discovered the overwhelming power of the written word. The late Abe Hill and Langston Hughes helped to guide us. Lou Peterson, Ted Ward, Alice Childress, William Branch, Lofton Mitchell, and Lorraine Hansberry took on the mantle and created outstanding work for the American theatre. The 50's nurtured outstanding actors such as Sidney Poitier, Harry Belafonte, Hilda Simms, Lou Gossett, Estelle Evans, William Greaves, Ruby Dee, and Ossie Davis. I don't want to make this a shopping list, but I do want you to know that many contributions to Black theatre did not begin in the 60's. I want you to know of the contributions of Rose McClendon Players, Harlem Suitcase Theatre, and American Negro Theatre. On the campuses we had the great ones like Dr. Randolph Edmonds, Owen Dodson, Dr. Ann Cooke, the Fisk Jubilee Singers who carried our message all over the world, making it possible to deliver this anthology to you. These are contributions we must look on with great pride. Then, we have contributors who span three or four decades, like the late Paul Robeson on the performing side, James Baldwin on the literature side, and James Earl Jones on the acting side. The politics of Robeson bordered on the radical left; James Baldwin on the side of Nationalism. James Earl Jones stays out of politics altogether. These three samples of Black politics in the arts are fairly representative. But let's look on the repercussions of these actions as they relate to other Black people and some white people.

The politics of the radical left suggested an overriding need to integrate with whites of similar persuasion. Looking on this, younger Blacks of the 60's saw an integrationist philosophy at work. With the onslaught of the Black Power movement and the Nationalist movement, whites of the radical left turned to Blacks of the radical left for answers - answers about these Nationalists, by the way, to questions many Blacks of the radical left had avoided over the years. Many Blacks of the radical left really believed Nationalism would soon fade from these Black upstarts. What is worse, they really hated much of the literature and the art of the 60's as well as the politics. Many could not work in the Black theatre. Some of these conflicts have been described in Harold Cruse's *Crisis of the Negro Intellectual.* Note James Baldwin's conflict with Richard Wright in Baldwin's essays *Alas, Poor Richard* and *Everybody's Protest Novel,* and the conflicts between the Negro Ensemble Company and the New Lafayette Theatre. One Uptown - one Downtown? That wasn't it at all. It was simple: radical left versus Nationalism.

Yet, all the contributions of these individuals and these institutions are so major it would be impossible to talk of the Black struggle without mentioning them. And the struggle continues. The writers herein continue that struggle.

Herein we will meet (and I hope not for the last time), Elois Beasley, Pearl Cleage, Nubia Kai, P.J. Gibson - all very young, but certainly not young in the craft of playwriting. We will read anew the fine work of Bill Harris, Ben Caldwell, Paul Carter Harrison, Amiri Baraka, Oyamo, Richard Wesley, Ntozake Shange. All these fine writers are represented here with plays never anthologized. Many of these plays were not produced outside New York City and/or the cities in which the authors reside.

It seems to me all these Black writers have one thing in common. We feel it; sense it. They love Black people; therefore, the characters are not stereotyped into the old traditional roles we see on television. The characters move and talk as if they are moving out of the 1980's into the 90's. We hope the characters will sound exactly the same in the year 2000 - only twelve years from when this introduction is being written. Not so very long to fight for liberation since we've been at it since 1677. A new day for a new reader/producer!

In my work on many college campuses, in so many theatres I find Black students humiliated by subtle racism - racism that only another Black person can really see; yet, neither student nor Black professor can run to the head of the university or NAACP and cry wolf. They are not only minorities, they are in the minority. For example, at almost every large white university, fewer than five Black students are drama majors. One would be lucky to find a Black professor in the drama department. We would certainly be amazed to find a tenured Black drama professor at that university. So, what happens? The white professors and the white drama students select seasons of drama from the traditional repertory of Shakespeare, Ibsen, Shaw, Albee, O'Neill, Williams, Miller, Shepard, Mamet, and the current crop of hot young white playwrights. The Black acting student will, at best, be rewarded with a role not worth his time and tuition. We hope these plays will change all this. We hope professors and drama students will read these plays and realize they are easily producible; that the small cast will make each and all easy to cast.

In the early and middle 60's with the founding of the Negro Ensemble Company and The New Lafayette Theatre in New York, along with the Free Southern Theatre in New Orleans, and Concept East Theatre in Detroit, Black theatre set its position alongside the Black Power Movement. Immediately joining this awareness movement were PALSA and the Inner City Culture Center in Los Angeles, the reawakening of Karamu in Cleveland, and certainly the many Black professional Chicago theatres. What began to emerge were Black professional managers, directors and playwrights. The literature had already been there; now we had playwrights who could put all of this in a beautiful artistic form. From the early to middle 60's, Black theatre molded itself from the fervor and passion of the Black Power Movement and the Black Arts Movement. It did have classic plays as bench marks; certainly *A Raisin In The Sun* by Lorraine Hansberry (1959), *Take A Giant Step* by Louis Peterson (1956), *Trouble In Mind* by Alice Childress (1955), *Our Lan'* by Theodore Ward (1947), and *Striver's Row* by Abe Hill gave us all direction.

Many of the playwrights in this anthology were active in both the Black Power Movement and the Black Arts Movement of the 1960's. I've begun to understand this as the playwright's exploration of Black themes begin to emerge in the decade of the 70's. Look at any of the plays of Don Evans, Elaine Jackson, Charles Gordone, Richard Wesley, Bill Gunn, Ntozake Shange, Paul Carter Harrison, and Melvin Van Peebles, to name but a few. Therefore, the plays of the 1960's have a base deeply rooted in the Black Power Movement and in the Black Arts Movement; i.e., Ed Bullins, Ron Milner, Ben Caldwell, Amiri Baraka, Alice Childress, Oyamo, Langston Hughes, James Baldwin, etc. The playwrights in this anthology who emerged in the 1980's had to face the challenge of both the 60's and the 70's. These playwrights are, in a sense, pioneers. They had forerunners to set the stages for them. *Hospice* by Pearl Cleage and *Parting* by

Nubia Kai are filled with images from the 1960's. The young lovers in *Parting* are in turmoil because the male role in the struggle for liberation was misconstrued. The mother in *Hospice* is a poet/artist of the 60's who could not be the shadow of her revolutionary husband. The father in Ntozake Shange's *Daddy Says* dominates because his values and his lifestyle are out of that period. In all these plays, however, new voices emerge from the other male and female characters who were either not yet born in the 1960's or were too young to know or care about the passion and the fervor Black people had as it related to freedom and liberation.

Woodie King, Jr.
New York City
August 1988

Song

A PLAY IN ONE ACT

by Amiri Baraka

Amiri Baraka is the subject of the recent PBS film *In Motion* by St. Clair Bourne.
He is co-editor of *Confirmation: An Anthology of African American Women*, with his
wife Amina Baraka. He is the author of the classic works *Dutchman*, *Blues People*,
Slave Ship, *Daggers & Javelins*, *Essays 1974-79* and *General Hag's Skeezag*.

SCENE: *A big elegant, roomy house with much good wood.*
TIME: *Afternoon moving toward evening.*

CHARACTERS:

OLD MAN (PROFESSOR WOOGIE)
POST MAN (BOOGIE)
SIGNIFYING MONKEY
BR'ER RABBIT
BLUE HOT*
BLUE COOL*
MRS. WOOGIE

(*can double as* SM & BR)

SETTING: *In a chair in front of a door, the room empty otherwise, a
black man, dark, with white hair and red staring eyes, sits, staring at the
door. After awhile, we hear suddenly the sound of drums thundering, like
an African master drummer, or a group of them, shattering the silence.
The man sits up with a start, then takes out his pocket watch and punches
the button down. (The drums were an alarm on the watch.)*
*The man shakes the watch after stopping the drumming, looks at it and
seems to note the time. He looks up beseechingly in the air, and at the*

1

audience. *He seems edgy but pitched so deeply into a pit of solitude and waiting that the edge subdues itself. As he seems to almost, at times, pick up out of the chair, and at other times, merely to slump forward. But still expectant.*

A bell rings finally as the lights seem to go down like it is evening and the man has been waiting a long time. The bells are oversized like there would be in a cathedral. The man again moves suddenly, brought to a start by the big bells. He looks around at the audience. But he is smiling now, taut, stretched tight.

Finally he gets out of the chair. He is hunched almost like he has a hunchback. He is limping. He seems to be struggling to get to the door. The bells keep ringing, each blast louder than before.

Finally he gets to the door and painfully swings it open. He waits, then peers out. He turns to face into the room, visibly depressed that no one has rushed in. He swings the door slowly shut. At this point there is banging on the window or walls, a thumping heavy and insistent. He drags himself over to the window, hunched and in pain. He peers up and out, looking, but the knocking stops when he arrives to look. He turns again even more deeply depressed. Looks at his watch and moves toward the chair.

Now the ringing at the door starts again, the bells even louder, even more disruptive. The man pulls himself as quickly as he can toward the door, but is still slow and agonizing seemingly. He swings the door open, and a man dressed as a postman comes in.

The POSTMAN *is younger, more athletic. He has his postman hat cocked on the back of his head. He is whistling and tries to whistle even while he speaks, which is difficult.*

POSTMAN: You the ol' red eyed man what gets the mail?

(OLD MAN *shakes his head.*)

POSTMAN (*whistling*): Were you expecting some mail, ol' red eyed man?

(OLD MAN *shakes his head, yes.*)

POSTMAN: I don't have any mail, ol' red eyed man. Don't have any mail. No mail.

(OLD MAN *is deeply appalled, shocked.*)

POSTMAN: No mail, old red eyed man. Why you want mail anyway? You too old for mail. What you expecting in the mail, old red eyed man? What you think gonna be in it? You too old for mail. (*Whistling.*) Don't nobody know to send you no mail.

OLD MAN: No mail?

POSTMAN: Naw, old red eyed man, no mail. Ain't nobody gonna send you no mail neither. People probably think you dead.

OLD MAN: No mail? (*Pondering.*) I ain't dead. I could get junk mail. I could get circulars and posters and coupons and give-aways. There's plenty mail I could get. I could get mail marked "Resident" or "Present Occupant." Wouldn't even nobody have to know me as me.

POSTMAN: People think your house dead too.

OLD MAN: House ain't dead. Gotta bell. Good bell. You ringed it. You come in here. You don't even know me, call me old red eyed man. Eyes ain't red neither. And if I ain't got no mail, why you come in here? Why you ring that bell and come in here callin' me red eyed man?

POSTMAN: I supposed to do all this. It's civil service. I'm civil service, do what I'm told. Don't have nothing to do with you. You dead, house dead, I come anyway. I'm told to come. Red eyed man. That's what you is, that's what I called you.

OLD MAN (*looking at him*): OK, leave now. You've done what you were told, now go. Didn't bring no mail. Didn't do nothing. I pay your salary, you know. You can leave.

POSTMAN: Can't leave just yet, haven't finished.

OLD MAN: What now? No mail. Call me names. Stand in my front room taking up time. I don't have no time to mess around. I'm busy.

POSTMAN: If you ain't dead and don't get no mail and are busy, (*Whistling.*) busy doin' what, (*Squints at man.*) doin' what?

OLD MAN: Creatin' stuff in my head to do things for people. Creatin' things. In my head. To populate darkness and light it up. (*Shyly laughing.*) Something like that.

POSTMAN: That's why your eyes red. In here creatin' and doin' stuff. That's why your eyes red. That's why you didn't get no mail.

OLD MAN: I get mail all the time. You ain't the regular mailman. This your first day. That's why you don't know me, don't know my house, and don't know I get mail.

POSTMAN: I'm a new mailman. I'm the mailman you couldn't know 'cause I started after you died.

OLD MAN (*stands looking at the* POSTMAN *then the audience - head cocks to the side - looking him up and down; he takes a couple back steps*): OK, you said all that, now you can leave.

POSTMAN: Leave? I told you I can't leave. I'm not finished. You not interested in hearing about what I just said?

OLD MAN: No.

POSTMAN: About how I'm the postman that begins this route after you dead and your house dead.

OLD MAN: No.

POSTMAN: You not curious about any of that?

OLD MAN: No. No more than if I runned into a drunk or staggering nut in the dark. A wild sound in the mist, I might turn for a moment and look off that way. It's minor. You forget little stuff like that. Even like you. (*The* OLD MAN *starts to drag himself toward the door to open it.*) Besides, you boring me. I bore easy. And I'm busy. Got to get back to my work. I thought you'd have mail. Word from somewhere. From friends of mine. Colleagues. But you don't have nothin' but lunacy.

POSTMAN: You don't wanna hear the rest of what I got to say?

OLD MAN: It's leavin' time for you.

POSTMAN: Can't leave, red eyed man. My civil service calls for me to start a new route. To finish all the unfinished business, then start a new route. You ain't on this route I go. You and your house was long gone by the time I come. Either I'm dreamin' you (*Laughs suddenly.*) or I'm a figment of your death stupor, a twilight lingering image somewhere between life and afterlife. (*Giggle, trails into pointed squeak, then dust-like sharp silence - frightening.*)

OLD MAN (*stands still watching, pulls himself a little straighter; his eyes glow a little more red; he bobs his head slowly up and down like a yes song, like he is feeling the rhythms of a yes song*): Hmmm. You have some complexity to your lunacy. This is not a chance call? You intended to come? And to see and confront me?

(POSTMAN *is whistling, nodding yes.*)

OLD MAN: And so you have. And more to say, now?

(POSTMAN *is whistling, nodding yes.*)

OLD MAN: Are you supposed to kill me or something? Are you some corny messenger of death? Some high falutin' mythological being from some dyin' culture?

POSTMAN: Ahhh. A dialogue. Yes, all that. I am a messenger. I bring the mail. (*To audience.*) You see, how symbolical and allegorical.

OLD MAN: As if someone were interested in that. We've video games for all that. And video series. Transmogrified light, elliptical illusions, and I've got my ax to while away the hours. We don't need you. You, in a manner of speaking, are also quite dead. Daid.

POSTMAN: Dialogue. Ahhh. Dialogue. It's what I thrive on. Confrontation. Yes and No.

OLD MAN: No dialogue now, it's late. I'm busy. I've much to do. No time to waste. No time to waste. You've taken up quite enough of my time, unproductive ego. (OLD MAN *swings open door.*) Goodbye! Adieu!

POSTMAN: You're making me into a murderer, old man. (*Pause, slow whistling.*) I come as told, to inform you of my task. That is your mail, if you could see. I am the mail man. Mail in the form of a man, if you will. I bring the only message you'll get today. Your last message. The last message to you or your house. The message is GOOMBYE!

OLD MAN: The countermessage is myself ushering you out. And you leaving and trailing off where you come from, the post office, the civil service bureau. In a sense, it is the same message, but to you and yours.

POSTMAN: You make me out to be a murderer and I am just a messenger. A postman. My message in the form of me to you, a message from the higher ups, from those in the Bureau of All Concern, the Bureaus of All Sensitivity, is GOOMBYE! to you and your house. You've had a good life. A rich life. You filled up spaces with faces, you clogged up drafts with laughs but, in the last resort, GOOMBYE! Your house, already past, is called by us, "The Last Resort."

OLD MAN: So we are at an impasse. Here you go. Out the do'. And you say, you stay. So what's it mean this constant babble of murder and murderer? Are you from some wild agency that kills old people like in a horror story that would be on the *Times'* best seller list?

POSTMAN: I'm a mailman.

OLD MAN: Then with no mail sail off into the night. Don't continue to bother me.

POSTMAN: I'm gonna be straight with you, ol' man. You supposed to be dead and if you ain't already dead I'm supposed to take you out somewhere and kill you.

OLD MAN: What? (*Shocked, but still in the throes of this as a joke.*) Hey, will you get outta here with this. You ruin what could've been a perfectly ordinary productive day with some off the wallism - quickly boring - wow - it's dull - get out - no dullness - get out - I heard it - get out.

POSTMAN: You don't believe me?

OLD MAN: Believe what? Get out. If you some kinda sick killer just kill me - if you can. (*A sudden other element the* OLD MAN *adds.*) ...This allegory of message and mailman and house dead and that stupidity. I'm not interested in no bogus fairy tales. Why are you still in my house?

POSTMAN: To be utterly clear, you are past usefulness to the users and we've abused you as long as we could with disinterest, and now you have become boring to <u>my</u> employers...

OLD MAN: Your employers are my annoyers...

POSTMAN: Precisely.

OLD MAN: The ones that make the crank calls in the middle of the night and breathe.

(POSTMAN *shakes head yes.*)

OLD MAN: The ones that shout obscenities over the phone and send death threats.

(POSTMAN *is animated happily at recognition.*)

OLD MAN: The ones that write articles in newspapers and magazines slandering reason.

(POSTMAN *shakes head up and down more rapidly.*)

OLD MAN: The uniformed marchers, the hooded terrorizers, the slimy sermonizers, the degenerate moralizers...

(POSTMAN *is shaking head up and down, dancing a little at the ecstasy of being recognized.*)

OLD MAN: One thing I can say about them, they must be rich!

POSTMAN: Yes, yes, yes, you know them. Of course. My employers. Your annoyers. How precisely said.

OLD MAN: Now go. I've no further use for this. I only wanted mail. Something of interest and information, some help perhaps. So much work to be done. We're still so close to the ground. The buildings stop so suddenly. All that expense of unknown sky. (*Re-*

focusing on POSTMAN.) Please, please don't linger now with poisonous boredom - go off somewhere and think!

POSTMAN: And as you see, I'm a negro, like you. I'm not white nor am I Asian nor some mixture of anything, except of what made me me and we. I'm a negro like you.

OLD MAN: Hah, a draft coming in the room and the wind from your mouth. How can I get you to leave?

POSTMAN: I'm a negro like you.

OLD MAN: I'm not a negro, mailess mailman from my annoyer. Boring person. Taker of precious time with dull ego. Messenger from what does not need to send messages, please leave.

POSTMAN: Not a negro? Hah. I used to think that, that I wasn't a negro, but thinking you're not a negro when you are a negro is precisely what makes you a negro. Or as my employers might say, that's what makes you negro. Isn't that grand, not a negro but negro. Somehow its so deepening. Deepening. Are you negro? (*Laughs.*)

OLD MAN: Leave, leave, leave! You want me to throw you out?

POSTMAN (*laughs and whistles, whistles and laughs*): This is getting tedious. (*He reaches in his pocket and pulls out a gun.*)

OLD MAN: Are you some kind of crazy person? Crazy sunofabitch pulling out a gun. You really are some crazy ass person. What's this? (OLD MAN *extremely concerned wants to understand.*) Hey, waitaminute. You're <u>actually</u> some kind of nut?! You actually want to kill me. Who are you? Why the fuck you come in my house?

POSTMAN (*laughs mirthfully*): Now you see my importance. I'm not just a crank. No, you still think that. I told you I was a mailman come to give you the message. GOOMBYE. That's <u>really</u> who I am. Really and truly, that's who I am. Really, no bullshit. I really and truly am a messenger sent by the Bureau of Most Concern to get rid of you because you have no more use for the community. That's really really true.

OLD MAN: But you're...foolish looking...silly talking and acting. You're a goddam joke.

POSTMAN: Of course, (*Laughing, whistling.*) of course. How else could I get in to people's houses?

OLD MAN: But this is comic anyway, manic somehow. This is not the way things are done. All this is too paranoid and funny. That's not the way these things are done. All this talk and surreal fantasy. A nut dressed like a postman with some symbolic bullshit

7

jargon - Jesus - you're some nut from the street. Some frustrated poet or something. Wants to bore people at bars showing their poems or something. Your name is probably Alphonso or something dumb. You've probably just escaped from the booby hatch, now you want to fuck with me. (*Rhetorically.*) Don't Fuck With Me, Frustrated Poet Escaped From The Booby Hatch! I'm busy.

POSTMAN: Not any more, that's why I'm here to get in the way of all that. I'm here to interfere. Is that clear?

OLD MAN: That's what I thought, Alphonso, after all!

(*They both laugh sharply, clearing the air, then silence juts in suddenly.*)

OLD MAN: And the gun is real?

POSTMAN: It will kill you. (*Shoots randomly, destroying a vase the* OLD MAN *has sitting on a table.*)

OLD MAN (*pushes the door half closed and backs away from it; he is cocking his head from one side to the other - as if trying to see the* POSTMAN *with more detail, studying his face*): A mouth full of stupid shit like that. A fool with a gun. A fantasy situation. But a real gun. A gun that shatters my artifacts. That vase was from Monomontapa; it was almost two thousand years old. A thing of exquisite beauty you've destroyed just to show me your gun works.

POSTMAN: I thought it'd be a convincing gesture. (*Whistling.*)

OLD MAN: But things, I insist, don't happen like this. This is too comedic and manic, too stupid and nonsensical. Probably a nut, and why me is my cry, why me? A goddam nut.

(POSTMAN *shrugs, still whistling.*)

And so now what, what are you waiting for, nut? Why stalk in here with a mouth full of boring nut shit then stand around and break up my artifacts, take up my time, standing around whistling. If you want to kill me as you allege for some fantasy bureau, why don't you do it? Why are you waiting? Perhaps you've been sent to bore me to death? Alphonso!

POSTMAN: You're right. It's about that time, ol' red eyed man. Just one further offense. I've said you've lost your use to the community. But also just this, I'm a negro like you. Weren't you interested in why I said that?

OLD MAN: No! I thought you were bragging. Like nuts do.

POSTMAN: It was just to slap you with this, that when I kill you, take you out, for the good of the community, I want to leave you with that striking phenomenon of social construct, dear red eyed man, that it is a negro that takes you off planet number three. (*Laughs.*) Isn't that ironic?

OLD MAN: No, it's not ironic. Whole lot of negroes work for anybody. It's your employers who are doing; you're nobody. A goddam messenger. Probably Alphonso anyway.

POSTMAN: My employers are negroes too! (*Whistles, laughs.*)

OLD MAN: So? What's that mean? Ultimately we know who runs this, it's not no negroes either!

POSTMAN (*laughs ironically*): But, old red eyed man, don't you understand? The first negroes were not colored. The first negroes were white people! (*The* POSTMAN *laughs and whistles. The* OLD MAN *looks in his mouth, his eyes seem also to wander a bit away from the* POSTMAN *and quickly around the room.*)

OLD MAN: I see. Yes. An important point.

POSTMAN: Yes. Yes. Very important. Try to savor it as you go, as you fly on your endless journey away from this speed, this mote in the heavens nestled near some tiny bit of light over near the edge of the universe.

OLD MAN: Alphonso!

POSTMAN: Yes.

OLD MAN: Is that all, now? No further explanations of what I've done to deserve this murdering?

POSTMAN: No, you know all already. Any explanation would be fantasy. Let the *Times* explain. *The Amsterdam News*. Let *Jet* carry a picture of you. And the *Afro* a misspelled, misinforming story with the wrong picture. I gave you enough, as much as you'd get in a James Bond movie.

OLD MAN: And now I'm going to die, and you're not Alphonso.

POSTMAN (*raises gun*): I'm a messenger, from a powerful state bureau, not Alphonso.

(OLD MAN *backs up, hands scrambling across a desk; as if panicked, he grasps papers.*)

How uncharacteristic for you to panic, how totally uncharacteristic. If we'd known that, perhaps you cd've got off. But they said you were cold except for the glowing red eyes. And they knew that meant further trouble, further agitation.

OLD MAN: But it's always been so. Why now? Like the messenger of gloom, are you death like in old novels, the devil, Alphonso?

POSTMAN: Why now? Because you're alone. Old and alone. In an empty house full of sounds and memories. Now you're vulnerable in ways you've never been vulnerable before!

OLD MAN: Family's gone. That's what you mean?

POSTMAN: Where's your children an' the old woman?

OLD MAN: You're from some heavy bureau, you already know. Children gone off in the world like they should, doing their own searching. Their own studying. I hear from them from time to time. That's why I looked forward to the mail. My wife was driven away from me by my own craziness, I guess. I was always...(*Ponders*.) busy. I had things to do. Things to make. Bringing things from inside my head to light up the world. I <u>was</u> busy.

POSTMAN: Now you're alone. And vulnerable. Now I'm here.

OLD MAN: And so let's see how you work with these, my man. (OLD MAN *waves the papers, rustles them, and in a crackle, a MONKEY appears. A chimpanzee with boater hat, and dressed up. He carries a cane, a boutonniere in the lapel of his blue blazer. He has white linen pants. The* POSTMAN *turns and jumps back whistling, pointing the gun at the chimp.*)

POSTMAN: What?

OLD MAN: Monkey, what's up?

MONKEY: What's up with y'all? I was in the neighborhood, thought I'd materialize. A man with a gun, that's no fun! A smirking face, a baleful eye, but the gun pointed still. What is the use of all this, my friend? (*To* POSTMAN.) And you, sir (*To* OLD MAN.), is he one of your creations, as well? A killer or a laughing maniac, which is it?

POSTMAN: Is this a pet of yours, old man?

OLD MAN: In a way.

MONKEY: I am something, aren't I? You never seen a monkey like this? You never been inside nobody's head with dressed up monkeys? You look kinda weird anyway. You don't look like your father. Who is your father, anyway? You got a father? Your father probably don't resemble nothing too tough. You don't resemble nothing too tough. In that burnt out postman's suit. How you get to be a postman? They must not have to take a test no more to be a goddam postman. No wonder the mail always gets lost. Postman be off somewhere sticking up people.

POSTMAN (*trying to adjust*): A proper messenger always brings the message necessary.

MONKEY: Dude can't even talk straight. Talk like a slot machine. Talk just like his mother. She cdn't talk neither. Mama babble like a drug addict too. I knew that bitch when she was on the bowery selling pussy. But didn't nobody buy none, bitch went bankrupt. That's why this motherfucker a mailman, mama cdn't sell her nasty pussy to nobody. Thought they was the bourgeoisie and shit. Nasty pussy bitch. Didn't nobody want nonna that nasty pussy. Smell like Nixon's breath. Nasty bitch. Boy, yo' mama a nasty bitch and everybody know it.

POSTMAN (*laughs*): What makes you think I play...

MONKEY: Don't play, you can pat your foot...whole family look like death...Had one sister was a bulldagger, a brother used to sneak around under bridges and try to suck dogs off. All of 'em be in *Ebony* all the time!

POSTMAN: Your pet is something like you I guess, like your head...

MONKEY: Talk shit, narrow ass sucker, moldy mouth cocksucker, smell like crocodile shit.

POSTMAN: But what do you think that'll do?

MONKEY: Do? I'll do you silly nigger, you betta get on yo' horse and ride the fuck on outta here. Take that gun and shove it up your narrow ass.

OLD MAN: Let's see what it'll do. (*He crackles the papers, waves them some more. A* RABBIT *appears. In designer jeans, a jacket. A large* RABBIT, *with dark glasses, smoking a reefer.*)

BR'ER RABBIT: Yoicks! What is it, gents? (*Slaps* MONKEY's *hands.*) Brother man, what it is? (*Struts over, pats* OLD MAN *on the back.*) Professor Woogie, long time no see. What's the word?

OLD MAN: My man over here with the piece. (*Gestures at* POSTMAN.)

RABBIT: Hey, slick Willie, the gun waver...what's with you, home? Ain't seen you since...(*The* POSTMAN *extends his hand to shake and the* RABBIT *neatly takes the gun out of his hand with a quick movement.*) Well, awright. (*Gives the* MONKEY *and the* OLD MAN *the "high five."*) Awright.

MONKEY: See, that brother the Rabbit is slick and quick.

RABBIT: Yeh, you talk shit and I do shit. (*They slap hands again.*)

MONKEY: All courtesy of my man over here (*Gestures toward the* OLD MAN.) Prof. Woogie.

POSTMAN (*stunned, but trying to maintain composure*): Another pet, old man? You are an interesting type for all your used up qualities, your uselessness.

OLD MAN: Interesting, I'd say. It's all you need to be to distinguish you in this sodden world, interesting. I can't say the same for you!

(*The* MONKEY *and the* RABBIT *start to do a step, a tiny march-like strut, in unison, back and forth. Now it turns into a kind of Monkish bop, back and forth, stepping elegantly. They are dancing for their own pleasure and invention.*)

MONKEY: Talk shit! (*Repeat.*)

RABBIT: Do shit! (*Repeat.*)

(*Their refrain goes back and forth between the two. The* OLD MAN/ PROFESSOR *looks at his watch to adjust it, noting the time, and the African drums punctuate the hip animals' dance.*)

POSTMAN: Yet, I don't have to be interesting, not at all. All I have to be is correct. Realistic. Scientific. A result of some rationalized planning, some systematic analysis. I don't need to be interesting, just effective.

OLD MAN: But now you're nothing, not even effective. You might just still be Alphonso too.

POSTMAN: No, I am the lonely representative of a huge bureau. This bureau demands your life be ended, and so I am the messenger of that idea. The doer of that act. I don't have to be interesting. Just effective.

OLD MAN: So explain your impotence?

POSTMAN: You explain yours, old man. (*A sleight of hand, the gun reappears in the* POSTMAN's *mitt.*)

OLD MAN (*surprised, shocked*): What? (*Papers fall from the ceiling, the room suddenly is lost in papers and bright light. The doorbell rings now loudly, the heavy chimes of a church. When the papers stop falling and the light stops beaming the two animals have disappeared.*)

POSTMAN: We are where we were, where we in fact, never left. I am here with a gun pointed at your head, ordered to kill you. And well I shall. You are here alone, lost under sheaves of papers. Nothing more. Just papers and more papers. Alone.

OLD MAN: Monkey, Rabbit?

POSTMAN: In your head, and for all that, dead. But not I. I'm not in your head. I exist in the real world. This gun does. The bullets in it. My orders. The message I bring. They are all real. And you too are, for the moment, real. But now is the time you leave. And in a few seconds you will be real no longer.

OLD MAN (*looks through his papers futilely*): Monkey, Rabbit, my children, creations...?

POSTMAN: Paper only, abstractions, old man. The myths of a dying people, a nation that never was! Hence your uselessness to the one that is.

OLD MAN: The one that is?

POSTMAN: Negronia. All stripes, no stars!

OLD MAN: Oh.

POSTMAN: Peaceful.

OLD MAN: Quiet.

POSTMAN: Grey.

OLD MAN: National Anthem?

POSTMAN: Atomic Bye Bye - it was once known as Mairzy Doats!

OLD MAN: Oh.

POSTMAN (*raising the gun again*): Goodbye (*Aiming.*), old man, adieu...(*The doorbell chimes start to bang insistently and there are thumps against the window.*)

POSTMAN: Too late for more pets my friend, old red eyed Professor Woogie. They cdn't stop anything. At best an amusement for a race no longer amusable. That, finally is your problem, you don't laugh enough and not at enough different things. (*The chimes and knocking go on.*) Your laughter is acid and dangerous. It's blue and hot or cool or hard or slick. But always blue laughter.

OLD MAN: Someone at the door! (*Trying to stall, animated.*)

POSTMAN: There's no one there, it's all in your head. No one there at all, just some more idleness and uselessness.

OLD MAN: No, it's not me. There is actually someone out there banging, trying to get in!

POSTMAN (*laughs uproariously*): Well now, as a last favor, a last resort, I'll cool for a bit and let you see the final emptiness of your own creation. The vacuum, the importance of your thought. The deadness of that blue laughter.

(OLD MAN *goes to the door and swings it open, peering. Two young men sweep in. One dressed in muted soft subtle colors, a sly grin on his face. The other in the latest fashions of the day, like Teddy Pendergrass, with a big strut, hand held stiff. They greet the* OLD MAN/PROFESSOR *together.*)

BLUE HOT: Pop!

BLUE COOL: Dad. Old Prof, how are you? (*They all embrace.*)

BLUE HOT: What's happening?

BLUE COOL: How are you?

BLUE HOT (*looking at the* POSTMAN *who stands now with the gun drooping a little - turns quickly to shout at the door*): Mama, don't come in here just yet! Who's this dude? Why is this scene going on?

BLUE COOL: Who are you, mister? With a gun pointed at my father? Are you crazy?

OLD MAN: Your mother is here? (*Looking out the door.*) Your mother...(*He goes to the door. A black woman about the same age as* PROFESSOR WOOGIE *comes in shyly.*)

BLUE HOT: Mama, stay back...

(PROFESSOR *steps forward to greet his wife. They embrace despite the* POSTMAN, *whose arm is slowly coming down.*)

BLUE HOT: Who're you, man? What's your story? Why are you in here? You better have something very interesting to say - very, very interesting. (*The* POSTMAN *is backing up as the two young men coordinate their attack, moving on the* POSTMAN *slowly and cautiously. Meanwhile the* OLD MAN *and the* OLD WOMAN *have moved slowly back out of range of the gun, yet closer to the audience so their dialogue can be heard. The two boys are moving toward the* POSTMAN.)

BLUE COOL: At least interesting, what you gotta say better be enlightening! (*Shouting back at father.*) Who is this fool, dad? Is this crazy Alphonso you wrote about, some nut? How'd he get in here? Alphonso, you better put that damn gun down.

BLUE HOT: Naw, don't let him put it down, let me have to take the motherfucker from him and wear him out. Naw, let him keep it till I get hold of his behind. (*They back the* POSTMAN *upstage into shadows so we can only hear them talking to him.*)

OLD MAN (*to wife*): How'd you get here?

14

WIFE: The boys said they were paying you a surprise visit on your birthday...

OLD MAN: My birthday...?

WIFE: Yes, it's your birthday, you forget that too? You still too busy even for reality?

OLD MAN: And you said you'd come too?

WIFE: I thought I'd see how you were doing. I wanted to see were you still crazy.

OLD MAN: I'm still crazy, but I think on this birthday I'm getting better. I'm much better in fact. Why did you leave me?

WIFE: Why did I leave you? Why do you always turn things around? You acted like you didn't need me...

OLD MAN: I was a fool...abstract, silly, vainglorious...

WIFE: The same things I said, exactly, the very same things...

(*They laugh and embrace.* BLACK.)

The Fallen Angel

by ELOIS BEASLEY

Elois Beasley is a native Chicagoan. She grew up on the city's Southside and attended Dunbar Vocational High School. After high school, Ms. Beasley left Chicago to attend Stillman College and the University of Alabama in Tuscaloosa, Alabama. There she majored in English and psychology. She later returned to Chicago and graduated from Columbia College. Ms. Beasley has several plays to her credit, including: *An' 'Long Came A Bumblebee, 1851, The Marriage* (an African-American love story) and *The Gold Shop,* which won the 1986 Patrons' Choice Award from the Chicago Cultural Center Theatre. Ms. Beasley is a recipient of the Albert P. Weisman Fellowship in playwrighting and a 1983-87 recipient of a grant from the Chicago Office of Fine Arts.

CHARACTERS:

K.C. IRVING - *a young woman in her mid to late twenties.*
KATHRYN SMITH - *K.C.'s friend, about the same age.*

SETTING: *Bedroom, K.C.'s apartment. The room is large, furnished stylishly, with a comfortable effect. As the scene opens, the phone is ringing. K.C. is walking the floor; she is very nervous. After a moment there is a knock on the front door. K.C. exits quickly from the room. After a moment she reenters almost running. She takes a seat on the bed as if it might break, looking anxiously towards the door. KATHRYN appears at the doorway and stops, looking the room over. The phone rings; K.C. begins to squirm, staring at the phone. KATHRYN watches her until the phone is quiet; she steps inside the room and gets out of her coat. K.C. springs up from the bed and begins to pace. KATHRYN lays her coat on the back of the chair and sits down; she waits.*

K.C. *(pacing, as if she's rehearsed it)*: This is what happened...I swear to god...(*Long pause.* KATHRYN *shifts her position, unimpressed by* K.C.'s *approach.*)...I know I'm stupid, I know this is stupid, but you got to believe me, Kathryn...(*Pause.*)...Okay, this is what happened:

17

a couple days ago...You really don't know what I've been through, Kathryn...

KATHRYN (*unimpressed*): I see I'm about to get the rehearsed version. You got something to drink?

K.C.: Wait! (*She rushes from the room. KATHRYN waits. The phone rings. K.C. rushes back to the room with a bottle of wine and a glass. She shoves it onto KATHRYN's lap quickly and goes over to the phone, standing in front of it as if to hide it. It stops.*)

KATHRYN (*ignoring her behavior*): You got a cork screw?

K.C. (*watching the phone as if it might come alive*): No...

KATHRYN (*examining the bottle*): It's gon' be hell trying to get this wine outa here. (*K.C. laughs a phoney laugh. KATHRYN sits the bottle on the floor.*) I need a drink, K.C.

K.C. (*preoccupied*): I know...I know...(*She turns to KATHRYN, looks at her innocently.*) The reason this phone keep ringing is because somebody is trying to call me. (*She goes over to the bed and sits down. Then pleasantly...*) How you been?

KATHRYN (*patient but puzzled*): Okay. I can't complain.

K.C. (*jumping up*): Let me turn on the radio! (*She rushes from the room; the radio comes up softly from the other room. The phone rings. KATHRYN gets up, goes to it, picks up the receiver.*)

KATHRYN (*into the receiver*): Hello? (*She listens; she appears confused. K.C. enters quickly, takes the phone from her hand and slams it down. KATHRYN stands with her hand in the air as if she were still holding the phone.*)

K.C. (*in a panic*): Don't do that!

KATHRYN (*annoyed*): Do what?! Was that you on the line?!

K.C. (*moving away from her*): It was not! It wasn't me!

KATHRYN: What am I deaf?! I know your voice when I hear it, K.C.!

K.C. (*defensively*): It wasn't me...it was a tape! (*Pause.*) What did you hear?

KATHRYN (*flatly*): Are you going to tell me what's going on?

K.C.: Okay...I'll tell you...

KATHRYN (*sitting*): I'm listening!

K.C.: I'm going to tell you...gimme a minute...(*She pauses, takes a deep breath.*)...There's this man...He wants me to work for him...

KATHRYN (*suspiciously*): Work where?

K.C. (*foolishly*): Broadway and Fifth.

KATHRYN (*shocked*): Broadway and Fifth?!!

K.C. (*smiling foolishly*): Broadway and Fifth...

KATHRYN: I <u>know</u> Broadway and Fifth. What I want to know is why he thinks you would be interested in working Broadway and Fifth.

K.C.: Because of the tape - you got to help me, Kathryn!

KATHRYN: What am I suppose to do? If he thinks he can make a hooker outa you, he ain't going to think twice about making one outa me!

K.C.: There's more to it than just that! You ain't even heard the whole story...

KATHRYN: Then why don't you tell me the whole story!

K.C. (*embarrassed*): He's got this tape...

KATHRYN: You said that.

K.C.: ...Okay, here it goes...Okay...I met him on my way to the store...I called a cab, and he was the driver - Kathryn, I don't know what happened...(*Quickly.*)...but I hadn't planned on nothing like that happening, never! Not in my whole life! Kate, I was sitting in that cab, waiting for the store to open, and we started talking and getting along, and somehow the conversation ended up...(*She stands.*)...at his place, in bed. (*She looks at* KATHRYN *for a reaction.*) How could I do it? I don't know what came over me! (*She stares at the floor.*) I don't know how it happened!

KATHRYN (*amused*): You sat in that cab too long. That's what did it.

K.C.: Will you stop it! (*She takes a deep breath and continues.*) Anyway! (*A bit less nervous.*) That's not the worst part of it! He taped it! The bastard taped it! When I heard that tape, my heart stopped. (*Very seriously.*) You know, Kathryn, I talk too much...(*She makes a cutting gesture in the air with her hand.*)...period! Ain't no excuse for it. I don't drink. I just start talking and I don't know when to quit! You should have heard me! I told him my last name, who Bruce works for, and all kinds of things about Bruce and our personal lives!

KATHRYN: That was stupid.

K.C. (*flatly*): Thank you, Kathryn. I needed you to tell me that.

KATHRYN: Anytime. When did you find out he had the tape?

K.C.: I was trying to leave, and he kept pulling me back, saying he wanted me to stay longer, and I said something like...(*Mocking tone.*)...I have to go home to my cold, unfeeling husband...

KATHRYN: On tape?

K.C.: Everything - all of it.

KATHRYN (*amused*): What did you think you were doing, K.C.? You got me on this one.

K.C.: I couldn't believe what I was doing...

KATHRYN: What does he want from you, money?

K.C.: That's what I thought, but I think he's some kind of pervert! He claims it would be "morally improper" to take money my husband earned.

KATHRYN: So he wants you to go out on the streets and earn it?

K.C.: Yes...

KATHRYN: What's this person's name, K.C.? Where's he live?

K.C.: I don't know!

(*There's a short silence between them. KATHRYN laughs.*)

KATHRYN: You don't know?! What's he look like?!

K.C.: A little bit like Bruce...kinda tall, thick hands, sensitive eyes, full face...

KATHRYN (*amused*): I would say you got a good look at mister wonderful. What did you do - keep your eyes on him all the way to his bed? Don't you even know where he took you?

K.C. (*attempting to remember her whereabouts*): I don't really know... I know it wasn't far from the store, but I wasn't looking, and hell, my sense of direction is pitiful!

KATHRYN (*giggling*): Only you could find a cab-driving pimp that looks like your husband...

K.C.: I was nervous too!

KATHRYN: I can imagine! So what's the plan? You going to tell Bruce?

K.C. (*mildly hysterical*): No!

KATHRYN: I don't see that you have any other choice.

K.C.: I have a plan. (*Short pause.*) That's where you come in. (*Looking at her.*) Kathryn, you know I can't go out on the street and hustle no johns...

KATHRYN (*teasing*): Bruce might catch you.

K.C.: Kathryn, could you please control that ugly in you long enough so I can tell you this?! (*Annoyed.*) I'm serious!

KATHRYN (*controlled amusement*): I know.

K.C.: Then could you stop?

KATHRYN (*giggling*): I'm sorry, K.C., but this is funny!

K.C.: It's not funny to me. I'm serious!

KATHRYN: Okay, I'm sorry. Go ahead.

K.C.: I don't have five thousand dollars - that's what he wants, five thousand dollars! He claims I could make that much money in a week on the streets! I've been racking my brain trying to figure out where I can get that much money on my own...

KATHRYN: Don't look at me. I don't have five thousand dollars.

K.C.: I know that and I didn't ask you for no money. I need your help. I already asked Billy; he won't help me, so it's just you and me.

KATHRYN (*amused*): You tell Billy what you told me?

K.C.: I had to tell him something.

KATHRYN: What he say when you told him?

K.C.: He was all indignant about it! Never mind my problems, the bastard!

KATHRYN (*teasing*): What you tell him, how you say it?

K.C.: I just said it. I said I needed him to help me get rid of a man that was bothering me.

KATHRYN: What he say?

K.C.: Tell Bruce.

KATHRYN: What you say?

K.C. (*embarrassed*): I just said I couldn't tell him, and he wanted to know why...I said because if I told him, he'd leave me. (*Pause.*) Nigguh wants to know what I did.

KATHRYN: You tell him?

K.C.: ...I told him that I slept with somebody...

KATHRYN (*laughing*): Were you sleeping, K.C.?

K.C.: You go to hell, Kathryn. I wasn't going to tell him the truth, not all of it anyway. Billy is my brother; he is supposed to be on my side. It's not like I do this kind of thing everyday!

KATHRYN: I don't see why you thought Billy would help you in first place! I'm surprised he hasn't told Bruce!

K.C.: I was desperate! Plus I don't have time to worry about Billy. I have to deal with this pimp person...(*Pause, seriously.*) Kathryn, I want you to help me kill him.

(KATHRYN *laughs, thinking that her friend is in no way serious about her last remark. She looks at her friend who is not laughing and regards her in a firm, serious manner.*)

KATHRYN: You may as well be laughing too because, as far as I'm concerned, your mind has taken leave and your mouth is in control, and, of course, it doesn't know what it's talking about.

K.C. (*ignoring her*): I gave this a lot of thought, Kathryn. (*She paces, thinking.*) I have tried to reach this person. I have begged him to leave me alone. I have cried, offered him money, every nickel we have in the bank. He will not leave me alone. (*Pause.*) I have sweared to him up and down and have offered to bring you along to verify that I have never, never cheated on Bruce before. He's crazy! He won't even listen to me! He wants me out on the street tomorrow morning, and I simply cannot do that! I have no other choice. WE have to kill him! That's final!

KATHRYN (*laughing foolishly*): We?!

K.C.: Yes we!

KATHRYN: Not me!

K.C.: Who else am I going to get?

KATHRYN: I don't care who you get, I ain't helping you kill nobody!

K.C.: Kathryn, I'm scared to death! If I don't get that money - his way, he'll play that tape for Bruce! I can't reason with him!

KATHRYN: Then tell Bruce!

K.C. (*nearly hysterical*): I can't! He'll leave me!

KATHRYN: Are you crazy?! You are talking about murdering somebody! You talking guns and bullets and blood, girl! I can't help you kill nobody! (*Moving to the arm of the chair.*) You ain't going to kill nobody either, so stop saying it!

K.C.: I don't see why you getting all upset about it! I'd do it for you!

KATHRYN: What'd you talking about?! I wouldn't ask you to do it for me!

K.C. (*sarcastically*): I suppose that's because you're above cheating on Ben! I know how much you love him!

KATHRYN (*calm but firm*): Oh, we're talking about me now?

K.C.: Whatever, Kathryn!

KATHRYN: Whatever ain't gon' get it! It ain't enough to make me get a gun and shoot somebody!

K.C.: This is!

KATHRYN: Then you do it by yourself! (*Standing.*) I knew the minute I walked in here I should have stayed at home! When was the last time you called me just to talk to me - weeks! Then you call me with this! And look at how you putting it! I <u>got</u> to help you! I ain't got to help you shoot nobody!

K.C. (*as if she hasn't heard* KATHRYN): We don't have to shoot him...(*She rubs her palms together nervously.*) He's coming over here tomorrow in his cab. He's going to blow, and I'm suppose to go down there - I won't. I'll make him come up here and try to drag me down. He knows Bruce is at work, so he'll get ugly and try to push his way inside. Now, I've got this poison...

KATHRYN: You think after what's-his-name breaks down that door - that door lined with steel - you think he's going to be in any mood to sit down and drink your poison? (*Annoyed.*) Where did you get poison anyway?

K.C.: What difference does it make? I got it! So, when he's inside, you hit him...

KATHRYN: Me again? You take a bunch of liberties with my person, don't you?

K.C.: Yes! You're more capable than me!

KATHRYN (*annoyed*): What the hell is that suppose to mean?!

K.C. (*realizing she could lose any support she might have gained*): It's just that you think faster than me. You know <u>better</u>; you <u>know</u> what I mean.

KATHRYN: Yes, I know what you mean. You just remember who's talking about murdering somebody.

K.C.: <u>We</u> are talking about it...

KATHRYN: Do you hear anything I'm saying?!

K.C. (*ignoring her*): When you hit him, we could pour the poison into a beer or something and give it to him while he's out...

KATHRYN: That won't work, K.C.

K.C. (*snapping*): You got a better idea?!

KATHRYN: I don't have any idea! I know that you couldn't be thinking right, or you'd see that it won't work! First of all, your friend...

K.C.: What'd you mean, my "friend?" I'm telling you that this man is bothering me! I'm telling you he's crazy! I'm telling you he's got to die! He's not my friend!

23

KATHRYN (*calmly*): For lack of a better description - your friend is not going to come charging through your front door to drag you out to some corner over on Broadway. Second, he's not going to drink anything you offer him. I wouldn't if I was him, and besides, I can't see him giving you time to offer him some refreshments! Why would he even turn his back to you, K.C.? Let's face it. The man is not stupid! All he has to do is mail the tape to Bruce. You told him where Bruce works; he knows where you live; he's got your phone number; he doesn't have to take any chances. You go and make a move like trying to poison an unconscious man, and you'll go to jail!

K.C. (*angry*): You may think this is real funny and that I'm not serious about this, but you wrong! I'm going to kill him whether you help me or not! I will kill him!

KATHRYN: I'm not making fun of you, K.C. I want to help you, but I don't know what to do.

(*The phone rings; KATHRYN goes to it and lifts the receiver. K.C. becomes nervous, moves toward her in an effort to stop her from listening. KATHRYN is too quick; she picks up the receiver and lays it on the table.*)

K.C. (*childishly*): You can stop making fun of me and help me!

KATHRYN: Look, I'm sorry. (*She goes back to the chair, picks up the bottle of wine, examines it.*) I cannot listen to this kinda talk in my right mind. You sure you don't have a cork screw? I would love to be very drunk. You should try it, K.C. It makes more sense than this murder stuff.

K.C. (*stomping her foot in a childish manner*): I can't drink my way outa this! This is serious! I'm talking about my life! (*Points to the phone.*) Bruce hear that tape and he'll go! (*Angry.*) I helped you that time you had that abortion behind Ben's back!

KATHRYN (*raising an eyebrow*): Right you did, didn't you, right after you damned my soul to hell. Made a special trip to church, too, as I recall.

K.C.: I did it for you! So what how I did it! It all amounts to the same thing!

KATHRYN: Just how do you figure that?

K.C.: Murder is murder.

KATHRYN (*pissed*): Oh, I see. You still got that racing around in your attic; I'm a murderer anyway, so one more dead body won't mean nothing to me, heartless bitch that I am. Is that right, K.C.?

K.C.: That's not what I mean, and you know it.

KATHRYN: What do you mean?

K.C.: Not that.

KATHRYN: You mean that the reason you haven't called me since I had that abortion is because we haven't had nothing to talk about?

K.C. (*angry*): What was there to talk about? You did what you wanted to do. I don't remember you asking my opinion or permission to do away with somebody I could love.

KATHRYN (*angry*): Somebody?! What somebody?! There was no somebody.

K.C.: To me there was a person!

KATHRYN: Where K.C.? Where did you see a person?!

K.C. (*going to her, puts her hand on* KATHRYN's *stomach*): Right there. Why do you always have to oppose me? Why can't you just believe what I'm telling you?

KATHRYN (*gets up from the chair, moves over to the bed and stands looking at* K.C.; *firmly*): Because you lying K.C. Why do we have to go through these changes?! Why do you lie to me before you get to the truth! You did it when we were little and you doing it now!

K.C.: I told you everything!

KATHRYN: You ain't told me nothing! You never said <u>what</u> was on that tape! Look at the way you acting; it's got to be more to it than what you saying!

K.C.: So, I don't get no credit? I'm lying and that's that.

KATHRYN: If what I heard is all that's on that tape, then you don't have a thing to worry about! I couldn't even make it out! Look at the way you snatched it outa my hand...

K.C.: I didn't snatch it!

KATHRYN: You did. You almost took my arm off! And another thing, I don't see how you figure what I did to myself has anything to do with what you're talking about now!

K.C.: That's because neither one of <u>these people</u> mean anything to you, that doesn't mean they didn't mean anything to me. I went with you because I wanted to go. I would have gone if you hadn't asked me to go. That don't mean I have to like it! It would have been nice to have a baby around.

(*There's a short silence between them.*)

KATHRYN: I suppose you're right, like you said, murder is murder, right?

K.C. (*looking at her, then quietly*): Kathryn, I didn't mean to say it that way...

KATHRYN: No...no...no...you are right...find me a drink and let's talk about it.

K.C. (*fully recovered, she jumps up, excited*): We got beer! Tons of it! You can have every damn can we got! (*She dashes from the room but returns in an instant, pokes her head inside the door.*) You mad?

KATHRYN (*calmly*): No, I'm not mad.

K.C. (*disappears and returns a little less excited; she stops in front of* KATHRYN, *extends one can of beer*): This is it.

KATHRYN: What happened to all those tons you was talking about. I can't get drunk on no one beer.

K.C.: Bruce got to it after I went to bed. You don't need to be drunk anyway.

KATHRYN: I can't plot no murder on no one beer!

K.C.: Start with it, Kathryn. I swear I'll tear up this place if I have to to get that cork screw! I'll have it before you finish! Swear! (*She raises her hand.*) Swear.

KATHRYN (*takes the beer; pops the top, teasing*): How you going to make any babies if you going to bed without Bruce?

K.C. (*annoyed*): What's it to you?

KATHRYN (*amused*): Nothing. (*Short pause between them.*) Funny how you can comment on my stuff, but I can't comment on yours. How come?

K.C. (*sitting on the floor, back to the bed*): How come what?

KATHRYN: You know what? How come you ain't sleeping with Bruce? You all fighting?

K.C.: I wish I could get that kind of rise out of him. We're having some problems, and they're bad enough without adding anything else. He won't talk about it; he just plays the hell outa the piano.

KATHRYN: How you gonna work things out if nobody's talking?

K.C.: We don't.

KATHRYN: Ah! Now, I understand the cab driver.

K.C.: I know this was a mistake, but I love Bruce and I don't want him to leave me. I really love him, Kathryn. (*Pause.*) You think I would consider killing somebody if I didn't love him?

KATHRYN: Yeah, but murder, K.C. I think you might be over-reacting...

K.C.: Don't tell me that! Damn it, Kate, he's got that tape! I know he's got it and I know he'll use it! Why would he go through the trouble of taping it? What's the point of the calls?! He's giving me no choice; he's got to die! (*Becoming nervous, she moves back up on the bed, rubbing her palms together.*) So, what's the plan, Kathryn? What'd you think?

KATHRYN: I think I'm running out of beer.

K.C.: Well, slow down.

KATHRYN: I'm going as slow as I can. If you want a plan you got to find the cork screw. I have to have something to loosen it all up!

K.C.: You drink too much anyway.

KATHRYN: Yes, I do. I drink too much. We established that. Locate the cork screw, missy K.C., and let's get on with this! (*There's a short silence. The radio plays something soft, soothing.*) Jesus! Listen to that!

K.C. (*sarcastically*): Want me to turn it off, ole cool Kathryn?

KATHRYN (*amused*): No. I want you to locate the cork screw.

K.C.: Okay. (*She starts to look around the room, in the drawers, etc.*) Help me look.

KATHRYN (*without moving*): What'd you looking in here for?

K.C.: Why not? I don't know where it is. Bruce drinks. He leaves his cans and bottles all over the place, in the bathroom, on chairs. Look under that cushion. (KATHRYN *doesn't move.*) Under the bed...

KATHRYN: Why you all buy wine with corks anyway? What's wrong with the kind that have the tops that screw off?

K.C. (*pulling back the blankets*): It's cheap.

KATHRYN (*smiling*): Oh well! Well! Well! I didn't know you had taken up wine tasting!

K.C. (*throwing a pillow*): Bruce is the wino - he says it's cheap. You gon' help me look?

KATHRYN: I'm not suppose to look. I'm the one with the brains, the "quick thinker."

K.C.: It better be good and it better work.

KATHRYN: You issuing ultimatums and you ain't found that cork screw. I'd watch it if I were you.

K.C. (*gets up and goes to the bedroom door*): Let me check the kitchen. (*She exits. After a moment, the phone rings. K.C. yells from the other room*): Let it ring!

KATHRYN (*to herself*): Your phone. (*Yelling.*) You got that cork screw?!

K.C.: No!

KATHRYN (*teasing*): You don't find it, I'll listen to that tape!

K.C. (*teasing*): You do and I'll kill you!

KATHRYN: You got nothing to hide from me! (*Picking up the receiver, holding it away from her ear.*) It could be anybody calling!

K.C. (*tensing*): Kathryn, you got that phone?!

KATHRYN (*phone to her ear*): Yes. (*Yelling.*) You told me everything! (*She moves to take the phone away from her ear, but something catches her attention. She listens a moment, then eases the phone back on the cradle and moves away from it. K.C. rushes to the room, cork screw in hand. She stops in front of the phone, stares down on it, then looks up at KATHRYN.*) I see you found it.

K.C. (*giving her the cork screw*): You got the cork screw - what's the plan?

KATHRYN (*drains the can of beer*): We'll shoot him. I figure somebody with all his morals should die with a few holes in him. (*Pause.*) You got a gun?

K.C. (*drily*): No. (*Thinking quickly.*) Bruce has one! (*She goes to the closet, fumbles around on the bottom, and produces a shoe box. KATHRYN stands slowly, becomes very tense as K.C. moves towards the bed with the box extended arm's length in front of her. She lays the box on the bed. They stare at it.*) It's in there.

KATHRYN: Let's see it.

K.C. (*rubbing her palms together*): There it is right there.

KATHRYN: Is it real?

K.C. (*a bit snappish*): Yes, it's real.

KATHRYN: Take the top off.

K.C.: You do it.

KATHRYN: It's your gun; you do it.

K.C.: It's your plan.

KATHRYN (*there's a stand off; she moves back to the chair to get away from the box*): What kind of gun is it?

K.C. (*rubbing her palms, hard*): A gun! I don't know! It's big and I think it's black...

KATHRYN: Well, I really don't need to see it now. Let's talk about it some more first. you can put it back in the closet now if you want to.

K.C. (*there's a short pause; she lifts the box carefully and sits it down quickly on the night stand*): I'll just leave it right here for now...(*Moving backward away from it.*) We can look at it later...

KATHRYN (*feeling the paper from the bottle nervously*): I don't know about that gun, K.C. I don't think we should borrow your husband's gun to kill nobody.

K.C.: Then where we going to get one?!

KATHRYN (*she plunges the cork screw into the cork, twisting it*): I don't know. Let me think about it. (*Working with the bottle.*) Isn't this suppose to come right out?

K.C. (*annoyed*): You can't work it?

KATHRYN: No. I don't use cork screws. My tops screw off. Can't you work it?

K.C.: You hounded me until I found it and you can't even work it?

KATHRYN: I said I couldn't. Can't you?

K.C.: No.

KATHRYN (*going to her, pointing to the hole*): See it?

K.C. (*looking at it*): Get the glass. (KATHRYN *does.* K.C. *shakes the wine, turns it upside down in the glass.*) What'd you do to it?

KATHRYN: I tried to open it.

K.C.: You broke it. What if I just push it down in there? (*She taps the bottle with the cork screw.*)

KATHRYN: Don't do that; you'll break it.

K.C. (*hits it even harder; the bottle breaks*): Damn it!

KATHRYN (*taking the bottle*): Look what you did! I told you you would break it! I can't drink this.

K.C. (*reaches inside the night stand drawer, takes out a handkerchief*): Gimme the wine. (KATHRYN *gives her the bottle.* K.C. *spreads the handkerchief over the glass and strains the wine through the handkerchief.*) You need a glass. (KATHRYN *steps from the room, returns with a glass, gives it to K.C. who strains a glass full of wine and gives it to* KATHRYN.)

K.C. (*smiling as she listens to a song on the radio*): Remember that?

KATHRYN (*moving to the sound of the music*): You got to be kidding! That is the love theme from the days with tall, lanky, burnt orange, brown-eyed J.W. Crawford! That man walked all over my feelings, broke my heart, and kept me smiling the whole time, and he wasn't even good-looking! (*Laughing.*) You remember that time he left us at that concert and we had to walk home in the rain?

K.C. (*remembering*): I don't remember it being funny. As I recall, that was a rainstorm we was walking in, and the only reason we had to walk is because he didn't wait for us after we saw him with that girl. He thought you was going to go off on him.

KATHRYN (*stands, begins to dance*): He explained it all so well. (*She laughs, spins around.*) Remember that little mole he had on his face, right by his left eye? It used to move all distracting and shit! (*Imitating J.W.'s dance style, she is happy, spirited.*) Remember this?!

K.C. (*half smile*): Yeah...

KATHRYN: And this?! Is this J.W.?

K.C.: That's him! Do Bruce!

KATHRYN (*imitating Bruce*): Here go Bruce!

K.C. (*laughing big*): That's him! That's him! Do that thing he do with his shoulders!

KATHRYN: What thing?

K.C.: You know how he do it! (*She attempts an imitation from her seat.*)

KATHRYN (*switching back to J.W.'s style*): Nope...(K.C. *sits the bottle on the bed and joins* KATHRYN *on the floor, imitating Bruce.*) That's him! (KATHRYN *laughs.* K.C. *dances a moment longer, then goes back to the bed and flops down.* KATHRYN *changes her dance style; her movement is tighter, more confined.*)

K.C.: Who's that suppose to be?

KATHRYN: You.

K.C.: That's not me!

KATHRYN (*laughing*): It is you!

K.C. (*annoyed*): It's not!

KATHRYN: I knew you were going to say that!

K.C.: Because it's not me. I don't dance like that!

KATHRYN: Yes, you do. (*She switches back to her imitation of J.W.; she is again happy, spirited, caught in her memories. K.C. watches.*)

K.C.: I ain't never seen you that strung out on nobody.

KATHRYN: That...(*She turns, whirls.*)...is because I have never been that strung out on anybody!

K.C. (*purposely putting a damper on* KATHRYN's *fun*): Not even Ben?

KATHRYN (*she stops dancing, looks at* K.C.; *annoyed*): Not even Ben.

K.C.: J.W. hurt you.

KATHRYN: If he hadn't, I couldn't stay with Ben. I wouldn't have the patience. (KATHRYN *takes her glass slowly and sits on the chair quietly.*)

K.C.: But you don't even love him and you don't cheat on the man.

KATHRYN: What is it with you, K.C.? (*Simmering.*) If you want to start comparing the two, I guess I don't. So, what's the point?

K.C.: You ain't happy.

KATHRYN: You ain't neither.

K.C.: But I love Bruce!

KATHRYN (*quietly*): But - I think you can't see that great big forest for that long, lean tree standing in your eye. Everybody that gets married don't do it for love; you know that. Ben married me for his own reasons. I don't know if I would call it love, but that's what he calls it, and it makes him happy. I married him, as you well know, because I was lonely and I needed somebody. Ben takes me out of that. I give Ben so much more of myself, parts of me that J.W. didn't even know existed. I'm satisfied. (KATHRYN *examines her glass. There's a short, reflective pause between them.*) Is this safe?

K.C. (*sits the wine and the cloth aside and raises her glass to the light*): At your own risk.

KATHRYN (*peering inside her glass*): You drinking?

K.C. (*gulps down half her drink*): That answer your question?

KATHRYN (*examining her drink even closer*): For the moment.

K.C. (*quietly*): You think I should let him go, don't you? (*Drinks what's left of her wine.*)

KATHRYN (*looks away thoughtfully, then back at the wine glass*): It's hard to say, K.C. I can't say what I'd do...What'd you asking me for? What'd you think?

K.C.: I need him, Kathryn. What am I going to do out there by myself? I don't know how to deal with being by myself.

KATHRYN: Something has to be wrong for you to do what you did. Instead of being so secretive about everything, why didn't you talk to Bruce about it?

K.C.: I told you he's not talking to me.

KATHRYN: Then why didn't you call me?! I don't know about this secrecy and shit; you didn't used to be that way.

K.C.: I didn't know I needed somebody until I was there, honest to god! I mean, it's one thing to start out with that kinda thing on your mind, but it wasn't like that. I didn't know until I was there and involved! (*Disgusted.*) Kathryn, I liked it! I enjoyed every minute right up until he played that tape. How could I?!

KATHRYN (*seriously*): Horney is horney.

(K.C. *laughs in spite of herself.* KATHRYN *smiles, watches as* K.C. *strains a drink.*)

K.C. (*tearfully*): I have spent the past five years being perfect! (KATHRYN *clears her throat;* K.C. *shoots her an ugly look but continues.*) Five years I have been right here where he can reach me! Right here! (*She stands to avoid the tears.*) You know how it's been, Kate! Everything I ever needed was right here...I thought...I don't know! Everything was perfect until I went out there! (*She looks at* KATHRYN.) I fell off my own cloud...

KATHRYN: You were pushed.

K.C.: You been pushed.

KATHRYN: You ain't me. I don't have no wings or no cloud to rest on. I'm a ripple. I'm what's left of the wave. I'm the ripple that washes up on the sand after the wave is long gone.

K.C.: You can't hold a ripple. I wanna be held.

KATHRYN (*into her drink*): Bruce can't do that?

K.C. (*long, hard pause*): No...

KATHRYN: There, you said it.

K.C. (*suspiciously*): What did I say?

KATHRYN: Just what you said...You wanna be held and Bruce can't do it.

K.C. (*eyeing her*): I said won't.

KATHRYN: Won't, can't - what's the difference? You need him, and he's not needing you back...

K.C. (*flatly*): You listened to that tape.

KATHRYN (*looking inside her glass, she finishes her drink*): I
didn't...

K.C. (*sits her glass down*): I been knowing you since you was five.
You lyin', Kathryn. Look at your face! I knew you was listening! I
knew it! You listened!

KATHRYN (*quietly*): Okay...a little bit.

(K.C. *takes one of the pillows from the bed and begins to hit* KATH-
RYN *with it. She is outraged, afraid that* KATHRYN *knows the truth.*
KATHRYN *gets up and moves quickly away from her.*)

K.C.: You listened after you said you wouldn't!

KATHRYN: K.C., stop! (*She makes her way to the bed, takes a pillow and defends herself.*) K.C., quit! Quit it!

K.C.: What did you hear?!

KATHRYN: Nothing!

K.C. (*hitting her hard*): You heard everything!

KATHRYN (*fed up*): Damn it, K.C.! Yes! I heard, and you should
have told me Bruce was gay!

K.C. (*painfully*): No!

KATHRYN: So what if I heard?! So what?! Who am I going to
tell?! Who would I want to tell? (*They hit each other with the pillows.*
KATHRYN *stops first; she's had enough.* K.C. *hits her again and runs
across the bed to the other side. They stare at each other, huffing and puffing.*) I'm getting too old for this...I haven't had a pillow fight since
me, you and Billy broke your mother's lamp that time...

K.C. (*spitefully*): You broke it!

KATHRYN: I did not! Billy kicked the damn thing off the table
'cause we took his pants!

K.C.: You broke it! (*She throws the pillow at* KATHRYN. *It lands
on the floor.*)

KATHRYN: I'm sorry, K.C...

K.C. (*angry*): You heard everything?!

KATHRYN: No...just a little bit...

K.C.: Which part?

KATHRYN: The part about Bruce...

K.C. (*impatiently*): I wanna know which part?

KATHRYN: The part about...when you said he was a neutral
person and...K.C., you know what you said. Why you wanna make
me tell you...(K.C. *waits; she looks as if she might strangle* KATHRYN.

The pause is long.)...and he asked you what you meant, and you told him about Bruce...that he's gay...(*More silence.*)...I'm sorry...K.C...

K.C. (*hysterically*): I could kill him! I could do it!

KATHRYN: K.C., you're upset now, but -

K.C.: You think I can't?! You think I'm scared?! (K.C. *moves towards the box holding the gun.* KATHRYN *moves around the bed in an attempt to get the gun.* K.C. *lifts the box from the table at the same time the phone rings. She jumps, startled, dropping the box. They scream as the gun discharges; both scramble for cover.* K.C. *ends up pinned to a wall near the door with her back to the audience;* KATHRYN *is behind the bed on the floor. The phone continues to ring. They wait, both frozen. After several more rings, it stops.*)

KATHRYN: K.C.?

K.C. (*whispering*): Kathryn?

BOTH: It stopped...

(*A short silence.* KATHRYN *laughs;* K.C. *joins her. Neither moves.*)

KATHRYN: It stopped?!

K.C.: I don't know, did it?!

KATHRYN: It's not ringing! It must have stopped!

K.C.: Then how come I still got ringing in my ears?!

KATHRYN: Maybe you dead! Am I?!

K.C.: I don't know; I'm too scared to move!

KATHRYN: Me too!

K.C.: Where's the gun, Kathryn?

KATHRYN: Over there by the wall...Who the hell put bullets in it?!

K.C. (*calmer*): I don't know.

KATHRYN (*coming from behind the bed slowly*): You can get off that wall now.

K.C. (*without moving*): Where you say that gun was?

KATHRYN (*moving around the bed on her knees, she spots the gun, points to it*): There it is, right there. (*She gets up and goes to where* K.C. *is standing, stopping to get her wine glass. She turns* K.C. *around and extends the glass to her.*) You okay, K.C.?

K.C. (*allowing* KATHRYN *to lead her away from the wall, she is still shaken; she seats herself on the chair and gulps the wine*): Hell no...

KATHRYN: I think that if your friend walked in here right now, I could shoot his ass myself!

K.C. (*sarcastically*): You'd have to pick up the gun to do that...

(KATHRYN *takes an imaginary gun and stalks around the room aiming it in front of her.*)

K.C.: Talk about crazy...

KATHRYN: Me? I'm not crazy, I'm hysterical!

K.C. (*collecting the wine bottle and cloth, she goes back to the chair and strains herself a drink; she is keyed up, nervous*): What's the difference?

KATHRYN (*aiming at the bedroom door*): Bang! You're hysterical too! (*She jumps up on the bed; aims again at the door.*) Bang! Bang! Bang!

K.C. (*sipping her drink*): You missed.

KATHRYN: See, I told you you were hysterical - I never miss!

K.C.: You just did; he ducked.

KATHRYN: Where is he?!

K.C. (*getting involved*): There he is, behind you!

KATHRYN (*jumping from the bed, turning, aiming*): Bang!

K.C. (*pointing towards the door, she slips out of the chair and gets up on the bed*): There he is! Get him! He's running for the door!

KATHRYN: Bang! Bang! That was for J.W.!

K.C.: You got him! Shoot him a couple of times for me!

KATHRYN: Bang! Bang! Bang!

K.C.: Bull's-eye! (K.C. *runs to the door, drops to the floor.*) Okay, help me!

KATHRYN (*joining her by the door*): He almost got away. (*Lightly.*) Is he dead? You think nine bullets was enough?

K.C. (*whispering*): I don't know. Feel his pulse.

KATHRYN: You do it; I shot him.

K.C. (*pretends to feel a pulse; she raises her arm as if she's dropping a limp arm*): He feels dead.

KATHRYN (*lightly*): You sure?

K.C. (*looking up at her*): You wanna shoot him again?

KATHRYN: He's dead.

K.C. (*she's now involved to a point that seems unnatural*): Grab one of his legs. Let's get him outa here.

KATHRYN: Why take him anywhere? He broke in, remember? I don't know the man, do you?

K.C. (*thinking*): No...I don't know the man, but I don't want him here. I'll have to answer questions!

KATHRYN: So what?

K.C.: I don't want to look at him! Kathryn, help me. He knows! (KATHRYN *takes the sheet form the bed and takes it to K.C. She spreads it on the floor as if she were covering a body.*) Get the gun! There it is on the chair! Get it! Bring it to me!

(KATHRYN *goes to the chair, takes the gun up and brings it to her.* K.C. *takes it with two fingers, wipes it clean with the edge of the sheet.*)

KATHRYN (*tiring of the game*): All that ain't necessary.

K.C. (*looking around*): Bring me that pillow case!

KATHRYN (*strips the pillows*): He broke in! We shot him; he fell! If we move him someplace else, then they'll know we're guilty.

K.C. (*snapping*): This is necessary! I'm not admitting anything! He's got nine bullets in him! What kind of accident is that! I have to hide it! You going to help me or what?!

KATHRYN (*pause, concerned*): K.C...

K.C.: Help me, Kathryn! I have to hide this! Grab his leg!

KATHRYN: K.C...no!

K.C.: I have to hide this! I don't want anybody to know! I don't want him to go! I can't let him go, Kathryn!

KATHRYN (*angry, frightened for her*): He's gone, K.C.!

K.C.: No!

KATHRYN (*watches as K.C. wads the sheet into a ball, bends to get the pillow slips; KATHRYN moves to take them away from her*): K.C., I'm sorry!

K.C.: No...

KATHRYN: Yes! (*Snatching the sheet away from her, throwing it to the floor.*) He's gone! Damn it! You know it! I know it! Why do you wanna be miserable?! He's gone! Take his body out of here!

K.C. (*picking up the wadded sheets*): Help me, Kathryn!

KATHRYN: No.

K.C. (*yelling*): I helped you! It's heavy...I can't...

KATHRYN: Then what'd you gonna do? You gonna hold on to something that's too much for you?

K.C.: I'm tired...dead bodies are heavy...

KATHRYN: Then get rid of it, K.C.!

(*There's a short silence between them. K.C. reposits the linen, takes it to the door and drops it. The phone rings. K.C. looks at KATHRYN. She is frightened. The phone rings a few more times, then stops.*)

K.C.: It's over? (KATHRYN *nods. The phone rings again as the lights fade.*)

Birth Of A Blues!

A SATIRICALLY-SPICED "SLICE-OF-LIFE" ONE ACT/ONE SCENE PLAY

by BEN CALDWELL

A Harlem-born playwright, Ben Caldwell is the author of more than 60 one-act plays, numerous essays and skits and several screenplays. The subject matter of the works varies from political/social criticism to satire and comedy. He is a recipient of the Harlem Writer's Guild Award (1969) and Guggenheim Fellowship for Playwriting (1970-71). He is also an original, creative graphic designer and illustrator.

CHARACTERS:

A BLACK BLUES SINGER - *a man in his late sixties or early seventies.*
A WHITE REPORTER - *early thirties.*
CAMERAMAN - *never in view; presence is sometimes indicated. This is a two character play.*

SCENE: *Sidewalk setting. We hear street traffic sounds - human and mechanical. Seated on a folding chair is an elderly Black man. Not as shabbily dressed as a beggar but not as well-dressed as a banker. He's wearing mirrored lens sunglasses. He's playing slow, mournful, "blues" sounds on his harmonica, accompanying himself on the guitar. He does not - I repeat, does not - pat his foot to the heavy rhythmic accents of the music he's playing. A young white man approaches him, trying to come as close as possible without straining the cord to the microphone he's holding.*

REPORTER: Sir, I'm from WICU-TV. I'd like to conduct an interview with you. (*No response, so he speaks much louder.*) Excuse me, sir, I'm from WICU-TV. I would like to interview you.
BLUES SINGER (*stops playing*): You talking to me? What you say?
REPORTER: I said, I would like to interview you, sir.

BLUES SINGER: Interview me for what? I ain't looking for no job.

REPORTER (*still talking loudly*): Not a job interview. I'm from WICU-TV. I want to interview you.

BLUES SINGER (*shouting*): Why you talking so loud? You hard of hearing?

REPORTER: I'm sorry, sir. I want to interview you. WICU-TV, a public service station which carries educational programming, is doing a series on all the great blues singers of the 20th century.

BLUES SINGER: Oh, and you want me to tell you what I know about them. Well, me and Muddy Waters was...

REPORTER: No, I don't want you to tell me about them. I want you to tell me about yourself. We consider you one of the greatest blues singers of the 20th century.

BLUES SINGER: Me? One of the great blues singers of the 20th century? Boy, the 20th century ain't even over yet. And the few years that's left is liable to produce some blues that'll make them old blues sound like "Happy Birthday!"

REPORTER: Well, that's besides the point. You call yourself B.B.B.B.B. King, is that correct?

BLUES SINGER: That's correct if you said five B's. I don't just call myself B.B.B.B.B. King, that's my name. My real name. They used to call me "Leadfeet" 'cause of how slow I walk, but my real name is B.B.B.B.B. King.

REPORTER: Don't people confuse you with B.B. King?

BLUES SINGER: Man, how-in-the-hell you gon' confuse two B's with five B's? You really got to be stupid to do that. He's B.B. King. (*Counts on his fingers.*) I'm B.B.B.B.B. King!

REPORTER: I read someplace that the two B's in B.B. King's name stand for "Blues Boy." What do your five B's stand for?

BLUES SINGER: B.B.B.B.B. stands for "Baddest Black Blues Boy Ever Been Born!"

REPORTER (*repeats the name*): "Baddest Black Blues Boy Ever Been Born!" Shouldn't there be an "E" in there?

BLUES SINGER: No - that'd mess up the rhythm I want. You know what I mean?

REPORTER: But wait - "Baddest Black Blues Boy Ever Been Born!" There seems to be six B's, not five.

BLUES SINGER (*slightly annoyed*): Oh yeah? Then call me B.B.B.B.B.B. King, goddamit! OK?

REPORTER: Are you, by any chance, related to Dr. Martin Luther King, Jr.?

BLUES SINGER (*still annoyed*): No! Is this a interview or a investigation? Which is it?

REPORTER: An interview, sir. I thought that was a pertinent question.

BLUES SINGER: Well, I thought "No" was a pertinent answer unless you wanna know why I'm not related to Dr. King. There's a whole host of King's I'm not related to. Do you want me to name some of 'em? King Tut. King Kong.

REPORTER: That won't be necessary. Where were you born, sir?

BLUES SINGER: Right here.

REPORTER: Right where, sir?

BLUES SINGER: Here! Coonkill, Mississippi! Don't you know where you are?

REPORTER (*hasty change of subject*): Have you been blind all your life, sir?

BLUES SINGER: I ain't never been blind. Hope to God I never will be.

REPORTER: But the sunglasses...I thought...

BLUES SINGER (*amazed*): You mean you think everybody wearing shade glasses is blind? I can see. You wearin' a blue tie and...

REPORTER (*another hasty change of subject*): Could you tell me something about your early life?

BLUES SINGER: Ain't nothing worth telling, much less worth hearing!

REPORTER (*more enthused*): My audience of blues aficionados would love to hear everything about your life, sir.

BLUES SINGER: "Blues aficionados?" What is that?

REPORTER: That means they appreciate the blues!

BLUES SINGER: If they appreciate the blues, they must not have ever had 'em, huh?

REPORTER: I don't know. What I mean is they understand the blues.

BLUES SINGER: Can't understand 'em if you ain't never had the blues, either.

REPORTER (*slightly annoyed*): Please, just tell me about your childhood. We're about to run out of tape.

BLUES SINGER: Well, how much tape did you bring for my whole life story? See how much you got left, so I can tell how much more I can tell you.

REPORTER (*to offstage*): Sam, how much tape? We have enough tape. Now, please tell me a little about your childhood.

BLUES SINGER (*brusque response*): I worked in the cotton fields before I could walk or talk. I ran away from home as soon as I learned to run. And I worked in a whorehouse for...

REPORTER: You played music in a whorehouse?

BLUES SINGER: No. I emptied ashtrays and changed sheets. Nobody wants to hear no blues-singing in a whorehouse! You wanna hear blues-singing when you fucking? I don't wanna hear nobody moaning and hollering but me or my bed partner.

REPORTER (*disappointed*): OK - you changed sheets and emptied ashtrays in a whorehouse. Where did you go from there?

BLUES SINGER: Well, after I changed the sheets, I went home. Sometimes I would hang around and watch the action, but you soon get tired of watching other people fuck...

REPORTER: I meant a next step, or phase, in your life.

BLUES SINGER: Oh, I see what you mean. I went on the chain gang.

REPORTER (*renewed enthusiasm*): The chain gang!? Did you kill someone? Robbery? Rape? What did you do?

BLUES SINGER: Nothing. I volunteered. Chain gangs is good experience for blues singers.

REPORTER (*quickly overcomes disbelief*): Is that where you learned to sing the blues?

BLUES SINGER: Where?

REPORTER: On the chain gang?

BLUES SINGER: What?

REPORTER: Did you learn to sing the blues on the chain gang?

BLUES SINGER: Oh, no! I was singing the blues long before that. When I volunteered for the chain gang, I did so so I could teach. I taught the blues to some of the prisoners who didn't catch on too fast. No, I didn't learn 'em there. I been singing the blues since I was born. Most babies come out thei' momma crying - I came out singing, "SeeSee Rider, see what you done done..."

REPORTER: Can you define the blues?

BLUES SINGER: Can I do what to the blues?

REPORTER: Why do you sing the blues? What is the blues?

BLUES SINGER (*thinks for a moment*): The blues, to me, is tight shoes. The blues is when the only pair shoes you got is too tight. That's why I sing the blues!

REPORTER (*questioning pause*): That's all? The pain, the suffering we hear in your songs is influenced by your hurting feet?

BLUES SINGER: Man, if you ever wore a pair of tight, cheap shoes, that's enough! I even wrote a tune called, "Shoes Blues!" Wanna hear it?

REPORTER: No. What is your favorite blues song? Is it something you wrote? Is it one of the famous Black blues classics? Something by W.C. Handy? Blind Lemon Jefferson?

BLUES SINGER (*in a confidential manner*): Quiet as it's kept and strange as it might seem, my favorite, it's written by a white man. And a foreign white man, at that.

REPORTER: Something written by a foreign white man? What famous blues song is that?

BLUES SINGER: Aw, you know the song and you know who wrote it. I thought by my saying "a foreign white man" that would give you a good hint. He's a Englishman.

REPORTER (*thinking hard*): Well, The Beatles didn't write blues. Let me see...

BLUES SINGER: You know who I'm talking 'bout. That English boy with the big mouth.

REPORTER: Mick Jagger?

BLUES SINGER: That's who I'm talking 'bout!

REPORTER (*puzzled*): Which song by Mick Jagger do you consider a great blues song?

BLUES SINGER: Which song? He only wrote one song as far as I'm concerned. The song says it all, about living in this society here. and it was the way Otis Redding sang it that made me feel it! I didn't feel it the way "Jagged" sang it. The way Otis sang it was what made it great! (*He sings stanza of* "I Can't Get No Satisfaction" *in his own inimitable style.*) Now, that's what I call a all-purpose blues song!

REPORTER (*moved to applaud*): I'm inclined to agree with you. How did you come to sing the blues for a living? How did that happen?

BLUES SINGER: Well, I was on this very same corner playing my guitar and hollering. Whoooo! Ooow! Oooohoh, Lord! And this young white lady comes over and says, "My, that's such a beautiful sound!" I thought she was crazy.

REPORTER: You sang on this corner, but you didn't do it for money?

BLUES SINGER: Let me tell the story! She listen a little while, then she say, "Is that the blues you're singing?" I said, "Lady, I ain't singin'. I'm in pain, and I'm complainin'. My shoes is too tight. My feet hurt!" She said, "Do you always play the guitar when you complainin'?" I said, "Yeah!" She said, "Why?" I said, "So nobody knows I'm in pain and complaining. Everybody thinks I'm singing the blues and enjoying myself." She said, "Why don't you take those tight shoes off?" I said, "It hurts too bad! I haven't touched my feet in fifteen years! I'm gon' wait 'til they wear off!" She said, "It's so beautiful to see someone suffer in so creative a fashion." And I said, "Yeah, I do the best I can." So, the next day she comes by; I was still in pain and complaining. She had a young white man with her. He said, "Jane, here, told me all about you. Come to New York, and I'll make you a millionaire." I said, "Oh, yeah? What do I have to do?" He said, "I want you to get on stage and sing the blues like you do on this street corner." I said, "I'm not singing. I'm in pain, and I'm complainin'." He said, "Well, your complaining is most entertaining, and people will pay to hear you complain that way." I said, "OK!"

REPORTER: A very interesting story.

BLUES SINGER: You think so? Well, anyhow, I went to the big city - complaining every step of the way. People really did pay good money to sit down and eat and drink and listen to me holler in pain. They seemed to really enjoy it - 'specially white people. They'd applaud, and jump up and scream for more. I had a whole lotta fun, but I ain't made no million dollars like them magazines say.

REPORTER: Did you ever sing anything besides the blues?

BLUES SINGER: Oh, yeah. I used to do a few love songs. One comes to mind. I wrote it. Recorded it, too.

REPORTER: What was the name of the love song you wrote and recorded?

BLUES SINGER: It was called, "When You Gon' Gimme That Pussy, Gal?" It was a beautiful ballad-type thing. I would've loved to hear Perry Como sing it. Coulda been a big hit, but they wouldn't play it on the radio. Only time you heard it was if you came to hear me in a club, or caught me hollerin' it at one of them fine gals used to walk by the club all the time.

REPORTER: You made dozens of recordings, but do you recall your first recording session? Was it special, or significant in any way?

BLUES SINGER: Oh, yeah. The first album; it's the technique I remember so well. That album was called, *Screamin' The Blues!* This same young white man - he called himself my producer and manager, now - he put me in this studio, in front of a big orchestra; I b'lieve it was Count Basis, or somebody. They put a whole bunch o' microphones in front of me; then this same young white man stomped on my foot as hard as he could. Boy, I do thirty choruses of what we named "Screamin' The Blues!" (*Describes.*) The band's saxophones was doing this riff (*Demonstrates.*) that sounded just like my throbbin' big toe felt! We did another number called "Blues For The Right Foot, Only." It was some of the best, loudest, blues anybody ever heard north of the Mississippi! Album was number one in Chicago for three years - but I ain't seen no million dollars.

REPORTER: You didn't make a million dollars. Did you make much money at all?

BLUES SINGER: You see I'm still wearing the same cheap, tight, shoes. If I'd have made anywhere near a million dollars, I'd have had these "bad boys" removed surgically!

REPORTER: You would've had your feet amputated?

BLUES SINGER: Naw! - just the shoes. I'd 'a' had a doctor cut 'em off! They got foot doctors up north, you know, that don't do nothing but treat feet! My feet hurt if I look at them too hard, much less touch them.

REPORTER: Do you believe you were cheated?

BLUES SINGER: Cheated? Oh, you still talkin' 'bout the money. You white folks sure do worry 'bout whether a nigger makes any money, and what he do with it. But, cheated - I don't know. I know I ain't seen no million dollars. I know a lotta money changed hands, but not much reached my pockets. That same young white man owns one of the biggest record companies in the world. I had a whole lotta good times. White gals loved me! I had so many gorgeous white gals, it took my mind off my feet for a while. That was during the time when it was a crime to even think of a white lady, much less doing what I did to some of 'em. (*Laughs.*) But, who knows, maybe I was cheated.

REPORTER: Having been cheated, exploited, is your music now a reflection of all the sorrowful things you've encountered, and now know about life? Is that now the inspiration for your blues singing?

BLUES SINGER: No, man, it's still about my feet. My feet still hurt. Excruciatingly! (*Sings.*) "But the sun's gonna shine in my back door one day..." Won't be long, now, before these raggedy so-and-so's wear clean off my feet, and I'll be all right! Probably sing like Frank Sinatra, then.

REPORTER: With your feet in that condition, how do you get about? Do you ever leave this corner?

BLUES SINGER: That's another long, slow story. You got enough time and tape?

REPORTER: I'm sorry, no. (*Extends his hand.*) Mr. B.B.B.B.B.B. King, thank you for the interview.

BLUES SINGER: Don't thank me, thank my feet. I owe it all to my feet. Oh oh! Here come one of them sharp pains, now!

(*As* REPORTER *exits,* BLUES SINGER *starts to sing a song composed of moans and hollers. A strong wind causes him to stop and huddle for warmth. Fade to black.*)

Hospice

A PLAY IN ONE ACT

by PEARL CLEAGE

Pearl Cleage is a prolific writer who works in a variety of forms and currently makes her home in Atlanta, Georgia, where she is a playwright-in-residence at Just Us Theater Company. Her plays include *puppetplay, Good News, Porch Songs, Banana Bread, Essentials* and *Hospice*. First presented by Woodie King, Jr., as part of The Women's Series at Henry Street Settlement's New Federal Theater, *Hospice* won five AUDELCO Awards for outstanding achievement off-Broadway in 1983. Ms. Cleage's *puppetplay*, which premiered at Just Us Theater in 1981, went on to open the seventeenth season of The Negro Ensemble Company. Ms. Cleage's performance collaborations include *A Little Practice* at Just Us Theater, *My Father Has A Son* at Nexus Contemporary Arts Center's Club Zebra and *Love and Trouble* at Seven Stages Theater. She has also published a book of short fiction, *One For The Brothers*, and her book of poetry, *We Don't Need No Music*, was published by Broadside Press in 1971. Ms. Cleage has received grant support for her work from The National Endowment for the Arts Expansion Arts Program, The Fulton County Arts Council, The City of Atlanta Bureau of Cultural Affairs, The Georgia Council for the Arts and The Coca-Cola Company.

CAST:

ALICE ANDERSON - *a black woman, age 47.*
JENNY ANDERSON - *her daughter, age 30.*

(The time is early morning. The set is a small house with upstairs and downstairs. The downstairs area is the main playing space, but the upstairs must be large enough to accommodate the bed, dresser with mirror, etc. This is ALICE's bedroom. JENNY sleeps downstairs, but her bed is not visible. The house is small and crowded with the accumulated paraphernalia of a lifetime. The walls are full of framed photos of dead family. There is a couch with a comforter or soft, warm coverlet of some sort thrown across the back. A coffee table in front is piled high with

newspapers, books, mail, papers and medicine bottles. On the table also is a vase holding a dozen beautiful, long-stemmed red roses. In the corner of the room is a small table piled almost as high as the coffee table with papers of various kinds. Somewhere in the middle is a typewriter. This is the area where JENNY writes. Tucked next to the table is a small suitcase. There is also a record player surrounded by record albums in and out of their covers. It is not an expensive, modern stereo, but has surprisingly good quality sound for its age and size. There are several brimming bookcases, some potted plants in various states of well-being, etc. The feeling of the room is cluttered, but not claustrophobic.

An elaborately carved wooden cane sits against the record player. It is morning. Early. The light is that thin early morning kind that lets you know the sun is still undecided. As the lights come up, we hear the sound of a typewriter clicking away. The daughter, JENNY, is hunched over her work. There is a floor lamp burning over her, creating a small pool of light in the eerie morning gloom. JENNY is thirty years old and very pregnant. She is frowning at the page which is still dangling from her typewriter. Re-reading over what she had just typed, she rips the page out and adds it to the small pile of crumpled balls at her feet. She shifts uncomfortably in her straight-back chair, and placing both hands behind her, arches her back, massaging the kinks out of her spine. She has been up for awhile. She shakes her head, and resumes her typing. Upstairs, her mother stirs and turns over in her bed restlessly with a soft moan. Hearing the noise, Jenny stops typing suddenly, listening. There is no immediate movement upstairs. She leans back to her work and is suddenly irritated by the fact that her very pregnant belly keeps her from getting as close to the table as she wants to. It is awkward. She tries turning sideways which means she has to type across her stomach. This is even more awkward. She tries several more approaches, but nothing works. During this process, the mother, ALICE sits up slowly. She is in obvious pain. The upstairs light is always blue and dim. The impression is of silhouette and shadow. ALICE almost doubles over when she sits up, but straightens slowly and with great effort. She is thin and very frail. She is dying of cancer and her head is bald or very lightly fuzzed over with hair from chemotherapy. Her head should not be covered during the course of the play. Slowly and painfully her back straightens, her shoulders are square, and she finds the strength to push the covers off and slowly swing her legs over the side of the bed. She is wearing a long cotton nightgown with sleeves. The effort of sitting up has been very great. She remains motionless, seated on the edge of the bed.)

JENNY (*loudly*): Well, damn! (*She has spoken more loudly than she meant to and looks guiltily upstairs. ALICE's head looks up in the direction of the curse. When there is no follow-up sound, she droops again. JENNY rises and goes to the bottom of the stairs, listening. No sound from ALICE. JENNY seems obviously relieved and crosses back to sit down at her typewriter. She pours herself a cup of tea from the pot near her. She sips the tea slowly, reading over the page that is in the typewriter and absentmindedly stroking her belly. Suddenly, JENNY drops the pages and begins to pant rapidly. She is having a contraction. When it ends, she checks her watch and crosses slowly to the phone. She is excited, but trying to contain it. She dials quietly.*) Alexis? I'm sorry! I know its early, but I think it's happening! Yes! Since early this morning...No. I'm okay...Yes...Alright...I'll call you later.

(*Upstairs, ALICE stands quietly and walks to the dresser. It is an old-fashioned wardrobe with a full-length mirror on the door. She slowly takes off her nightgown and looks at herself naked in the mirror. We see her in shadow, but it is clear that she is gazing at her body. She folds the nightgown and lays it on the bed. Downstairs, JENNY finishes her tea and resumes typing. ALICE dresses slowly. Underwear, long socks, long skirt, sweater buttoned over it all. She slips on her shoes and makes her slow, painful, laborious way down the stairs. Holding the bannister tightly, she manages it, but the effort to do it with such a straight back and measured gate is immense. JENNY is typing loudly, continuously, and is thoroughly absorbed in her work. She does not look up when ALICE reaches the bottom of the stairs and stops to catch her breath. After a moment, ALICE turns to look at JENNY. JENNY, typing furiously, is oblivious. ALICE walks slowly over to the record player and puts the needle down on the record already on the turntable. It is not the first cut on the album, but she goes right to the spot as if she'd done it a thousand times before. With sudden and unexpected richness, the strains of Leontyne Price singing Puccini's "Madame Butterfly" fill the room. It is "Un Bel Di." JENNY jumps, startled out of her reverie by the blast of music. ALICE moves slowly but with determination over to the couch and sits down slowly, eyes closed, listening to the music and trying not to give in to the pain.*)

JENNY: God! You scared me! (*She moves to turn down the record. No word from ALICE.*) I thought I heard you get up. (*JENNY moves to her desk and carefully takes her work out of the typewriter and puts it face down on her desk. No response from ALICE. Her eyes are closed. She is listening intently.*) Are you okay? (ALICE *looks at her, and* JENNY *looks a little guilty at what could be a loaded question.*)

ALICE (*sarcastic*): Never been better. What were you cussing about?

JENNY: What? Oh. I'm sorry. I got stuck in the middle of something. You know...

ALICE: I didn't mean to startle you. I wasn't ready to wake up yet.

JENNY: Did you sleep much?

ALICE: No.

JENNY: Me neither. I try to lie on my back, but after awhile, she gets so heavy, I feel like I'm smothering.

ALICE: Well, it won't be long now, as they say.

JENNY: As they say. You want some tea? I just made it a few minutes ago. (ALICE *nods but doesn't answer. She is listening. Eyes closed.* JENNY *goes for the tea.*)

ALICE: Turn it up a little, will you? (JENNY *stops at the record player and turns it up. The rest of "Un Bel Di" is sung by Leontyne Price as* JENNY *gets the tea and ALICE leans back, eyes closed, while she listens.* JENNY *brings the tea, standing quietly until the song finishes and then turns off the record. ALICE sits motionless for a few moments as if in a trance, then comes back to reality and sits fully erect, eyes open, back in touch with the world around her.* JENNY *hands ALICE her tea and goes back to her work.*) Deadline?

JENNY: Not really. I told them I wasn't going home to work. I was going home to have a baby! (*Laughs at her own determination.*) I knew I could get away with it. They've never had a black film critic before. (*Evasively.*) I'm working on a couple of things, but it's hard when the only deadlines are self-imposed.

ALICE: I've always found those to be the hardest ones to miss. Well, I hope you're not blaming this lack of discipline on me. This is your choice, you know. Just keep that in mind.

JENNY: Don't worry. I accept full responsibility.

ALICE: You should.

JENNY: I have.

ALICE (*a beat*): I envy your confidence, but I wish it didn't make you start typing quite so early in the morning.

JENNY (*very controlled*): I think you completed your bad night by getting up on the wrong side of the bed this morning. I said I'm sorry I woke you. I'll say it again, only because I really mean it. I'm sorry.

ALICE: Me too.

(JENNY *rises, stretches, and sits down Indian style on the floor. She has the soles of her feet together and is bouncing her knees toward the floor, pushing them down closer with every bounce. She continues as she speaks, trying to make "neutral conversation.")*

JENNY: Daddy laughed when I first started doing movie reviews. He thought it was the perfect job for me. We used to go to the movies all the time. It gave us something neutral to talk about. No matter how many demonstrators the police locked up, Katherine Hepburn was going to marry Cary Grant; Norma Sherer was going to smile that sweet, sad smile; and Natalie Wood was gonna do Juliet all over Spanish Harlem.

ALICE (*putting her cup down with a smash, irritated by* JENNY's *chatter and her bouncing knees*): Do you have to talk about that now? (JENNY *stops abruptly and sits perfectly still.* ALICE *winces, recovers quickly, and looks fully into* JENNY's *face.*)

JENNY (*softly*): You ought to take something.

ALICE: Like what?

JENNY: Like something for the pain. There's no shame in that.

ALICE: Shame? (*She laughs and shakes her head.*) You've been watching too many of those Hollywood movies. No real sick person gives a damn about shame.

JENNY (*reaching for the medicine*): Then take something. (ALICE's *hand on hers stops her abruptly and with finality.*)

ALICE: I'm not myself when I take something.

JENNY: Then, by all means, take two.

ALICE: Touche, Sister. Touche! (JENNY *extends a pill and pours a small glass of water from a pitcher on the table.* ALICE *relents and swallows the pill and several more. She leans back again, waiting for the medication to take effect.* JENNY *lays down on her back near the couch and takes a long, deep Lamaze cleansing breath. She sucks in as much air as she can, holds it, then lets it out with an extended "whoosh!"* ALICE *opens her eyes and watches her.* JENNY *places her hands very lightly on either side of her stomach and breathes in and out, using the Lamaze method.*) What is that supposed to do?

(JENNY *holds up a finger to indicate that she has to complete the cycle before breaking the breathing to respond. She accelerates her breathing*

*until she is panting rapidly and loudly. She stops after a minute, takes
another deep cleansing breath, and lets it out.)*

JENNY: I've tried to explain all of this to you before. Why do you
always wait until I'm in the middle of it to decide you want to listen?

ALICE: I'm easily distracted.

JENNY: It's supposed to minimize pain during labor. Redirect
your energy or something.

ALICE: It's not your energy you're going to be concerned about.
Trust me.

JENNY: No horror stories please! I can't stand it when people
tell a pregnant woman horror stories, especially when I'm the pregnant woman!

ALICE: You've already heard all the horror stories I know.
You've probably written them all down, too.

JENNY: You're very closed mouthed with your stories, now that
you mention it. Horror or otherwise.

ALICE: But the few gems I've let slip have not escaped your attention. You've probably made a few notes, just in case.

JENNY: I probably have. Would you mind?

ALICE: I'm not sure. I guess not. It's not like I'm going to use
them for anything. You're not, are you?

JENNY: Going to write about you? (ALICE *waits but does not
answer.*) Probably.

ALICE (*laughs*): God! That isn't really fair, is it? Why write about
me now? Another dreary tale of a cancer-ridden mother attended
by her long lost, but dutiful, daughter. The last days of Acid Alice.
(*Laughs bitterly.*) Not the stuff best sellers are made of, Sister. Not
this year. Not this color.

JENNY: I'll risk it.

ALICE: Don't fool yourself. You're not risking anything. It
would probably be great therapy at the very least. (*A beat.*) I'm
sorry. I'll be better in a minute. Soon as this pill decides which pain
to concentrate on first. Is there anymore of that sweet wine we had
around here the other day?

JENNY: I stuck it away someplace.

ALICE: What are you writing about that makes you start cussin'
so early in the morning?

JENNY (*hedging; sheepishly*): I'm trying to create a portrait of the "the new woman."

ALICE: Is there such a creature?

JENNY (*laughingly*): That's the problem. I've read endless magazine articles about her. I've gone to conferences dedicated to her and read novels supposedly written by her about herself. But...

ALICE: Different costumes, Sister, same character.

JENNY: Voila!

ALICE: I can't stand the taste of sweet wine. I've never liked it, but it's the only kind that doesn't upset my stomach. Probably just another part of the penance. It's true, you know.

JENNY: What's true?

ALICE: About your not risking anything. It's true. I don't want you to fool yourself about that.

JENNY: I'll try not to. (JENNY *hands* ALICE *her wine and drinks some herself.*) Cheers! Getting pretty decadent around here, aren't we? It's not even nine o'clock in the morning, and we're already drinking wine.

ALICE (*draining her glass*): I'm your mother. It's okay.

JENNY (*suddenly concerned*): Is this okay for you to be drinking that with your medicine? (*She looks on the bottle label for possible warning label.*)

ALICE: Probably not. But what's the worst that can happen? It might kill me.

JENNY: I don't want all of our conversations to be about dying!

ALICE (*very quietly*): Then get out.

(JENNY *looks stunned as if* ALICE *had struck her.*)

JENNY (*looking for a neutral subject*): What happened to all of those old Billie Holiday records you used to have?

ALICE (*still calm and quiet*): I don't think you should be here, Jenny. I don't want you here.

JENNY: Your timing is lousy, mother. I'm having a baby any minute now, remember?

ALICE: I'm not asking you to go to the moon, Sister. It is my understanding that Prince Charming resides just across town.

JENNY: That's not open for discussion! And what difference does it make? I had a man and I don't have him anymore.

ALICE: I'm old-fashioned. I believe that if you ever have them, you always have them.

JENNY (*wearily*): We're not all as lucky as you are.

ALICE: Alright, Sister. Let's get the ground rules straight. This is my house. It was left to me, not to you, by my mother, not yours! I own it. Lock, stock and mothballs, and I came a very long way to get here in time enough to die in it.

JENNY: I wouldn't have moved in here if I had known you would be coming. It never occurred to me. It's not like you have a history of dropping in.

ALICE: It's not like I have a history at all as far as you're concerned, so why not just go wherever it was you would have gone if it had occurred to you that I might drop in.

JENNY: I want to stay.

ALICE: No, you don't. You think you ought to stay. Nobody wants to bring a new baby home to a death house!

JENNY: This is not a death house! I'm here, and I'm very much alive!

ALICE: I'm looking for a hospice, Sister. A place to die in peace, not in pieces. (*A beat. Wearily.*) It's just that I get so tired...

JENNY (*very gently*): I want to help you.

ALICE (*angered at her own vulnerability*): Why are you alone?

JENNY: Because I choose to be.

ALICE: Nobody chooses to be alone. You might choose your sanity, or your freedom, or some other wild thing that results in your being alone, but that's the fallout. The unavoidable consequences. Not the choice.

JENNY: Why can't you let me help you?

ALICE: You're not here to help. You're here to hide.

JENNY: I haven't got any reason to hide. I'm not ashamed of anything.

ALICE: Well, that's something we have in common. Shamelessness.

JENNY: I want to make the best of it.

ALICE: The best of this?

JENNY: The best of the time we have together.

ALICE: That's not one of my strong points, making the best of it.

JENNY: It's my specialty...

ALICE: You want to make a fairy tale out of it! You want me to tell you the secret of life and give you my motherly blessing. You want me to make up for twenty years of silence in two weeks. You want the two of us to play mother and daughter.

JENNY (*hurt and angry*): We <u>are</u> mother and daughter! (*Frustrated and confused.*) This is crazy! This doesn't make any sense!

ALICE: Is it supposed to make sense?

JENNY: Isn't it? I'm not a child anymore! We are two grown women!

ALICE: My mother used to tell me that once she was sure I understood what being grown meant, she'd never have to worry about me again.

JENNY: Is that why you came here? To see if I was grown?

ALICE: No. To see if I was. (*A beat.*) I'm dying, Sister. I'm only forty-seven years old, and I'm dying. I don't have the energy to figure out what you need to know and tell it to you.

JENNY: What are you talking about?

ALICE: You've been sitting around with that hopeful look on your face ever since I got here. You want too much, Sister.

JENNY: I don't want anything from you! You're my mother, and I'm your daughter. Isn't that enough?

ALICE: Yes, you are my daughter. (*A beat. The medication and the wine make her a little drowsy.*) My very own baby daughter. (*A beat.*) I'd like to have been better at this, Sister. But I just don't have any energy left for it now. I need all my energy for myself. I have to pay very close attention to what's happening up here. (*Taps her temple lightly.*)

JENNY: I understand...

ALICE (*sarcastic*): Do you?

JENNY: I think I do. (*She resumes her Lamaze exercises quietly.*)

ALICE: Well, then, you don't need any advice from me. You've got everything under control here, Sister. You've got it all organized. You've found a way to redirect your energies and feel no pain. You've even taken the guessing out of boys and girls.

JENNY: It's safer, that's all. I just wanted to be careful since she's my first one.

ALICE: It's a violation.

JENNY: No, mother. Nothing so dramatic as that. It's a simple test that lets you know in advance if your baby is going to have two heads and by the way reveals the gender. It just gives Alexis a lit-

53

tle more information to work with. There's a certain amount of risk in having a baby when you're as old as I am.

ALICE: I can't tell you anything about that. You and my eighteenth birthday arrived neck and neck. Is thirty late? Women used to have babies from nine to ninety.

JENNY: It's late for a first one. What are you talking about anyway? (*Laughs.*) You sound like a pioneer woman. "Nine to ninety."

ALICE: It's all different now. Your doctor doesn't even sound like a doctor.

JENNY: Alexis?

ALICE: How can you call your doctor Alexis?

JENNY: That's her name, mother. Don't act so shocked. You're not so old that ought to shock you.

ALICE: No, I guess not. (*A beat.*) I don't even know if the doctor who delivered you had a first name. Dr. Stewart. I never heard anybody call him anything else. Young Dr. Stewart. That was it.

JENNY: "Young Dr. Stewart"...sounds like a soap opera doctor.

ALICE: He only delivered babies at the Catholic hospital. The whole time I was in labor with you I had to look at all these bleeding crucifixes. Nails in the palms, a sword in the side, and a great big bleeding valentine right in the middle of his chest.

JENNY: Want some more wine?

ALICE: No. Yes, I guess so. I'm on to you, Sister. You think I'll get high and reveal those secrets you think I'm guarding so closely.

JENNY: No, I don't. I'm hoping you'll get a little high and remember where you put those Billie Holiday records.

ALICE (*irritated*): They're down there with the rest of the records, or they should be. Where else would I put them? Upstairs in my room? It's been awhile since I was in any condition to be playing Billie Holiday in my bedroom!

(JENNY *rummages through the records looking for Billie Holiday.*)

JENNY: I told someone once that the music of Billie Holiday ran through my early life like a leit motiv.

ALICE: What did he say?

JENNY: Why do you assume I was talking to a man?

ALICE: It's a seduction line, Sister. I'm not that sick. What did he say?

JENNY: He said, "What's a leit motiv?"

(*They both laugh.*)

ALICE: You know what your father said when you were born?

JENNY: What?

ALICE: I thought he might be disappointed because you weren't a boy, so I said I'd heard that sometimes kings divorce their wives if the firstborn is female. And he laughed and shook his head. "Not in my tribe," he said. "Not in my tribe."

JENNY (*delighted*): He never told me that!

ALICE: It's not a man's story. That's a story women tell each other. (*A beat.*) You see how you're looking at me? You're doing it again! I shouldn't have told you anything! It's only going to make you think you were right about those secrets. Forget it, Sister! It's only the way this medicine (*holding up the wine*) and this medicine (*taps medication bottle*) make my mind wander. There are no secrets. (*A beat.*) Well, maybe one.

JENNY: And what's that?

ALICE: That there are no secrets! (*A beat.* ALICE *is exhausted. She closes her eyes.*) How was it...for your grandmother?

JENNY: I think the memory loss was the worst part, for her and for me. She thought the nurse's aides were her daughters. Once when I went to visit, two of them were helping her pick out the earrings she was going to wear that day. She had about five pairs spread out on the sheet, and they were talking as seriously as if she had been getting ready for a night at the opera. (*A beat.*) Sometimes she would make me sit right in front of her and hold my face in her hands and look real hard. (*A beat.*) Sometimes she would remember that I was her granddaughter. Sometimes she could remember my name, but all of that went after awhile.

ALICE: What did they decide?

JENNY: Decide about what?

ALICE: The earrings.

JENNY: A pair of carved gold hoops with ram's heads. They were so heavy they pulled her earlobes down long. Stretched them out like a Watusi woman. She laughed when they held up a mirror so she could see herself. "There now," she said. "That's better."

ALICE: I gave her those.

JENNY: I wondered what she was doing with earrings like that.

ALICE: She used to tell me that the only women who wore big gold hoops in their ears were gypsies or prostitutes.

JENNY: She kept tossing her head so they would bump against her neck. The were very beautiful.

ALICE: When I sent them, I wrote and told her she was too prim ever to be mistaken for a gypsy and too old to be mistaken for a prostitute, so I thought it was safe for her to wear them. She wrote me back and said she was still my mother, and some things didn't change.

JENNY: God! I wish I knew what those things were!

ALICE (*sarcastic, but gently*): Oh, you know, Sister. The right way and the wrong way of doing things. What makes a "lady" and what does not.

JENNY (*finds the record*): Well, here's the only Lady that matters...in full gardenia!

ALICE: Don't play that now!

JENNY: Why not? (ALICE *does not respond. A beat.*) When she died, the paper said it was a drug overdose, and you were furious. You told me it wasn't the drugs that killed her. She died because she had to feel everything. Every time. You said nobody could live that way. Not for long.

ALICE: I was wrong, Sister. It's the only way you can tell you're still alive. (*A beat.*) Your father never liked Billie Holiday.

JENNY: I know. He said she made him feel lonesome.

ALICE: He wasn't the only one. You know she had a song that they made them stop playing on the radio because every time they did, the suicide rate in the city would go through the ceiling.

JENNY: Which one was that?

ALICE: "Gloomy Monday." Is it on there?

JENNY (*checks the label*): Yep.

ALICE: Well, don't play it! Lord knows we don't need any additional depression around here.

JENNY: What do you want to hear?

ALICE: How about a poem or two?

JENNY (*startled, covering*): I'm a journalist. You're the poet, remember?

ALICE: There's no journalist in the world who gets up at six in the morning to work. Journalists work late at night. Poets work at dawn. Don't fool yourself.

JENNY: That's the second time you've said that this morning.

ALICE: If I say it three times, believe me. That probably means it's good advice.

JENNY (*hesitantly*): Well, I have been working on something new.

ALICE (*raising eyebrow*): You're writing poems now?

JENNY (*nervously, fingering the pages*): Well...sometime...I hardly ever show them to anybody though. They can't help comparing mine to yours. (*She laughs ruefully.*) You're a hard act to follow.

ALICE: Then don't try it. And on second thought, don't read anything to me either. If I'm a tough act, I'm probably an impossible audience. Where's Butterfly?

JENNY (*disappointed*): Again?

ALICE: Indulge me. If you're going to stay and keep watch at my death bed, the least you can do is indulge me.

JENNY: I should have told that kid Puccini ran through my life like a leit motiv.

ALICE: No. That would only have added insult to injury.

JENNY: I used to be so embarrassed when you played this stuff.

ALICE: You have no shame about being the unwed mother of a fatherless child, and you were embarrassed at lovely Leontyne singing "Un Bel Di?"

JENNY: She has a father. Besides, you have to admit the Puccini was not exactly the dominant musical influence in our neighborhood. Our driveway was the only place where you had to be careful or you might get hit by a blast of "La Boheme" in the middle of a serious handball game. Everybody else was playing The Supremes! (*Laughing at the memory.*) I remember one day I was trying to get you to at least turn it down a little, and you made me listen to "Un Bel Di" all the way through. You told me to see if I could hear the same thing in it that made me love Smokey Robinson. You said forget about Italians and operas and just try to hear the passion.

ALICE: You looked at me like I was crazy, but you closed your eyes and listened. (*A beat.*) Ten years old...trying to hear the passion.

JENNY: I used your analogy a couple of weeks later when Dwan Johnson asked me what was playing at our house. I told him it was "Un Bel Di," and when he asked what it meant, I said, "one fine day." And he said, oh yeah? Just like the Chiffons!

ALICE (*laughs gingerly*): You know I hate the idea of taking these damn pills, but they do help.

JENNY (*a beat*): You know, when I got to college half the girls in my dorm had your books. It was a weird feeling. I had never seen them before, and they would come up to me and ask me about you. It was like some of them knew more about you than I did!

ALICE (*a beat*): I guess I should eat something.

JENNY: What would you like?

ALICE: There's some jello in there, I think. (*She shudders at the thought.*)

JENNY: How about some soup?

ALICE: I don't think so.

JENNY: It's just broth. I don't think it will upset your stomach.

ALICE: Maybe later. It's bad enough to be babbling like this without being nauseated too!

JENNY: There should be something in there that will appeal to you. Let me take a look. I'll put this on to entertain you while I'm gone.

ALICE: I don't want to be entertained. That's what I've been trying to tell you!

JENNY: Alright, alright. I stand corrected.

ALICE: Oh, hell. What's the difference? (JENNY *sets the record on and exits to the kitchen. It is "In My Solitude." ALICE winces a little in pain now that she is alone, but she quickly straightens and takes several more pills rapidly.*)

JENNY (*calling from the kitchen*): I've got some plain yogurt too. What do you think? (ALICE *leans back listening, eyes closed. She reaches out to touch the beautiful roses. JENNY enters with a small tray. She has to balance it precariously on the pile of stuff already on the coffee table. She fusses over the food until the song ends.*) If I thought taking heroin could make me sing like that, I'd be a junkie with no regrets.

ALICE: You can't sing like that without some regrets, Sister. Don't you know that yet? You better put some sugar in these roses.

JENNY: Sugar? Why?

ALICE: Flowers always live longer if you put some sugar in the water.

JENNY: I guess everything does better with a little sweetening.

ALICE: The woman who told me that was a fiend for roses. She was beautiful, and her boyfriends always sent her roses. Red only! Her apartment was full of them. The scent would choke you when you went to see her. She had so many roses she used to float their petals on her bath water.

JENNY: I tried that once. It sounds beautiful, but it feels like a tub full of hot, sticky rose petals.

ALICE: You know, this place looks very different.

JENNY: It needed a lot of work. Renovations, repairs. I did most of it myself. It took longer than I thought it would. I made a lot of mistakes. Do you like it?

ALICE: I'm not sure yet. (*A beat.*) I sure went the long way around to end up sleeping in the house I was born in.

JENNY (*a beat*): I can't believe you're really here.

ALICE: That makes two of us, Sister. (*A beat.*) The quiet in this house used to be so strong it was a part of the conversation. Mother and Daddy were so calm about everything. They never raised their voices. (*A beat.*) I used to wonder if I was their natural child. I used to study them, looking for clues. They were so damn certain! (ALICE *closes her eyes and leans back.* JENNY *watches her and then suddenly has a contraction. She handles it calmly, blowing out for a few seconds Lamaze style.* ALICE *speaks without opening her eyes.*)

ALICE: You're not going to start that again, are you?

JENNY (*out of breath*): No. I'm going to pack. (*She begins putting things in the large suitcase near her desk.* ALICE *opens her eyes and watches.*)

ALICE: What all are you taking to the hospital, Sister?

JENNY (*laughing*): Not much. This is the only bag I have.

ALICE: I've got a carpetbag. Very bohemian. I guarantee there'll be nothing like it on the ward.

JENNY: Sounds wonderful. Where is it?

ALICE: Look upstairs.

(JENNY *goes upstairs and rummages around to find the carpetbag, still talking.*)

JENNY: I wish I had a bed jacket to take with me. I love those scenes in the movies where the new mother is always propped up on lace pillows in a pink satin bed jacket. (*As* JENNY *rummages and talks,* ALICE *rises stiffly and wanders rather aimlessly around the room. She stops to touch a picture frame here, a piece of furniture, but all very absently. She is not looking for anything. She is simply moving around restlessly. She moves to* JENNY's *desk and sees the two pages* JENNY *was working on this morning. She picks up the pages slowly and reads a little. Upstairs,* JENNY *finds the carpetbag and opens it to look inside.*) They don't hardly make bed jackets like that anymore. I guess they...(*She seems to be surprised by what she sees and reaches in to withdraw a cheap wig. She realizes that* ALICE *may have worn it as a concession to vanity when her hair started to fall out.* JENNY *is embarrassed to have found it.* ALICE *is aware that* JENNY *has stopped in mid-sentence. She breaks off her reading and looks upstairs.* JENNY *puts the wig back in the closet and starts talking again nervously, coming downstairs.*) I always like that scene in "The Women" where Joan Crawford and Norma Sherer are getting ready to have it out and the store lingerie model keeps sweeping through saying "Try our new one-piece foundation. Zips up the back and no bones."

ALICE (*watches* JENNY *with irritation as she crosses to sit down again, wincing slightly*): I don't care, you know?

JENNY: About what?

ALICE: About what you think. About your crude efforts to capture my madcap phase in your schoolgirl poetry. Hardly a fitting memorial. (*A beat.*) It just doesn't matter, Sister. Can't you see that?

JENNY (*stung and hurt*): What does matter to you?

ALICE: My own heartbeat. The way my blood feels rushing through my veins. The parts of my body that are going to start hurting again in a few minutes. All of that matters. (ALICE *winces, and* JENNY *moves toward her.*)

JENNY: Are you okay?

ALICE: Stop asking me that! I'm not anywhere in the vicinity of okay, and I'm not going to be for the rest of the time you know me. (ALICE *leans back and takes a pill wearily.* JENNY *has retreated and started transferring her things from her big bag to the carpetbag. She realizes there is still something in it. She withdraws a small packet of things: papers, photographs, etc., bound up with string.*)

JENNY (*cautiously, but curious*): What's this?

ALICE (*wearily*): What?

JENNY: All this "stuff"? (JENNY *hands the packet to* ALICE *who holds it delicately in her hands.*)

ALICE: Some old photographs. A poem or two. Your father's letters.

JENNY (*startled*): He wrote you?

ALICE: Yes.

JENNY (*surprised*): When?

ALICE: For years.

JENNY: He never showed me your letters!

ALICE: I didn't say that I wrote to him. I said he wrote to me.

JENNY: You never wrote back?

ALICE: No.

JENNY: Not once?

ALICE: Not once. If I had had anything left to say to your father, I wouldn't have been in Paris.

JENNY: How long did he write to you?

ALICE: I told you for years.

JENNY: But how many? How many years?

ALICE: Until he died.

JENNY: Where are the rest of them?

ALICE: I burned them.

JENNY: You burned them? God! Don't you ever think about anybody but yourself? You could have given them to me!

ALICE: He asked me to burn them! Besides, they were my letters. Nobody else's.

(JENNY *knowing this is true, but still hurt by the secret, turns away.*)

JENNY: What did he say about me?

ALICE: He never wrote about you. When I left he told me he wanted to write to me. I told him he could, but not to expect answers to his letters and that if he ever referred to you in any way, I would never open another letter that he sent to me.

JENNY: And he believed you?

ALICE: That's a child's question, Sister. Children can never imagine that their parents could sustain exchanges of over five seconds without discussing them. (JENNY *turns away, and* ALICE *begins to talk almost to herself.*) He wrote about almost everything. Books and politics. Gossip about people we knew and what they were doing. What he was thinking; ideas.

JENNY: He used to talk to me like that, too. Sometimes I felt like listening to Daddy talking was as close as words could ever hope to get to being music. He could start off with Langston Hughes, move to Stokely Carmichael, swoop down long enough to touch on whoever I fancied myself to be in love with at the time and finish up with Duke Ellington without ever taking a breath.

ALICE: He wrote me when Malcolm was shot down. He must have sensed how hard it was to be in Paris then. When something like that happens, you want to be around your own. It seemed like we all heard the news at the same time. We ended up gathering at the cafe where we spent half our lives, crying in our Pernod and trying not to feel so black and helpless and far away from home. But then we looked up the street and here comes this young brother who we know works at the American Embassy. That's all we knew about him because he never hung around with us, but here he comes in his dark blue, pin-striped suit with a step ladder under his arm.

JENNY: A step ladder?

ALICE: He walked right up in front of the cafe, opened the thing up and cleared his throat. Speaking the most perfect, diplomatic corps French, he invited us to express ourselves on the death of "our shining black prince." Then he stepped about halfway up that ladder, left the flawless French behind, and told us in good old Southside Chicago English how his heart was broken by what he had heard happened in the Audobon Ballroom. When he got done, somebody else got up and talked about hearing Malcolm at the Temple in Detroit, way back when, and I told about another meeting where he brought us all to our feet. Everybody had a memory of the man. (*A beat.*) We must have been there a couple of hours. When everybody had had their say, the young brother from the Embassy thanked us, folded up his ladder, and went on up the street.

JENNY: What was his name?

ALICE: I don't remember. I don't think I ever knew, really. He killed himself...

JENNY (*distracting* ALICE *from death*): What about pictures?

ALICE (*bemused*): Just some ancient snaps of the ex-patriot colored poetess in her prime. (*She hands the photos to* JENNY *who looks through them eagerly.*)

JENNY: Look at that dress! You look wonderful! Where were you going?

ALICE: Who knows? We are always...(*She catches herself suddenly, suspicious of being so unguarded.*) When are you planning to have this baby anyway?

JENNY: Any minute now!

ALICE: I want you to make other arrangements for after she is born.

JENNY: What?

ALICE: I don't want you to bring her back here. I don't want to see her.

JENNY: Not at all?

ALICE: No. Not at all.

JENNY: She's your granddaughter!

ALICE: We've been all through this, Sister. Why don't you just go home?

JENNY: This is home!

ALICE: Why don't you go to where home was before this was home?

JENNY: Because I can't.

ALICE: There's a big difference between can't and won't.

JENNY: Yes. I know. (*Picking up the snapshots again, hoping to resume the conversation.*) Who were you playing here?

ALICE: Probably a cross between Josephine Baker and Anais Nin. I had a lover who loved my "leetle 'ead." He had a lot of money, and it amused him to keep a black American poet. Poetess! That was the phase when I started calling myself Simone and wrapping my head round and around with silver ribbons. (*A beat. She looks at the photo.*) They told me my hair was going to fall out when they started the chemotherapy. They explain everything to sick people, you know, so we won't be surprised when the awful things that are going to happen actually start happening. They explain everything as they take you into those little dark rooms and sit you down. Then they ask you if you've got any more questions, and since they've just described the horrors of hell to you, you probably don't want to hear any more, so you say no, thank you. Then they ease the needles into your arm so that the poison can drip into you for an hour or so, and that's it. Sometimes you feel okay. A little weak, but pretty good. You might even eat something, which is usually a mistake because then you start throwing up. And your hair starts falling out, and pretty soon they tell you it didn't work, and you've

still got the cancer, and they're real sorry about...your...hair. (*A beat.*)
He used to love to rub my head, this European fool. I told him that
in the United States, black folks didn't tolerate white folks rubbing
their heads because we knew they thought it gave them good luck
and we needed all our good luck for our damn selves. He just
laughed. He didn't know what I was talking about. "You have such
a perfectly shaped leetle 'ead," he used to tell me. "Such a leetle
'ead."

JENNY: I shaved my head once.

ALICE: Bald?

JENNY: Completely.

ALICE: If there isn't a good story associated with that kind of
madness, there is no excuse for it.

JENNY: It's not much of a story at all really. It was during a time
when all the white girls at school were ironing their hair, morning,
noon and night. You couldn't walk into the laundry room without
bumping into Mary Jo or Susie Q. in their drawers with their hair
thrown over the ironing boards.

ALICE: Why didn't you tell them about Madame Walker and her
straightening comb?

JENNY: They weren't interested. I think in some weird way they
thought the ironing board thing was some kind of ethnic beauty
secret.

ALICE: Ethnic, maybe. But not black. There aren't enough of us
with hair long enough to throw across an ironing board.

JENNY: After a couple of months, things moved from fad to
fetish. All anybody talked about was ironing hair. The best temp-
eratures to use. The advantage of steam over no steam. Techniques
to do it yourself and tips on doing with a friend. It was silly, but it
started to get on my nerves. One day at dinner, I told them all I
thought hair - ironed or otherwise - was the most boring subject in
the world and to prove it I was going upstairs and shave all of mine
off. And I did.

ALICE: How did you like it?

JENNY: The look or the feeling?

ALICE: Both.

JENNY: It felt great. Cool and strange. Sensual. The look took
some getting used to, though.

ALICE: My Frenchman would have loved you! "Such a lovely leetle 'ead!"

JENNY: I liked what it did to those girls though. It made them keep their distance. They were intimidated by whatever it was that made me do it.

ALICE: Ordinary people often mistake courage for insanity. It frightens them. (*A beat.*) What did your father say?

JENNY: He never saw it completely bald. It had grown in some before I went home. It was still too short to suit him though. He looked at me real hard and then he said, "I don't think you've got the face for it."

ALICE: Your father never was one for the avant garde.

JENNY (*pulls some other papers from the packet*): What are these?

ALICE: Poems, Sister. Those are the poems. (*A beat.*) You recognize a poem when you see one, don't you?

JENNY: Can I read them?

ALICE: I should have burned them, too.

JENNY: Why?

ALICE: Because some things are better left unsaid.

JENNY: Are they about Daddy?

ALICE: Yes.

JENNY: All of them?

ALICE: Yes, Sister. They are all about Daddy. (*A beat.*) I was so young when I met your father that he was not just the only man I'd ever slept with, he was the only man I'd ever fantasized about. He was very gentle with me. Very tender. He knew I was a very young girl. He had been a man out in the world longer than I had been alive!

JENNY: "A man out in the world..." Listen to how old-fashioned that sounds!

ALICE: Those were different times. Black folks were a little more prim in the fifties just like white folks. Besides, I was only seventeen. I graduated from high school on Wednesday and married your father in the sanctuary of Plymouth Church on Friday night.

JENNY: Daddy said you looked so young to him when he looked into your face to say his vows that he was afraid you had lied and he was marrying a child.

ALICE: When we first got married, I used to write two or three serious love poems everyday. I used to write them on little tiny pieces of paper and put them under his pillow. Whenever he reached under there and found one, I'd read it to him. One night, I told him I wanted to send one of them to a magazine and he ate it!

JENNY: He did what?

ALICE: He ate it. Rolled it up in a little ball, popped it in his mouth, chewed a couple of times, and swallowed it right down.

JENNY: Was it your only copy?

ALICE: That's hardly the point, Sister. He told me those poems were a gift from me to him. He said my words went all down inside him and made him stronger. So I said, that's all very fine, but why did you eat my poem? And he just laughed and said, so the white folks wouldn't get it.

JENNY: Is that when you stopped writing them?

ALICE: No. I wrote them for awhile after that. I just had to memorize them, too. I didn't stop writing them until you were born. Then I didn't have...time. (*A beat.*) You want to know what I learned in Paris? Almost twenty years abroad and you know what I learned, Sister? (*She does not give* JENNY *a chance to respond.*) I learned that my name is Alice and not Simone and that the Left Bank is not as far from the West Side of Detroit as I was hoping it would be.

JENNY: It was as far away as another planet to me.

ALICE (*a beat*): I just don't have the energy to figure out what you need to know and tell it to you, Sister. I don't have enough time, and I won't pretend that I do.

JENNY: You never would pretend. Even when it hurt to tell the truth.

ALICE: It hurt you. It hurt me to lie.

JENNY: To lie about <u>what</u>?

ALICE: There was a voice screaming inside my head, Sister. After awhile, the only thing that mattered was to make her stop shouting.

JENNY: Did she tell you to go to Paris?

ALICE: She told me to go!

JENNY: Did she tell you not to take me with you?

ALICE: She never considered you at all.

JENNY (*recoils from this statement, but is silent for a moment. She stares at* ALICE): Is it such a crime? To want to know the things your mother knows?

ALICE: And what if I tell you that I don't know anything at all? What if I tell you that running around Europe playing the exotic...playing god knows what...What if I told you it didn't teach me a damn thing?

JENNY: I wouldn't believe you.

ALICE: Now you do sound like your father. Confront the man directly with an unassailable truth - a provable reality - and he would look calmly into your face and say, "I don't believe you."

JENNY: There's more than one reality.

ALICE: Multiple truths? No. Multiple fantasy, but only one truth.

JENNY: You're making this so hard on me.

ALICE: Join the club. Membership is absolutely voluntary.

JENNY: Even now, you just can't let it go, can you?

ALICE: Let what go? You're talking movie-speak again. Hollywood alone has created the myth of a secret guilt that torments the dying. Forget it, Sister. I let it go. I let it all go. Your father...the poems...

JENNY: Well, that's nothing new, is it?

ALICE: That's what I've been trying to tell you.

JENNY: I just...

ALICE (*interrupting angrily*): ...you just decided to leave your husband or your lover or your friend and move into your grandmother's house to have a baby, and you liked the whole idea so much you couldn't drag yourself away even when your long lost decaying mother arrived at the door? Give up, Sister! That sepia-tone photograph you've been carrying around in your head for twenty years hasn't got anything to do with me. I wasn't that way then, and I'm not that way now.

JENNY: You don't want to know anything about me at all. You've already drawn your own conclusions.

ALICE: I have drawn no conclusions. I have made no judgements. You are free to do whatever you please.

JENNY: At what price?

ALICE: We all have to pay for something.

JENNY: Why can't you just be my mother for once and not some world-weary, wisecracking, black caricature of a cynical ex-patriot?

ALICE: I am being your mother. This is what your mother is, Sister. A world-weary, wisecracking, black caricature of a cynical ex-patriot.

JENNY (*quietly*): That is not the answer.

ALICE: Don't try for answers, Sister. You don't even understand the questions.

JENNY: That's where you're wrong!

ALICE: Am I?

JENNY: Yes, you are. I understand all the questions. Every single one. (*A beat.*) Right after you left, Daddy sent me away to boarding school. He thought I needed...I don't know...stability, safety. There had been bombings, threats on his life. So he sent me off to Massachusetts where I'd be safe. I knew he was doing the best he could, so I didn't tell him how much I hated it. I thought that if he really loved me, he would know. Somehow, he would feel it and come and get me. (*A beat.*) But he never did. (*A beat.*) That's one of the questions, isn't it? How come people that love you can't read your mind?

ALICE: Why should they?

JENNY: So that they can love you better!

ALICE: There is no better or worse, Sister. You either do or you don't.

JENNY: You make choices.

ALICE (*outraged*): Choices? Okay, Sister. Take a look! My parting gift to you is a close-up look at the end result of all those choices you're talking about with such enthusiasm. Choices? Take a good, long look at me, and save your reaction to this terrible truth for the labor room. You can scream about the injustice of it all in there, and nobody will pay you the slightest bit of mind. All the ladies do it. They'll never know that your screaming is different. That yours isn't about the pain of your bones separating to let your daughter out. That yours is about the presence of injustice in the world! They'll never suspect a thing. And it doesn't really matter anyway. In spite of their feigned interest, nobody else really gives a damn if you do your birthing and your living and your dying well, or if you shriek and holler and cling to the nurse's arm.

JENNY: You left me?

ALICE: I did not see my future as the dedicated wife of the charismatic leader, dabbling in a little poetry, being indulged at cultural conferences and urged to read that one about the beautiful brothers and sisters in Soweto, or Watts, or Montgomery, Alabama. I just couldn't be that. The world is bigger than that. The world inside my head is bigger than that. Even now...I used to watch your father at rallies and in church on Sunday morning, and he'd be so strong and beautiful, it was all I could do to sit still and look prim in my pew. But he was committed to "the movement." He didn't have time anymore to lay in bed with me and improvise. I'd been a wife since I was seventeen, and here I was almost thirty, with a ten-year-old daughter, trying to convince your father to let me publish some love poems! But he couldn't. Or he wouldn't. The kind of love he had to give me now didn't allow for that. And I couldn't do without it. So I left. Not much of a story is it?

JENNY: I could have gone with you. I was old enough.

ALICE: I can tell you the day, the hour, the minute you were conceived. (*A beat.*) I couldn't stand to look at you. (*Changes her tone.*) And I'm selfish! You said it yourself. What was I going to do in Paris with a ten-year-old child? Besides, you were always more your father's child than you ever were mine.

JENNY: I didn't have much choice, did I?

ALICE: Neither did I, Sister. Neither did I. I've spent my life trying to heal a hurt I'm not supposed to have. I got so tired of being trapped inside that tiny little black box. No air, Sister. I couldn't get any air. Everybody was mad at somebody, or about something. (*A beat.*) My mother spent her life catching the bus downtown to The Anis Fur Company. Sitting there in that hot little back room sewing purple silk linings in rich white ladies sable coats. I went there with her once when I was little. There must have been thirty black women in a room smaller than this one. It was hot and dusty and close. I felt like I was smothering. (*A beat.*) No air, Sister. No goddamn air.

JENNY: Daddy never wanted that.

ALICE: No. He wanted exactly what I was looking for. A way out of that black box. It's just that I was prepared to admit defeat and let the white folks have this particular piece of ground since they wanted it so bad. But your father was different. He was not prepared to give an inch. He was always talking about survival, and I was always talking about love.

JENNY: You were happy once.

ALICE: But the moment passes, Sister.

JENNY: Does that mean it never happened?

ALICE: It means most of the time nobody's even listening.

JENNY: I was listening.

ALICE (*angry*): For what? So you could make up schoolgirl fairy tales about my exotic existence? So you could record my tragic demise for posterity? (*She picks up the poetry and waves it at* JENNY.) Read it to me, why don't you? No? Okay! I'll read it to you then. I used to be good at this. "Pretend it's Paris." (*Her voice is totally sarcastic.*) "For mother..."

JENNY: Don't! (JENNY *grabs the poem away and crumbles it in her hand.* ALICE *smiles cruelly.*)

ALICE: You're not a poet, Sister. You're a runner. Don't you even understand that? There are people who are runners, Sister. Runners who spend their whole life in flight. Sometimes the speed may have a kind of flash to it - a certain style - but in the end, it's nothing but a hard, scared run, and you end up somewhere panting and hurting and babbling over your shoulder into the dark. (ALICE *turns her back to* JENNY. *She is spent.* JENNY *speaks slowly but with confidence. Something in her tone makes* ALICE *turn as she speaks.*)

JENNY:
"you ration yourself out
like there was a war on.
In Paris, the soldiers threw
chocolate bars and silk stockings.
some people saved the sweets
and hid the stockings in a bureau drawer.
safe and sound.
not me. i was the one
in my stocking feet
with chocolate smeared
across my smile
dancin' and grinnin'
unsafe/unsound/undone.
there's more i can give
if there's more you can take.
the only thing
i wanna do
is make love
and drink champagne
in the middle of the day
and in the middle of the night

and sometimes in the morning
i am the one
in my stocking feet
with chocolate smeared
across my smile
dancin' and grinnin'
i am the one.
oh, yes, i am the one.
close your eyes.
take a deep breath.
pretend it's Paris.
pretend it's Paris.
pretend it's Paris...
(*They look at each other for a long moment.*)
ALICE (*quietly*): It's too late to be sorry, Sister, but I...
JENNY (*stops her*): Sometimes the love is enough. When it's all you've got. Sometimes just the possibility is enough. And we don't have to explain it. We just have to be here together and try. We only have to try! (*A beat.*) All I ever wanted to tell you was that I understood. I think I always understood.
(JENNY *and* ALICE *look straight at each other in silence.* JENNY *moves to* ALICE, *but then stops and winces slightly. She puts her hands to her stomach lightly, breathing through her mouth.*)
ALICE: What is it?
JENNY (*panting a little*): Contractions! I'd better call Alexis. (JENNY *goes to the phone and dials quickly.* ALICE *slowly picks up the crumbled pages of the poem, smoothing them carefully as* JENNY *speaks.*) Alexis? I think it's ...Yes. Pretty strong...Okay. I'll be ready. (*She hangs up.*) She's going to come by and pick me up.
(*They look at each other.* ALICE *touches* JENNY's *cheek lightly.*)
ALICE: I think when I married your father so young, my mother was afraid she wouldn't have time to get all the women lessons in before I was gone.
JENNY: Did she?
ALICE: She told me what she knew. I guess that's the best anybody can do. (*Suddenly.*) Forgive me, Sister. I did what I could.
(*They embrace each other very gently. Alexis' car horn blows outside.*)
ALICE (*breaking the embrace and urging* JENNY *to the door*): Don't try to be brave now, Sister. Scream as loud as you want.

JENNY (*stops at the door and looks back at* ALICE): I love you, Mamma.

ALICE: And I was always some place loving you, Baby. I was always some place loving you. (JENNY *exits.* ALICE *sits down slowly in the rocking chair. She looks down slowly at the poem in her hand and all the energy seems to leave her body. She drops the pages to the floor.*) Don't fool yourself, Miss Alice. Just don't fool yourself.

(*Lights go down slowly.* ALICE *remains in a blue spot in the dark and then it also fades.* BLACK.)

Konvergence

by P.J. GIBSON

Ms. P.J. Gibson holds a M.F.A. degree in Theatre Arts from Brandeis University and a B.A. degree in Drama, Religion and English from Keuka College.

Ms. Gibson was born in Pittsburgh, Pennsylvania and raised in Trenton, New Jersey. At the age of fourteen she became the student of J.P. Miller, author of *The Days Of Wine And Roses*. Ms. Gibson was awarded a Shubert Fellowship to study dramatic writing at Brandeis University. Her mentors have been Don Peterson, author of Broadway's *Does A Tiger Wear A Necktie?* and Israel Horovitz, author of *Indian Wants The Bronx* and *Author, Author*. She has been the recipient of numerous playwriting awards, including two prestigious Audelco Awards and a National Endowment for the Arts grant for playwrighting. She is a prolific writer, with twenty-four plays to her credit, and an abundance of poetry and short stories. Her works have been produced throughout the United States, Europe and Africa. Ms. Gibson's skills have led to several writing commissions. These opportunities led to a fine and productive working relationship between academia and the arts. This is an area of interest for Ms. Gibson who has taught on the university level for many years. She also teaches Creative Writing and related writing workshops to community organizations and penal institutions. Ms. Gibson's published works include " Long Time Since Yesterday" and "Brown Silk And Magenta Sunsets" in *9 Plays By Black Women*.

CAST:

DEREK - *Black man of thirty. Local politician; fashionable dresser of quality.*
NANYEL* - *Black woman of twenty-eight. Extremely fashionable dresser.*
Both characters are upward mobile oriented.

* Pronunciation: Nanyel - Non-yel, Nani - Noni

TIME: *Spring, late 1970's.*
SCENE: *Interior of vacation lodge in mountainous area. The lodge is rustic, accentuated by exposed wood. Its shades are those of earth tones.*

The playing area is that of living and dining rooms. Necessary items are those of sofa, bar, counter, and bar stools.

(*At rise of curtain,* DEREK, *man of thirty, places bottle of wine in refrigerator beneath counter. He reads note left with bottle of champagne. He sits focusing in on door. Enter* NANYEL *with luggage, wearing lightweight, all-weather coat. She stops upon noticing* DEREK.)

DEREK: Nani. (*Pause.*)

NANYEL (*direct*): Derek.

DEREK: You look good.

NANYEL (*dispenses with luggage and coat*): Thank you. (*Pause.*) You too, you look good.

(*Silence.*)

DEREK: Well, here we are.

NANYEL: Yes, here we are. (*Observes surroundings.*) Makes for a strange meeting, our being here. (*Pause.*) A year to the date. (*Pause.*) It looks the same, the place. (*Moves about lodge.*) You know, Jewel has no flair for adventure. She could at least rearrange things a little. And she's a pack rat. (*Indicates lodge. Leafs through magazines.*) I left this here last year. (*Holds up magazine.*)

DEREK: Why are you attacking Jewel?

NANYEL: I'm not attacking Jewel. It's this place; your sister-in-law keeps it like a museum.

DEREK: <u>My</u> sister-in-law.

NANYEL: She's your brother's wife. (*Quickly.*) Why are you doing that?

DEREK: Doing what?

NANYEL: Staring?

DEREK: Was I staring?

NANYEL: Yes, Derek, you were staring.

DEREK: Is there something wrong in looking at a beautiful woman?

NANYEL (*quickly*): That was a nice spread they did on your project.

DEREK: Thank you.

NANYEL (*talk sings*): "You can take Derek out of the ghetto, but you can't take the ghetto out of D.J." It's paying off. Seems the people are beginning to trust you.

DEREK: Some.

NANYEL: Derek the politician.

DEREK: Big Momma told me about your new position.

NANYEL: Umm, she told me.

DEREK: Like it? (NANYEL *nods "yes" and spins, modeling her attire.*) A real nine to fiver

NANYEL: Nine to five.

DEREK: I never thought of you as an administrator.

NANYEL: One among many you never thought of concerning Nanyel. Did you think I would play the blue jean save the community routine forever?

DEREK: What are you angry about Nani?

NANYEL: Angry? Who's angry? (*Pause.*) Tell me, who took my place in the door-to-door polling process?

DEREK: That's a low shot Nani.

NANYEL: Why? It's true.

DEREK: It implies you were primarily concerned with my career.

NANYEL: Remember, you said it. (NANYEL *crosses to refrigerator and brings up bottle of champagne.*) You?

DEREK: Jewel and Ron, they left a note.

NANYEL (*reads note*): Derek, stop staring.

DEREK: You've changed.

NANYEL: Some. (*Quickly.*) Will you stop doing that?

DEREK: Nani, it's been a year.

NANYEL: I know it's been a year. I was also a part of that year, remember? (*Crosses to window. Silence.*) It would have to rain. (*Silence.*) Silence, that's a new thing for you.

DEREK: People change.

NANYEL: People change. (*Pause.*) I take it the year must have been beneficial for you.

DEREK: You could say so.

NANYEL: That's good, considering that was the intention. (*Pause.*) Oh, thank you for the flowers and cards. I didn't know we could acknowledge birthdays.

DEREK: Nani, twice I tried to contact you.

NANYEL (*sarcastic*): Just twice? Um...

DEREK: Twice I wrote. Twice the letters were returned <u>unopened</u>. I left messages, each time no response.

NANYEL: As I remember it, the agreement specifically stated no contact for an entire year.

DEREK: I know what the agreement said. Alright, I was rough around the edges then and...

NANYEL: By then you mean you're not now?

DEREK: At least not consciously.

NANYEL: I see you're still careful in the way you phrase things.

DEREK: Nani, how long are we going to continue this?

NANYEL: Continue what?

DEREK: We're not strangers.

NANYEL: We're not? Are you sure? Or hadn't you considered that occurring when you concocted the idea. You do remember it don't you? Hum? You came up with this "fantastic" idea. (*Sarcastic.*) "We'll find ourselves." Together, but separate. You at point "A" and me at "B." Then a year later, to the day, we'd meet, same place, same station and hook it all up again. Providing, that is, that neither one of us changes too radically during our Siberian separation. Providing, that is, neither one of us falls in or out of love with ourselves or someone else. (*Pause.*) "Ourselves or someone else." I was in love with you Derek, who was that phrase for? No, you left me. Call it an idea, an agreement, whatever. You left me.

DEREK: I didn't leave you.

NANYEL: No?

DEREK: No.

NANYEL: Oh excuse me, it seems I'm not fully comprehending what actually happened. You didn't leave me?

DEREK: No. Nani, why are you making this dramatic?

NANYEL: I'm making this dramatic?! You leave me, our marriage for a year's sabbatical and you tell me I'm being dramatic? Derek, you...are...too...much.

DEREK: I needed to get some air, space to breathe.

NANYEL: To breathe, meaning I was stifling you.

DEREK: In a sense, yes.

NANYEL: How?

DEREK: By coming at me from all directions. (*Quickly.*) Don't look at me like that. You were closing in on me.

NANYEL: Closing in on you.

DEREK: Closing in and evaluating everything I did. I looked up and it seemed I couldn't do not one damn thing to please you.

NANYEL: So you accuse me of playing judge and jury.

DEREK: It felt that way. Nani, do you know what it was like then? Do you? I took a look at myself. There I was, young, intelligent, handsome...

NANYEL: Oh, your conceit.

DEREK: I'll overlook that.

NANYEL: Oh, by all means don't.

DEREK: You know, things didn't come easy for me...

NANYEL: They came easy for me? Be original Derek.

DEREK: Nani, you've got to understand how things were. Things were finally, finally beginning to take shape, solidify. I wasn't Big J's little boy anymore. I wasn't accountable to some institution's rules. I was my own free agent to make decisions for and about me.

NANYEL: And...

DEREK: And it seemed every, not some, but every decision I set into motion set something off in you.

NANYEL: That's not true.

DEREK: No?

NANYEL: No. (*Quickly.*) How?

DEREK: It was your eyes, always studying and evaluating me. You never once let up. In the middle of the night you'd lay there staring at the ceiling contemplating whether or not you'd voice your opinion about the "Changing Derek."

NANYEL: You were changing.

DEREK: I know I was changing. I didn't need to hear that from you.

NANYEL: No? Then tell me, what exactly were you to hear from me? We were suppose to have been two people in love who cared about each other. What was I suppose to do, sit by and let you become another chocolate-covered android of the system?

DEREK: You see, that's what I'm talking about.

NANYEL: What?

DEREK: "Chocolate-covered android." Just listen to that kind of thinking, android. Changing, yeah I was changing. You damn well better change if you want to live in this hell as system. And Nani, I want to live. You understand?

NANYEL: Your kind of rationale? No.

DEREK: Nani, ain't none of that rhetoric about justice true, you know? They say, "Go to school young Black man, and a prosperous future awaits you." For whom? I was out there bustin' my brains so I wouldn't have to break my back the rest of my life and what did I get from you? Disapproval. You were draining me.

NANYEL: Draining you. How, Derek, was I draining you?

DEREK: Making things claustrophobic. I was meeting that monster head on everyday. Waging a war, equipped with a zip gun, facing nuclear power and what did I get from you? "You can't afford to lose your sensitivity."

NANYEL: You couldn't and still can't.

DEREK: No?

NANYEL: No Derek, you can't.

DEREK: Nani, that's theoretics you're talking, and I'm talking about life. I'm not reading this from some book. I'm dealing in this madness and catching hell. I catch hell with the people, you know, our people.

(*Imitates street man.*) "Hey man, what you tryin' to prove to the folks uptown? We know you got that expensive alarm system. How come you livin' down here braggin' 'bout your gains?" I'm in that damn system and I still catch hell.

(*Imitates white collar man.*) "I must say it's commendable you're living with your constituents." Commendable. Nani, that system is rancid. It ain't got a bit of morals, no conscience, nothing. It's eat or be eaten, and all I heard from you was "Don't forget to keep your sensitivity in the struggle."

NANYEL: So because the system has no morals, no conscience, and is dog eat dog, I was suppose to sit by and watch you amalgamate and say nothing?

DEREK: No, you were supposed to understand.

NANYEL: Oh, excuse me for not having the ability to understand, but you see I believe that joining that rat race, and giving up your innate sensitivity justifies and validates all the bullshit that's been written in those damn libraries about us. "Supposed to understand." No Derek, what you did split us up.

DEREK: What I was trying to do was make it.

NANYEL: Well we didn't make it. We ain't together. What kind of power do you have now, hum? What do you have when the man and the woman can't get together? What's it gonna mean? You can't hang in that battle forever. What are you going to have when the Great White God calls time out? What are you gonna do Derek, get another Mercedes with vanity plates? You're a big man in the city now, politically, top of your world, king on your throne. What's it all gonna mean in the end, hum? No, what I saw you doing was lose too much of your natural warmth and kindness.

DEREK: Nani, that warmth and kindness will not pay the bills. It is not an asset in that system. The lines on the page read equality, but it ain't there. It says freedom for all men, that ain't there. None of it's there, and my natural warmth, kindness and sensitivity ain't goin' to keep me alive. You understand?

NANYEL: Derek, I knew that system fucked with you. I wasn't blind nor deaf. I heard them.

DEREK: Then you should have understood what I had to do.

NANYEL: Imitation and assimilation.

DEREK: Imitation, sometimes.

NANYEL: Imitation of what? A white man's Babylon?

DEREK: It would be nice if life were sweet and pretty. It would be nice if we could sit everyone down once a week and quietly talk out problems, understanding that this week this person's id or ego went off, but it just doesn't work that way. Baby, the name of this thing is money and politics. That's it, two words, all the rest is window dressing. (*Quickly.*) I know you don't agree with me, but that's the way I perceive it. And Nani, I couldn't make it being that type of sensitive man you envisioned.

NANYEL: You act as though I wanted you to walk out there naked. I wanted to see you deal in that battle with everything, strategy, wit, arms, armor, tanks, whatever. All I asked was that you leave that white man's vicious hostility, his destruction, his distrust out there, outside the door, us.

DEREK: Do you know what that sounds like?

NANYEL: No, what?

DEREK: It's schizophrenic. You're saying I should cut myself on here and off there.

NANYEL: You did it with me.

DEREK: How?

NANYEL: Oh Derek, you clicked me right off. You were there and you weren't there, and that made me feel schiz. I felt like a case study for Freud. The personification of schizophrenia. You had my world coming and going in circles so fast sometimes late at night I used to jump up and ask myself, "Why am I on this masochistic, sadistic merry-go-round?" You'd tell me you "love" me. Fine. It's exemplified via hugs, kisses and making love.

DEREK: You made your point.

NANYEL: No I haven't made my point, and I won't let you discharge this as if this were some kind of a political statement you don't want to hear. This is now, here and real.

DEREK: Real? What do you know about "real," the reality of power and making it in this world? You just stepped into the real world. You've got no more safeguard stages of moving from mommy and daddy to the university to Derek. There's no more protective umbrellas to allow you to brainstorm. This is real. The equation to this thing is: callousness and viciousness equals success and power, not your sensitivity. At least not the way you perceive it.

NANYEL: That is your opinion.

DEREK: The system's. And like it or not, we live in this system, and a sure way to die is to believe in the rhetoric of justice and equality and hold on to that "sensitivity." It's not only schizophrenic, it's suicidal.

NANYEL: So, we're right back where we started.

DEREK: Not exactly.

NANYEL: Not exactly? What is this a draw?

DEREK: Can we, just for the moment, put the past behind us, the accusations and establish some kind of...

NANYEL: Of what?!! (*Calming.*) Derek, I used to visualize this meeting. I visualized it many times, many, many times. I'd enter that door. Relive last year, every painful detail, every word...And you know, no matter how many times I had that instant replay, I could never decide whether we greeted with a handshake, an embrace, a kiss...I couldn't get that part.

DEREK: What do you want to do? (*Crosses to her.*)

NANYEL: I don't know what I want to do.

DEREK: Then let it happen.

NANYEL: Let what happen? What's left to happen?

DEREK: Us.

NANYEL: "Us." How can you say that with a straight face? What "us," Derek? Did you honestly think we'd kiss, forgive and pick up on the good old days when Derek was D.J. and Nanyel was Nani? Hum?

DEREK: Can you say that you don't want to be close to me? Can you?

NANYEL: No I can't, but that doesn't mean I will. I want you just as much as you want me.

DEREK: Then why are we playing games with each other?

NANYEL: Derek, did you step out of your mind for a moment, or is it me? This isn't a game. That year's separation hurt.

DEREK: It wasn't meant to hurt you.

NANYEL: Fine, it wasn't meant to hurt, but it did. You can understand that. I'm sure you can imagine the number of nights I cried myself to sleep, the number of mornings I called in sick because my face and eyes were too swollen to face the world. You can understand that kind of pain, can't you? (*No response.*) "It wasn't meant to hurt..." You just turned my world inside out. I managed to make you such an integral part of my life that you completely fucked it up. Completely. (*Pause.*) To think of the number of affairs I cancelled because I didn't want to run into you and one of your dates.

DEREK: You were free to see men.

NANYEL (*Mimics*): "You were free..." You know how sick that sounds? Do you? You got right in the midst of your no morals, no ethics, rancid "<u>system</u>." "You were free to see other men." I was your wife. Did it ever occur to you that I didn't want to see any other men? That I didn't need any other men?

DEREK: You did agree to it.

NANYEL: Agreed?! You're damn real I agreed. Didn't have much choice as I remember it. Agree or not to agree.

DEREK: Alright.

NANYEL: Alright, what?

DEREK: Nani, this isn't easy for me either.

NANYEL: It isn't? It wasn't my idea, remember? (*Pause.*) Okay, fine, fine, we'll put the accusations behind us. We're two consenting adults converging at the scene of the crime. Okay Derek, you had your year...

DEREK: Our. We had our year.

NANYEL: For the betterment of the fact, "our." A year separate. (*Dramatically.*) "A year to find ourselves, separately."

DEREK: That wasn't cute Nani.

NANYEL: No? Neither was last year to me. I loved you D.J...

DEREK: Loved? That's the second time you've referred to the past tense.

NANYEL: <u>Loved</u>. Despite all that shit you had rolled up in you, I did. But don't expect Nani to continue the game by waving a wand, dismissing the past twelve months, calling a stalemate and continuing on as usual. That year's off process to find myself found me.

DEREK: Meaning?

NANYEL: Meaning my life is valuable to and for me now. That I've had time to evaluate a great many things and I've made some decisions, <u>on</u> <u>my</u> <u>own</u>, which have been advantageous to both myself and my profession.

DEREK: Myself and my profession?

NANYEL: Myself and my profession.

DEREK: What happened to the our?

NANYEL: Well Derek, you were right. I can't get to the "our" until I get to "me."

DEREK: What's happening to you?

NANYEL: What's happening? I'm growing.

DEREK: Meaning?

NANYEL: Meaning I've made some important decisions.

DEREK: Singularly?

NANYEL: Yes.

DEREK: Affecting?

NANYEL: Me.

DEREK: Us.

NANYEL: Indirectly.

DEREK: Nani, we're not talking about some people, couple on TV; we're talking about us. "Important decisions for me." We're supposed to be making some decisions about us. That was the agreement.

NANYEL: Agreement? Derek, fuck that agreement. In fact, fuck the whole facade. Like you said, "It ain't about 'us' and 'we,' it's about 'me' and 'I'."

DEREK: Can't a man change his...

NANYEL: Change your mind? For how long? Six, ten months? Just how long will it be before that brain of yours comes up with another idea? How long will it be before you tell me I can "see" other men to justify your desire to check out other women? Hum?

DEREK: You make it sound like I set up this thing so that I could bed hop for a year.

NANYEL: Frankly Derek, I don't know what you did.

DEREK: Well I didn't screw every woman I met.

NANYEL: No?

DEREK: No. In fact, I don't even have a desire to be with any other woman.

NANYEL: I'd assume not. You've had a year to come to that decision. Ugh, ugh Derek, count this lady out. Out as in O-U-T. No more. I'm hanging in here with the best of 'um. "Straight up, up front, get in there, get yours and retire at a nice, young age." Sound familiar?

DEREK: Nani, that "me" and "I" does not work.

NANYEL: Why? Because you say so? Have you done a political study on it?

DEREK: Because I know it.

NANYEL: Thank you Mr. Authority on the subject. The information has been recorded.

DEREK (*crosses to her*): Nani, please... (*She retreats to window. Silence.*) What's that supposed to mean?

NANYEL: It means...I should have never come. I should have phoned, telegrammed or something.

DEREK: To say what?

NANYEL: To say I cannot continue with the farce. This was truly a growing experience and thank you.

DEREK: And good-bye. (*No response.*) Just like that. Separation and then divorce.

NANYEL: That is the way it's done.

DEREK: Not for us.

NANYEL: Why? Because we started this off in an agreement? What did you expect? You know Derek, you were right. This ain't TV. That melodrama of a man and woman, after having been happily married five years, separated under the guise of "finding themselves" meet, a year later to the day, race into each others' arms and saunter off into the sunset, ain't going to happen. (*Break of thunder and lightening.*) Rain. (*Silence.*)

DEREK: You used to like rain. (*No response. NANYEL crosses to table, crumbles empty pack of cigarettes.*)

DEREK: Nervous?

NANYEL: No. (*Searches through her purse and retrieves another empty cigarette pack.*)

DEREK: Need a smoke?

NANYEL (*sarcastically*): No.

(*Break of thunder.*)

DEREK: Lake Road should be flooded by now.

NANYEL: No shit. (*Searches through luggage.*)

DEREK: You're sure you don't need a smoke?

NANYEL (*slow turn, stare, silence*): Do you have a smoke?

(DEREK *crosses to his luggage where he retrieves a carton of cigarettes. He opens pack, offers cigarette to* NANYEL *and lights it. Lights in lodge go out.*)

DEREK: Well, it seems Lake Road's flooded along with the power. (NANYEL *curls up on couch with cigarette.*) You know where Jewel keeps the candles? (*No response. He searches for candles.*) Nani? (*No response.*) You're not still afraid of thunder and the dark?

NANYEL: No, I am not afraid of...(*Softly.*) thunder and the dark.

DEREK: Then help me find the candles...Please. (*No response or movement.*) Nani? (NANYEL *drags deeply on cigarette to obtain light.*) You're still afraid of lightening, thunder and the dark.

NANYEL: I am not. (*Lights another cigarette and sits it on its filter.*)

DEREK: You're sure?

NANYEL: Positive.

DEREK: Where could she have hidden the candles? (DEREK *exits into adjacent room.* NANYEL *lights two additional cigarettes and sits them on their filters as though they were candles.*) Remember that black out April 13th? You got caught in the attic getting Big Momma's spring linen. We found you sitting in a circle of lit cigarettes. (DEREK *enters with two lit candles.* NANYEL *is seated on couch facing a semi-circle of lit cigarettes.*)

DEREK: You're not afraid?

NANYEL: No, I thought this was a cute idea.

DEREK: Sure. (DEREK *places candles on bar and table. He gives* NANYEL *a second pack of cigarettes.*) This one is to smoke.

NANYEL: You're full of laughs.

DEREK: While you were being "advantageous to myself and my profession" you should have also considered your phobias.

NANYEL: I'll work on them this year. (*Drags on cigarette.*) When'd you change brands? (*Indicates cigarettes.*)

DEREK: I didn't. They're for you. Big Momma told me you'd started smoking again, heavily.

NANYEL: Sometimes Big Momma talks too much.

(*Silence.*)

DEREK: I see you're wearing make up now.

NANYEL: Yes Derek, I wear make up now. I have also taken to polishing my toe nails. Would you care to hear more?

DEREK: Nani...What's wrong with you?...You know, you're just being hateful and rebellious.

NANYEL: I am? Well tell me, have you changed from politics to psychology?

DEREK: Alright.

NANYEL: Derek, don't alright me like I'm some kind of a child. You don't like what you see?

DEREK (*blows out candle*): I can't see anything. Come here.

NANYEL (*lights candle*): Well now you can see, in person. Although I am quite sure Big Momma filled you in on all the incidentals concerning Nanyel and the past year.

DEREK: Are you finished?

NANYEL: Finished what?

DEREK: Being evil for the purpose of pay backs.

NANYEL: I'll ignore that.

DEREK: Nani, how long are you going to keep this up? Why don't we just make the best of it, at least until the weather clears.

NANYEL: By best of it you mean touching, holding, kissing, making love and with a little of the D.J. charm everything will mellow out? Well not tonight sugar, not tonight.

(*Loud crack of thunder followed by lightening. Silence.*)

DEREK: Then why'd you come?

NANYEL: Why?

DEREK: Why'd you come? It wasn't to please me, or because it was a part of the agreement. I mean Nanyel, that was made very clear, your feelings concerning the agreement. What did you say, "Fuck the agreement,"? Why did you come? (*No response.*) Why did you come? (*Break of thunder. He touches her.*) You still have soft skin. (*She becomes taut.*) Relax Nani. (*Kisses her neck.*) I've been thinking about you and this moment for a long time. You're still a beautiful woman. (*No response.*) You were always good at choosing sensual fragrances. It's nice on you. (*Break of thunder. Tautness continues.*) Come on Nani, relax with me. (NANI *quickly rises. Strong cross to coat, luggage, purse and makes strong cross to door.*) Where are you going?

NANYEL: I'm leaving. I shouldn't have come here. I didn't, don't, won't believe in that sick ass agreement of yours and I shouldn't have come.

DEREK: So you're leaving.

NANYEL: I'm leaving.

DEREK: You'll wade your car through Lake Road, right?

NANYEL: No, I'll paddle.

DEREK: Thunder, lightning, storm and all, right?

(*Flash of lightning, crack of thunder.*)

NANYEL: Yes...Lightning, thunder and all. (*Pause. Gathers strength.*) Good-bye Derek, it was truly an...experience. (NANYEL *opens door. Elements of major spring storm rush through door. Lightning can be seen in distance. She remains fixed in door allowing elements to enter. She gets drenched. Silence. She closes door. Belongings still in hand, faces closed door, no movement.*) Piss.

(*Silence.*)

DEREK: A gift from the Gods?

NANYEL: I don't think that's funny.

DEREK: You look funny.

NANYEL (*sarcastic*): Do I?

DEREK (*crosses to her*): You do. (*Reaches for her bags.*) Here, let me help you with these.

NANYEL (*moves away with belongings*): I can do it myself.

DEREK: I know you can do it yourself. I wanted to help.

NANYEL: Well Derek, I don't need your help. (*Discards coat.*)

DEREK: You're soaked.

NANYEL: No shit. (*Discards wet shoes.*)

DEREK: Want my robe.

NANYEL: I packed a robe just like you packed a robe. Thank you, no. (NANYEL *crosses to adjacent room with luggage.*)

DEREK: You don't dress in front of me anymore?

NANYEL (*from adjacent room*): No.

DEREK (*crosses to refrigerator where he retrieves chilled bottle of wine*): And you're not afraid to dress all alone in there in the dark?

(*Break of thunder.* NANYEL *enters in an attempted controlled state. She is in the process of adjusting lounge wear. It is sensual, becoming, and must not be gaudy. It represents her upward mobility.*)

NANYEL: No.

DEREK: You're beautiful. (*No response. He pours wine and crosses with glass to* NANYEL.) You're really beautiful.

NANYEL: Thank you.

DEREK: For the wine or the compliment?

NANYEL: For the wine. (*She drinks.*)

DEREK: I missed you. (*Pause.*) Oh Nani, the times I wanted to call and didn't, wanted to ring your bell and didn't.

NANYEL: Why didn't you?

DEREK: I don't know. I wasn't ready. I guess I just wasn't ready.

NANYEL: And you are now.

DEREK: I think so. Yes, I think so.

NANYEL: Ready. Ready to make sweet, gentle, passionate love, yes?

DEREK: Yes Nani, I admit I want to make love to you. I'd be crazy if I didn't, but that's not my only reason for wanting to be with you. I've had time to try and internalize that sensitivity thing of yours and I've put out a real effort to make it work for me.

NANYEL: You? Derek? Sensitivity? Well I guess an effort is a start.

DEREK: You know changing midstream isn't easy, it takes time.

NANYEL: "It takes time." Seems to be a consistent phrase with you these days, especially politically.

DEREK: You're leading up to something. Say it and get it over with.

NANYEL: You're right, I am leading to something. You see this all seems to befuddle my mind. You're making an attempt at sensitivity, but it takes time. Yet in taking time to be more sensitive you seem to be less sensitive to the needs of the people you represent. But then, that too might take time. Right?

DEREK: Get to the point, Nani.

NANYEL: Derek, it's only that this all seems to be incongruous. You, your sensitivity and time; the people, their needs, sensitivity and time...

DEREK (*frustrated*): Get to the point!

NANYEL: The Mason Hill Complex issue is the point.

DEREK: I'm doing a lot for the Mason Hill community.

NANYEL: By being sensitive to their needs.

DEREK: I'm doing the best I can for those people.

NANYEL: "Those people?" When did they cease being "our people" and become "those people?"

DEREK: Look Nani, are we talking about me and my personal endeavors or my political actions?

NANYEL: We're talking about you. Can't you see what you've turned into? You've assimilated. That blinking yellow light, which took time to install...That blinking yellow light does as much good at the base of that hill as a sauna in hell. What's happened to you Derek? And you talk to me about working at being sensitive. What about those people at Mason Hill? Will another little Black child have to fall victim to another racing truck through the community?

DEREK: Look Nani, I don't want to talk politics with you.

NANYEL: No? That's all you do anyway, talk politically. Why not deal with some real political issues?

DEREK: Because you don't understand politics. Understand that? You don't understand politics.

NANYEL: I understand that taking time and holding out on your endorsement bought a yellow light instead of a functioning red, yellow and green. I understand that you entered politics because you were sensitive to the needs of your people, that you knew instinctively what the people needed. "Instinctively" that was your word. You don't have any instincts, and sensitivity isn't something you table for the next meeting.

DEREK: Look Nani, I don't need a lecture from you, especially over an issue that's dead and over with.

NANYEL: You are the issue. Are you dead and over with? How can you continue to believe you can help others until you come to understand you've got to help yourself? Some politician you are. In fact, some man.

DEREK: Look Nani, I know you've got a lot of anger rolling around in you, and I know you like hitting below the belt, so I'll let that last statement pass. But...I don't want to talk politics with you.

NANYEL: What's left to talk about? Politics is supposed to make up, how did you put it? One hundred percent of your life. (*Fights tears.*) What do we share? We can't share physical space. We can't talk like two human beings. Platitudes...It's like we're sounding

boards to get things off our chests. You walk around polished, ready
to respond politically and then have the nerve to say, "I don't want
to talk politics with you."

DEREK: Alright Nani. (*Paces.*)

NANYEL: You haven't changed.

DEREK: Alright.

NANYEL: Have you checked yourself out lately?

DEREK (*crosses to bar*): Alright.

NANYEL: Don't you have any other words in your vocabulary?
You are the great politician.

DEREK: Alright! Christ!! Alright Nani, alright...I've been wrong
about some things...

NANYEL: Some.

DEREK: Some. The year's separation wasn't such a bright idea.
I was wrong. What else do you want me to say? I was wrong. At
least about parts of it.

NANYEL: What does "at least parts" mean?

DEREK: Are you sure you want to hear my side of it, or is this
to be the catalyst for another one of your tirades?

NANYEL: I'll ignore that.

DEREK: Fine, do. (DEREK *crosses to refrigerator for wine.*)

NANYEL (*calming*): What does "at least parts" mean?

DEREK: I didn't know you were still concerned.

NANYEL: Like you said, let's make the best of it.

DEREK: The blackout and storm wouldn't have much to do with
this change of mind, would it? (*No response.*) I thought not.

NANYEL: You had everything planned, didn't you? (*Indicates
wine.*)

DEREK: Didn't you?

NANYEL: Didn't I what?

DEREK: Have everything planned, down to the speeches.

NANYEL: They were not speeches.

DEREK: No? (*Pours wine.*)

NANYEL: No. (*Quickly.*) They weren't.

DEREK: "Myself and my profession."

NANYEL: That was not a speech. (*He gives* NANYEL *a glass of
wine.*) Thank you. (*Pause.*) What had you planned, besides seduc-
ing me?

DEREK: The blackout.

NANYEL: I believe it.

DEREK: Seriously, I'd hoped we could rectify some bruised emotions...

NANYEL: And we'd remedy them just like that? (*Snaps fingers.*)

DEREK: I'd hoped so.

NANYEL: What do you think now?

DEREK: I've abandoned my plans. No more games, Nani. No more ideas. I'm laying everything out.

NANYEL: Up front?

DEREK: Up front.

NANYEL (*holds up wine glass*): Up front. What was that before the electricity blew? Music? Yes, music, wine, a lodge in the middle of nowhere and rain. You truly have not changed.

DEREK: What did you think I did, consult the farmers almanac? (*Pause.*) What do you want from me? Blood? (*No response.*) Will that clear the air? (*No response.*) What is it? (*No response.*) A divorce? (*No response.*) You want a divorce, Nani?

NANYEL: Possibly.

DEREK: Possibly. You sound decided.

NANYEL: I didn't say I'd decided. I said possibly.

DEREK: It's either black or white. Either you do or you don't. Which is it? (*No response.*) Do you still love me? (*No response.*) Do you?

NANYEL: Derek, quit putting me through the third degree.

DEREK: Nani, this isn't a game. We're talking about us. Our future.

NANYEL: Well it's a fine time to think about an "us" and a "future."

DEREK: Nani, do you still feel something? Nani, do you still...

NANYEL: Yes!!...Yes, I still feel something.

DEREK: Then why don't we act like two sensible adults who love each other...

NANYEL: Because we are not two sensible adults who love each other. Last year was supposed to be sensible. Did it work for you?

DEREK: Somewhat.

NANYEL: Fine, then it worked for me.

DEREK: Are you sure?

NANYEL: Positive.

DEREK: You found yourself?

NANYEL: Yes.

DEREK: And you're happy?

NANYEL: Amazingly yes. You?

DEREK: No.

NANYEL (*sarcastic*): Because you miss me.

DEREK: Yes.

NANYEL: And you need me.

DEREK: Yes.

NANYEL: Since when has Derek Jerome needed anyone other than himself?

DEREK: Since this past year.

NANYEL: Sure.

DEREK: You need me too.

NANYEL: I do?

DEREK: Do you know what you're doing, Nani? Do you? You've got a new look, new job, new clothes, new you, and you're puffing out of both ears. (*Indicates cigarette.*)

NANYEL: This is my vice.

DEREK: And mine.

NANYEL: Why?

DEREK: Because I care about you. I love you. And I don't like what you're doing to yourself.

NANYEL: Fine.

DEREK: Look, enough's enough. What are we doing to each other? We're both miserable. I want this to end. I want to hold you.

NANYEL: I want...I,I,I. I have an "idea." (*Lights come on. Silence.*) Maybe Lake Road's drained by now.

(*No response.*)

DEREK: How long do you keep this over my head? I fucked up. I admit it. Damn it Nani, how far does this go? I make the first mistake. You initiate the second. Is that how it goes? On and on? (*No response.*) I'm trying to make that sensitivity and togetherness work for me, for us. I'm trying.

NANYEL: Well you needn't concern yourself with trying anymore. Nanyel, togetherness and sensitivity have bowed out indefinitely and turned over a brand new leaf.

DEREK: To do what? Go from jeans to dresses? Get in the system's main stream, pick up a nice, white-collar position and move to suburbia with the Black nouveau riche?

NANYEL: And get a Mercedes just like you.

DEREK: Can you believe it's just a car to me now?

NANYEL: Do you want the truth? How did you put it? "I needed a ride, Nani. A nice ride, something I wouldn't have to trade in before it fell in, so I got the Mercedes. And despite what you think, Nani, I got it because I liked it."

(*Silence.*)

DEREK (*exasperated*): Nanyel, Nanyel, Nanyel. Fine. It's yours. (*Pause.*) You want to end this? You want a divorce? Fine. Look, to make things easier on all concerned, I'll take the couch. You, <u>Ms. Lady</u>, may take the bed. Tomorrow, after the roads clear, we can get into our separate cars and drive our separate ways again. (*Silence. NANYEL takes luggage and crosses to adjacent room.*) You know what this means. (*No response.*) This won't be an arrangement to meet again a year from this date. Do you really not care anymore? Is that how you feel?

NANYEL: I don't know how I feel anymore. (*Pause.*) I just don't know...I hurt. That's what I feel, hurt. And yes, I care. I may even still love you. I just don't know. I just don't know.

DEREK: Nani. (NANYEL *crosses away.*) Don't turn away.

NANYEL: I can't. Don't you understand that? I can't keep up. I can't continue cultivating the worst of me to impress, to win you. I can't allow that hell out there to gnaw away the last bit of me. I can't do it.

DEREK: What are you saying?

NANYEL: I don't know! Does it matter?! Hum?

DEREK: You want us to talk? We can sit down and...

NANYEL: We've done enough cute, biting, political speeches for one evening to last a lifetime. Look at us. We can't communicate. God, when was the last time we talked to one another? Can you remember? We either bitch or lecture. I can't. I really can't, and this isn't Nanyel going off in anger.

DEREK: We just can't let five years of our lives go.

NANYEL: It's not "just." This has been rising and taking form for years. Why are we elongating the process? Why not just shake hands, bid each other good-bye and part?

DEREK: Because I need you. We need each...

NANYEL: Need? You can get your needs fulfilled via your politics, your constituents. You can even buy love now. What is it that I, Nanyel, have that will solidify Derek's world? What's the new thing you've come up with? What do we have? (*Pause.*) Derek, who are we? Who am I, you? How do we address each other when we're just two regular people? Do we make up a new set of nicknames to suit those momentary personalities?

DEREK: Do you want us to work?

NANYEL: It isn't that cut and dry. "Do you want us to work?" Yes, I want us to work. And if we follow through with the right dialogue we'll saunter off into the bedroom, make love in the rain and tomorrow? What happens then? There are too many unasked and unanswered questions.

DEREK: Ask them Nani and they'll be answered.

NANYEL: I don't know how to anymore. I don't know what's important anymore. I've learned to intellectualize everything, and now nothing seems valid after inspection, nothing. I don't even know how to express myself without being bitter.

DEREK: We can both start by just saying what we feel. We can get back to those simple days.

NANYEL: You believe that?

DEREK: We can try.

NANYEL: You know, not once, not once have you asked what really went on in my life these last twelve months. I know you well enough to know you're interested. I sure as hell am interested about what you did. I'm jealous about those moments you had away from me. Who were the other women? Did you fall in love with them? Could they offer you the kind of support I never seemed to?

DEREK: No.

NANYEL: No? Your career seemed to sky rocket. Why do you need me? Is it because we're this new class of Black folks who've educated themselves out of the ghetto and moved into a new world we're not sure we like? After all, when the day's over and we're through throwing around our fifty cent words, we can come home and be regular. Is that what we have? Common ground?

DEREK: Is that all you think we have?

NANYEL: The truth? I don't know what we have. I don't...Facade. That's what we have. All of this...(*Indicates lodge.*) Facade. Facade. (*Indicates her attire.*) The straight, controlled form of a man in front of me. You're a facade. Can you feel anymore? Can you? (*No response.*) Got damn it Derek, break!! BREAK!! I can't stand your being so got damn reserved. BREAK!! (NANYEL *attacks* DEREK. *He moves away from her, continuing to maintain his control.*) You're a phony.

DEREK: You're calling me a phony.

NANYEL: It's spelled p-h-o-n-y. It's a disease, and you've got it.

DEREK: And you're immune to it.

NANYEL: I'm working on a cure.

DEREK: Working on a cure. Your cure seems to have some discrepancy with the past and the present.

NANYEL: They're tools of the trade. You should know about that.

DEREK (*crosses to window*): What was that you drove up in, a tool of the trade? I mean a V.W. would have been sufficient.

NANYEL: It's not a Mercedes.

DEREK: Nani, what is it you have against my car? You want one? Buy one and get off my back!

(*Silence.*)

NANYEL (*calming*): You've gotten that far...Well, I guess if you're gonna take the plunge into materialism you might as well go all the way, in style. (*Pause.*) You don't want "us" Derek. You don't want a "marriage." What you may need is a good God-sanctioned bit of window dressing, but you don't need me.

(*Silence.*)

DEREK: What happened to the good old times?

NANYEL: We didn't try so hard.

DEREK: We had good times, you know. Being with you in those days was...I remember feeling like fire was running through my veins.

NANYEL: I had nothing to do with that fire. It was all you.

DEREK (*reflecting*): Good days...Sometimes when I'm shaving I look in the mirror and wonder who that strange face is staring back at me. Sometimes I even get a kind of coldness that runs through me. But you know what, Nani? I made it. Big J's little boy became a man and made it. My dreams, you, a home, my ride. Got to have it all. Still have most of it. I even got to help some of the people from the old neighborhood. Me, D.J., doing it. (*Pause.*) I didn't mean for any of this to hurt you. (*Pause.*) To change it, to be able to eradicate it. I don't know, I just ended up on a path of vicious cycles. It all made sense. It was logical. If plan "A" doesn't work, move on to "B," "C," "D," and so forth.

NANYEL: I'm not a plan you can put in a box and move on with.

DEREK: My focus went off. Can you understand that? I'm not justifying it, but my focus went off. I let the system I was trying to tear down...

NANYEL: Tear us down

(The following dialogue is to be done simultaneously. DEREK *and* NANYEL *begin dialogue facing away from one another. They end the dialogue talking to one another.*

DEREK: Nani, I can't do it alone. I can't walk out there day after day and buck that hell without you. I need you. I need your honesty, your insight, anger, your inputs...Nani, give us...

NANYEL: If it were just that easy. If I could say, "hold me," "let's try." But I've got real scars Derek, and they don't go away in five minutes.

DEREK: I'm asking you to give us a chance, to trust me, us again.

NANYEL: I'm afraid to trust. (*Silence.*) God, talk about facing all your fears head on. This past year was a real lesson packer for me.

DEREK: I learned a few things, you know.

NANYEL: Can you believe that? A real lesson packer. Something good came out of our sabbatical. Derek, I learned I can not only exist without you, I can live. I can live. That got my focus right in order. Me loving me.

DEREK: You loving you. That's what you've come to?

NANYEL: Me loving me. Believing and being honest with me. I don't need to force you into my world or my beliefs. Like me, you've got your own. I'm not desperate anymore. My life isn't contingent upon our staying together to keep me together. I'm working on loving me.

DEREK: Working on loving you. One lone woman against the world. What happens three a.m. in the morning?

NANYEL: Somehow it's not as lonely anymore. Fancy you should be concerned now.

DEREK: I need you Nani.

NANYEL: The nights I wanted to hear that. It's all so empty now, those needs. It's ironic the campus crusaders from the ghetto, Nani and D.J., the couple set out to make a change became a statistic.

95

Educated, professional, separated, distant, and <u>free</u>. We can't forget the free.

(*Silence.*)

DEREK: So what do we do? Drive away, set a date for lunch someday and...

NANYEL: That might be good. Spend some time getting to know each other, ourselves more. Who knows, we might even find we like each other. We might not have given away too much of our truth. (*Pause.*) A lunch might be good.

(*Lights fade to blackout.* CURTAIN.)

Every Goodbye Ain't Gone

A PLAY IN ONE ACT

by BILL HARRIS

Bill Harris began writing in the early 1960s. He wrote his first full length play, *No Use Cryin'*, while in the army. He received a Master's degree in Creative Writing from Wayne State University in 1977. He has worked as an arts administrator for the Detroit Council of the Arts, JazzMobile, Inc. and the New Federal Theatre. Mr. Harris has taught creative writing, humanities and adult education courses at Wayne State University and the Center For Creative Studies. His writing awards include the Tompkins Writing Award for Drama at Wayne State, the Mary Roberts Rinehart Foundation Grant for the completion of a novel, the Greater Detroit Motion Picture Council Merit Award for drama and the Paul Robeson Cultural Arts Award given by the State of Michigan for cultural contributions.

The play takes place largely in the mind and memory of FRANK. *The reality and time of any given place or moment is made specific by the actions of the actors, the lighting and a minimum of realistic or representational props. The areas remain the same throughout. They are...*

1) Hospital - with bed and chair
2) Downstage Area - with table
3) Nightclub - with microphone on stand; table with two chairs
4) Hotel Room - with writing desk and chair

It should be possible to isolate each of these areas by means of lighting.

RULA (*we see her isolated in what we will come to recognize as Hospital Area; she is wearing a hospital robe and is laying down in a fitful sleep*): Frank...? Hold me...(*She sits up suddenly.*) Frank! (*She lies back down, turns on her side and curls into a knot.*)

FRANK (*we see him in Downstage Area packing a small suitcase*): I got a call from a hospital in Cleveland. Rula's there. They said she collapsed while she was on stage singing. From exhaustion, they said. Said she needs rest. She asked them to send for me. (*Lights go off* RULA.) I guess all that proves is that I'm still the only some-body that she has, despite what we went through. Maybe that's why I'm going. Maybe it's to see if she's changed...Maybe...? Be-fore I wouldn't have even thought I would. (*Closes suitcase.*) But you never what you'll do until a situation presents itself. (*He puts on an army jacket and cap and picks up suitcase.*) It was Christmas Eve, and I was going home on leave when I met her. Waiting for a bus connection in this little club near the station. I was going more out of a lack of anywhere else to go than any sense of duty or desire to be there. (*We see* RULA *in the Nightclub Area.*) I don't remember what she was singing, but the songs were never important any-way. It was the feeling that was underneath.

RULA (*at microphone as if singing*):
Even if you don't know,
you feel it,
listen close and I'll reveal it.

FRANK: Regardless of the song, the message that came through was that she faced up to the fact that the world could be a cold and nasty place. Her singing was as open and honest as a Saturday night moan from a satisfied sinner lady pleased by her man, or a Sunday morning shout from a sanctified sister praising her maker. Every note and nuance was as deep in it as a mess of collards in bubbling pot likker.

RULA: You can love it, or me
or you can leave it,
but if you're honest
you must believe it.

FRANK: But despite how true she was to it, there was a tension that I couldn't put my finger on. And whatever it was it kept it from being as powerful as it had the potential to be. It was like the pow-er a mule exerts against a plow that is hung up against a root hid-den in the earth. You can feel the frustration of its not being able to break 'loose, but even so, just the effort of its straining and pulling was exciting.

RULA: My singing is what I have to do
to live, it's all in the world I have
to give.
I don't say that to apologize

      you can see that if you've got eyes.
      It's just the way I am,
      if you can't accept it
      I don't give a damn.

FRANK: But I could also tell that she'd be damned if she was going to give up. She was going to wrassle and tug and struggle until something gave.

RULA: You can love my song,
      or you can leave it,
      but if you're honest,
      you must
      believe it!

FRANK: The women I knew had so many fantasies of Prince Charming or Daddy Warbucks dancing in their heads it was either impossible to cut through all the nonsense or not worth the effort when you did. (*Moving to her.*) You might be real good one day.

RULA: I'm good now.

(FRANK *makes a gesture which says: If you want to believe that, fine, but I know better.*)

Didn't you hear how they applauded?

FRANK: All they wanted was to be amused. I doubt if any of them have any idea how close they were to really hearing you tell the truth about you and them.

RULA (*pleased, but uncertain*): The truth, huh? Most people think I'm trying to be some kind of arrogant bitch when I do tell the truth.

FRANK: Most people are afraid to hear it, or tell it.

RULA: Or accept it.

FRANK: You're trying, but something is stopping you from getting all the way into it.

RULA: How do you know?

FRANK: I listened.

RULA: I didn't know Uncle Sam had slots for listeners.

FRANK: Before I worked for Uncle Sam I wanted to be a musician. But I realized I could never be as good as I wanted to be, so I gave it up.

RULA: Yeah, you have to have somebody, somebody that you can trust, tell you you can do what you already know you can do. Otherwise you almost stop believing in yourself. Maybe you didn't have anybody to tell you that.

(FRANK *makes a gesture which says that is a possibility, but it is now a closed case.*)

And you think I could be good.

FRANK: If you be honest.

RULA: Sometimes I almost have it. I'm almost singing - me. But...Who are you?

FRANK: Usually I'm Frank Dandridge, RA 86678532, attached to Special Services. But at the moment I'm just an orphan in a storm, waiting for a bus.

RULA (*shaking his hand*): Rula Payton. A fellow orphan, for real. And I've spent a lot of time waiting to go somewhere, too.

FRANK: I'm sorry...I didn't...

RULA: Don't apologize; you didn't have nothing to do with it. But don't let nobody jive you, being an orphan ain't no comic strip. Oh, things would be cool on the foster home circuit 'til my "parents" got their bills caught up, or I said something their imaginary child wouldn't've, or moms caught pops looking at me a little too long...And then it was: "I'm sorry, but we're going to have to send you back." Like I was damaged goods or meat that was turning green. And it was pack my little stuff; then it be me and that damned sanctimonious social worker taking that ride "back." But it wasn't back at all. The only way you can be sent back is if you come from somewhere in the first place.

FRANK: But you'd have your little tough-as-nails attitude together, right?

RULA (*surprised and pleased that he knows that*): Like it didn't phase me in the least.

FRANK: Like you were just cruising to the corner for a double dip of chocolate.

RULA (*laughing*): Yeah. And you know what that taught me? That whatever I was going to be or do, I was going to have to be it, or do it, or get it by myself.

FRANK: So you rolled up your sleeves and you went to work.

RULA: You a mind reader for Uncle Sam?

FRANK: I heard it all in your singing.

RULA: Have to be more careful when you're around. Like they say, "Anything you sing will be used in evidence against you."

FRANK: Do you think that I would do that?

RULA: People do.

FRANK: My listening service is provided free of charge or fear of retribution.

(*They both realize they are at a juncture, with the option to continue or not.*)

RULA: I don't want to hold you up from catching your bus...

FRANK: Where have I got to go but home for Christmas?

RULA: Don't knock it. I don't have anywhere to go but back to a hotel room.

FRANK: You going to spend Christmas alone?

RULA: It's not that bad, once you get used to it.

FRANK: I'm looking for an excuse not to go home. I could hang around, practice my listening on you.

RULA: I'm a singer, not a talker.

FRANK (*moves down to address audience*): And then she proceeded to talk. It came bursting out of her like a John Coltrane solo. Chorus after non-self-pitying chorus, on themes of darkness, silence and rootless endings, beginnings and endings again. With counterpunctional variations of the rules, standards and ideals of countless benign benefactors, too immersed in their own ignorance or frustrations to even sense, let alone respond, to her longing for answers or the fulfillment of her need for confirmation of her existence or worth. And I had the feeling that most of what she was telling me had never been expressed before, other than as the emotional base for her singing. (*He looks back at her.*)

RULA (*who has moved to Hotel Room*): I always had to do it all by myself, by myself. (*Laughs.*) Like when I found out that boys were different than girls. I felt like Columbus coming over the horizon. I said to myself, "Little Miss Rula, you have discovered a whole new world here, girl!" But I wasn't like a lot of young girls, giggling in groups of twos and threes. I was out there on my own. And that "skating on thin ice," and "unlady-like" stuff they was peddling didn't mean no more to me than soup de jour to a dinosaur. I'm telling you I was sizzling; spicy as Tijuana tacos and hot enough to put Birdseye out of business. What I wanted was for them to know who I was. I wanted to thrill 'em and chill 'em in the day time and have them dream about me at night. I wanted to draw them like flies to honey or moths to a flame. I wanted them to whisper me their fantasies when they sat behind me in class, then break out in a cold sweat when I turned around and smiled at them.

I mean, I inspired and made poets out of them. I made them tell me how sweet I was, how soft and fine and whatever else I felt like hearing. But don't get me wrong, I wasn't getting up off nothing but petting and sweating. But don't think for a minute they wasn't glad to get that. And I'm telling you something else: when somebody said Little Miss Rula Payton, folks knew who was being referred to.

FRANK (*to audience*): It was Christmas morning before she began to wind down.

RULA (*laughing*): The lady at the place where I was a baby said she'd be jumping up all night trying to keep me covered up because I'd keep kicking them off. Hell, she could have just let me lay up there and kick. Ain't nothing like having your behind out to make you get your grits together. But then it still probably wouldn't have taught me nothing with my fast self.

FRANK (*to audience*): Strutting. But up under all that flip and hip and bluster it was like listening to the confessions of the lady the guy throws the knives at in the circus. Nothing about occupational hazards; her indignation was self-directed because she lacked the final courage to place herself in the position to make the knives come even closer. (*He moves back to her.*)

RULA: And now you know all of my secrets, you tell me some of yours.

FRANK: I'll tell you something that I don't think you've heard enough of.

RULA: And what's that?

FRANK: That you're a nice lady.

RULA (*caught off guard*): That shows how much you know.

FRANK: I mean it.

(RULA *knows he does.*)

Doesn't one good compliment deserve another?

(RULA *is uncertain.*)

Do you think I'm a nice man?

RULA: You might be all right.

FRANK: Then why don't you tell me so?

RULA: Maybe because I'm afraid.

FRANK: You? Tough as you're supposed to be? Afraid of a few little words?

RULA: It's not the words I'm afraid of.

FRANK: What?

RULA: You. Because all my life I have wanted somebody that I could talk to, tell stuff to - even be, you know, weak with, without being afraid they would hurt me, so I wouldn't always have to feel like I was some kind of arrogant bitch who didn't give a damn about anybody but herself.

FRANK: I understand. I never felt like I could afford to be a kid either. I used to have this teddy bear.

RULA (*gentle teasing*): Aww...

FRANK: I did. And everywhere I went: playing, going to bed, eating, even in the tub, teddy bear was right there. And then one day, I was four or five I guess, I gave it to my mother and told her to get rid of it for me because from then on I was going to be a big boy and I wouldn't need teddy bear anymore.

RULA (*touched by his story or his reason for telling it to her*): Got your little tough-as-nails attitude together...

FRANK (*trying to cover his feelings*): I used to say, "On my honor, I will do my best, to take what they give me and steal the rest."

RULA: You understand. I did what I could with what I was. And what I am is all I've got.

FRANK: I'm going to tell you something that I want you to remember. You've got me as your friend, now and whenever...OK?

RULA (*working up the courage*): Can I ask you a favor, as a friend?

FRANK: As a friend.

RULA: Asking for what I really need isn't easy for me.

FRANK: It'll be my Christmas present.

RULA: You gave me that by staying.

FRANK: Ask.

RULA: Hold me? (FRANK *does.*) I don't feel like I have to explain, justify or apologize for anything to you. The knot isn't there anymore. Almost to the point that it's hard to understand or remember why it was there in the first place.

FRANK: All the people who have hurt you are somewhere else. If they're here it's only because you let them be. (RULA *is silent.*) Where are they?

RULA: Somewhere else.

FRANK: And where am I?

RULA: Here...

FRANK: They're somewhere else, and I'm here - and will be as long as you let me.

(RULA *moves upstage and begins to prepare for the wedding ceremony*. FRANK *moves down to audience*.)

As a kid I'd never seen anybody who was married where it wasn't like a constant war - people who could only see themselves reflected in the dishwater dull mirror of their predecessors failures; who used each other as mental and emotional sparing partners out of an ingrained assumption of some predestination to act out the bluest of blues couplets. And I'd always figured if that's all there is to it, then who the hell needs it? But I guess you never know what you'll do until a situation presents itself.

RULA (*joins him and they pantomime the wedding ceremony*): Now I can forget about all them hot-mama games I've been playing and tell the truth about the love I sing about. (*They kiss*. RULA *moves up to remove wedding apparel*.) Forget about the real life, move over Cinderella, Rula Payton Dandridge is coming through.

FRANK: But...we couldn't forget about real life.

RULA (*in mid conversation*): I don't know, this doesn't seem real to me.

FRANK: What?

RULA (*indicating*): This. I mean, I know I'm here. You, and furniture and food in the refrigerator...

FRANK: You'll get used to it. People have been doing it since the beginning of the world.

RULA: But it's like a movie, and I'm just watching it instead of being part of it. I keep thinking the lights are going to come on and I'll be me again, the old me. And I keep thinking it isn't fair to you.

FRANK: Why don't you let me worry about what's fair to me? (*Turns to audience*.) But we both knew there was something...I've got to give it to her, she fought it. And she never bitched. But there got to be a restless silence. Then she got a gig, to sing in some of the lounges of the Webster chain. (*We see* RULA *packing a suitcase*.) Good opportunity for her. (*Trying to joke*.) And, like she said, all the towels she could steal. But...

RULA (*in mid conversation*): I used to tell myself I would quit wondering where I came from if I could find somebody like you, that understood...

FRANK (*apprehensive*): You need any help with that?

RULA: I've done it so much I can do it with my eyes closed. They used to tell me happy-ever-after fairy stories, and I would think to myself, "Yeah, OK. Maybe if you're a princess or something..."

FRANK: And you had a Prince Charming...

RULA (*determined*): Even the ones with orphans or poor little match girls or ugly ducklings, as much as I wanted to believe...

FRANK: You're not planning on coming back, are you?

RULA (*angry at his perception*): It's like you can see into me! Nobody else ever even saw me before, and you, you see everything, hear everything, know everything! I always feel like...

FRANK (*overlapping*): Wait. Let me see if I can say it for you. You found out you need the audience more than you need me...

RULA (*overlapping, anxious to correct him*): You know what you mean to me? I think about you and I say to myself, "Relax, girl, it's OK. He understands, and it's cool. So just relax."

FRANK (*trying to suppress his rising anger*): You relaxed now?

RULA (*avoiding a direct answer*): What I'm saying is that you're the highlight of my life.

FRANK: When are you going to get to the point?

RULA (*continuing, determined*): You know what the highlight of my musical career is? I was singing "Strange Fruit" in a beer joint in Out Of Step, Indiana or somewhere, and some "music critic" who slaughtered pigs for a living or something told me to shut up and show him my tits.

FRANK: There's no business like show business.

RULA: And when I showed him he told me to put them away and sing. (*A little laugh.*)

FRANK: So?

RULA: So, it's not about - competition between you and them.

FRANK (*hard*): Do you love me?

RULA: Yes, damnit!

FRANK (*harder*): And I love you, and I care about what happens to you!

RULA (*matching his tone*): I know how to take care of myself!

FRANK (*overlapping*): Big bad Rula.

RULA (*continuing*): Had to be that way all my life.

FRANK: Yeah. Right. You against the world.

RULA: The world against me. I didn't ask for it. Just like I didn't ask for the way I was born, or the way I had to be to survive. I just know I want to do what I want to do the way I want to do it.

FRANK: I know what singing means to you. Maybe better than you do.

RULA (*overlapping*): Maybe better than I did.

FRANK (*continuing*): I've never tried to or wanted to stop you.

RULA: I know that. You made me think it was all right to do what I was doing and the way I was doing it. I love you for that.

FRANK: You know as much about love as a baboon knows about beauty marks.

RULA: I know that love can mean stopping somebody from doing what they have to do.

FRANK: I told you I don't want to call the tunes you dance to.

RULA: That's not what I mean.

FRANK: Then tell me what you do mean, damnit. And tell me straight. I deserve that much, don't I?

RULA: Singing isn't just what I want to do, it's what I have to do.

FRANK: I told you...

RULA (*continuing*): I created myself out of nothing. All that I am, my strength is in my not depending on anybody but me - for anything.

FRANK: I heard all that in your song. But...

RULA: And you said that was what made me good.

FRANK: What's that got to do...?

RULA (*overlapping*): I tried. I swear I did. I wanted this to work. I want to be with you. But with you I'm not being me. If I love you I cut myself off from the only way I know to survive.

FRANK (*with fatalistic insight*): Rula alone, against the world.

RULA: I don't know if I'm Rula Payton, or Rula Dandridge or who the hell I am. When I'm singing I feel like I should be with you. And when I'm with you I feel like I should be...

FRANK (*interrupting*): I'm asking you not to go. Give me another chance to show there is another way.

RULA: I've got to. If you love me you'll understand.

FRANK: Understand that if I love you I have to let you go? I'm damned if I do, damned if I don't.

RULA (*closing suitcase*): That's the story of my life.

(FRANK *watches her.* RULA *moves away with suitcase.*)

FRANK (*moves to audience*): And she was gone. Off to sing her song. Maybe I could have stopped her, but what good would that have done? She wanted to go. Had to, according to...I couldn't change that by stopping her. She had to make that decision. I missed her. Maybe more than I had thought I would. Because she had reached and touched and completed a part of me that I had kept closed off. Secret. And my response was to want more, to be able to open myself to as much of it as I could, for as long as I could. And I wanted to give that back to her. I don't know if what I missed most was what she gave to me, or what I wanted to give back to her: that feeling, the chance to find a way to open up that thing in her, to loosen that knot that she talked about. No, it wasn't about stairways to the stars, or rainbows or June moons. It wasn't even about turning her on to what my feelings were, but allowing her to find what hers could be; would put her in touch with, whatever they might have been. I'd think about her and I'd get this flash of joy/pain through my stomach...But then after a while I felt it less and less, until I started to get letters from her. But never with a forwarding address - so I never knew where to write.

RULA (*we see her in Hotel Room at desk, writing*): Indianapolis; Fort Wayne; Peoria; Cat Puke, Pennsylvania - Going to a gig, riding by cute little houses with lace curtains off Main Street with that social worker all over again. But I tell myself I'm going to the corner for a double dip of chocolate.

FRANK: And I started to miss her all over again.

RULA (*writing*): But it all gets to be a blur. (*Rises, preparing to move to Nightclub.*) I woke up in a motel in Dayton and thought I was in Scranton because that's what the notchback cover said. The joke was on me. Ha, ha. Love, Rula. (*Moves to microphone in Nightclub.*)

FRANK (*from downstage, as* MASTER OF CEREMONIES): Ladies and gentlemen, the Naugahyde Lounge of the Toledo Hotel of the Webster Hotel Chain is proud to present - Miss Rula Dandridge.

RULA: Night after night I do my little show for audiences of double knitted salesmen and their ladies. But I'm just background for their b.s.'ing, bragging and bargaining. Nobody really listens, not like you used to. But then, like you told me, that's show business.

107

FRANK (*from downstage, as* DRUNK CUSTOMER): How do you like our little town, girly?

RULA: The K-Mart is just fabulous.

DRUNK: Sing "More Today Than Yesterday."

RULA: I still put my whole thing in my song, but it's all jumbled up. It's not just me in there now. There's you too. And I can't seem to get it straight. But don't worry - not that you were - I'll work it out. I always have.

DRUNK: "More Today Than Yesterday."

RULA: What's wrong with "Melancholy Baby?"

DRUNK: You do any Olivia Newton John tunes?

RULA: Never heard of her. How about some Dinah Washington?

DRUNK: Never heard of her.

RULA: Billy Holiday?

DRUNK: Wasn't she that dope addict in that movie?

RULA (*moving to Hotel Room*): Too tired to even cry, I go back to the room and order something from room service. Couples plan a night for it, but alone it's really not that hip. I leave the bathroom light on and go to sleep, counting trucks zooming by on the Interstate. I can hear you saying "I told you so." Smile. Not having a wonderful time. Wish I wasn't here. (*Lights go down on her.*)

FRANK: I read her letters. I could hear it again. Just like I'd first heard in her songs. But it wasn't just a moan or shout. It was a cry. And I heard it. I couldn't <u>not</u> hear it. And I thought, "It was my fault that I didn't make it work; that I didn't reach her, like she reached me; that I didn't turn that cry into discovery, or even love.

(*We see* RULA *in Hospital, as at opening.*)

I didn't reach her because I didn't try hard enough or reach deep enough or <u>give</u> enough to help her fill in the empty spaces - and fill in a few of my own. (*Takes suitcase and moves to her.*)

RULA (*sits up*): Frank.

FRANK: How you feeling?

RULA: You look like you're disappointed I'm not in a strait jacket.

FRANK: You're too tough to be crazy.

RULA: That shows how much you know.

FRANK: They said you asked for me.

RULA: It wasn't a lot of trouble, was it?

FRANK: I got an emergency leave. You are still my wife...

RULA: I didn't know if you remembered.

FRANK (*cautious*): I had to see how you are. If you...need anything. If you're going to be all right.

RULA: Thank you for coming.

FRANK: I got your letters...

RULA: You know how it is, lot of daytime to fill when you're on the road.

FRANK: There's always the soap operas.

RULA: My life is a soap opera.

FRANK: Why did you call?

RULA (*trying to joke*): Everybody's entitled to one phone call. (*Serious.*) Because I wanted you to listen to me.

FRANK (*trying to joke, but with serious intent*): Not for me to sweep you off your feet and carry you off into the sunset?

RULA: Does that happen in real life?

FRANK: If you let it. You want to tell me what happened?

RULA: I wish you could have come to hear me. Maybe you could have told me what was wrong. They applauded and said I was good, but you wouldn't've lied to me. Like when you said the first time we met that I'd never be a star.

FRANK: What I meant was...

RULA: It wasn't the same anymore. So it wasn't enough anymore. Before, I could stand all the bad times, the times in between when I wasn't singing because I knew that at least when I was singing it would make up for...

(*During this she has removed robe, gotten the suitcase and moved to Hotel Room. She takes magazines and bottle of whiskey from suitcase. She pours a drink, stopping occasionally to hold her head, trying to get herself together. Drinks with obvious distaste. Pours another. Makes a decision. Drinks. Gets a bottle of sleeping pills from the suitcase and puts them on table. Drinks, pours, delaying the decision. Flips through the magazines with irritated intensity. Puts them aside. Stands tensely for a moment. With sudden inspiration picks up the phone. Cradling it between ear and shoulder, she picks the pills up with one hand and drinks with the other. Then opens pill bottle, pours out a handful and one by one drops them into the whiskey bottle. She puts phone on table without hanging it up. Holds the bottle like a microphone, then grasps it with both*)

*hands and presses it against her forehead; the slowly pulls it down her
face, breasts, to her stomach and leans over it, moaning.)*

It's stupid. Stupid, stupid, stupid! To be...by myself in this...
Where the hell is this? Nobody that wasn't stupid and scared would
even be here. And for what? To sing a goddamned song. Why? Because I'm stupid. Dumb, ignorant, stupid. I need to quit I need to
get my hips up from here and...If you so hip how come you by your
dumb self all the time? Anybody with any sense would catch the
first thing smoking back. Anybody with a teaspoon of sense. But
not me. Not Rula. Not sad, stupid, disappointed, lonely little orphan Rula. Too stupid to just quit this simple gypsy nonsense.
Eating alone and sleeping alone. Being alone. Like some kind of
damn, stupid, simple gypsy-bird with no nest to flutter to. Other
people don't have to do it all by themselves. Ugly people, sick
people...*(She moves to Nightclub and grasps microphone.)* Why can't
I? What's wrong with me!? *(Stronger.)* I'm tired of it. I'm tired of
holding it in. I don't want to anymore. I can't hold it in forever. I
can't. It's killing me. I'm killing me. Ain't nobody doing it to me
but me. Don't you think I know that?! *(Stronger.)* I need him...I just
need him to tell me it's all right. Just take me and hold me and tell
me it's OK, baby...*(Stronger.)* I need to...to love. I need to love. I need
to love and be loved. And to know that I can and am! *(She has stag-
gered to him, and he holds her, soothing her until she begins to calm
down.)* It just suddenly came to me that I was tired of having it all
on me. All my life, having to figure things out for myself. Having
to do for myself. And right then it didn't seem like the singing was
enough.

FRANK: Right then. And what do you think now?

RULA: I'm not sure.

FRANK *(moving away)*: Let me tell you what I think is going to
happen. You're going to get through this, and it'll make you stronger and more determined.

RULA *(with favorable consideration)*: Maybe I can learn from it.
And it'll help my singing. Maybe it'll open me up to new things. If
I can get it straightened out.

FRANK: Maybe...

RULA: No, I know I can do it, if you'll be there; tell me it's all
right - that what I'm doing and the way I'm doing it is OK, I can
relax.

FRANK: And then the next thing we know you'll be back out there, better than ever.

RULA (*caught up in the possibility*): That's all I want. Just to sing my little songs, be your old lady, maybe get my name in Jet so I'll have something to back up my bragging as I sit and rock my grandbabies.

FRANK: But don't you see that won't work? Nothing's changed from before because you still think if you're not out there singing...

RULA (*suspecting she has fallen into a trap*): No...I was wrong before; wrong to think it and wrong to do it.

FRANK: But you don't just sing to live, baby. You sing not to die. Without it you don't think you even exist, no matter what or who else is around you or with you.

RULA: Don't try to punish me. Not now. I don't need that.

FRANK: You don't need anybody to punish you. You make it hard enough on yourself. The shame of it is it's all for the wrong reasons. You're still fighting a battle that you've won. You've got somebody to love you. All you've got to do is accept it.

RULA (*confessional self-realization*): I know that. I think what kept me from...doing it to myself in that hotel room was that I knew that you...

FRANK (*interrupting so as not to hear her reason*): The other thing is you can't split yourself. You've got to save it all to put in your song. That doesn't leave anything for anything else.

RULA (*her only defense*): I've always hurt me as much as I've hurt anybody else.

FRANK: That's fine if you're willing to pay that price. But it's a hell of a lot to ask of someone else.

RULA: Not if they love you like they say they do.

FRANK: I don't think there's anybody who can pay you back all the love you didn't get when you needed it most.

RULA: Right now is when I need it most. All right, let's don't call it love. Maybe I don't know what it is. Let's call it...charity, or anything you want to, but don't go.

FRANK: Until your song calls you again? And you tell me, "I'm sorry, but I'm going to have to send you back." And I'm left with nothing but the feeling like you had of having to take that ride "back" again.

RULA (*lashing out*): So what are you going back to? (*Derisive.*) The <u>army</u>? Well that's nowhere either. (*Taunting.*) Three meals a day and somebody telling you what to do and when to do it? Well, that's no better than those places they sent me to. And I'd rather be stuck by myself in an igloo in Siberia than in something like that, just so I'll <u>belong</u>!

(FRANK *is silent.*)

But why not, from somebody who gave up trying to be a musician because...what was it, you didn't think you could be good enough? Well, they tried to tell me that, but I am good enough. And I'm going to keep on being good enough. And I'm going to get better!

(FRANK *is silent.*)

Why'd you even have to come along in the first place? And open me up to a whole lot of...stuff I'd have been better off without? (*Sudden thought.*) And how come you came now? If you knew you were just going to...

FRANK (*interrupting*): I didn't know. I had to find out for sure. To see if I'd gotten over my fantasies of rushing in like Prince Charming to rescue you from the Black Magic spell you're under.

RULA: What happened to your promise to always be my friend?

FRANK: I will. I just can't do it and be with you, waiting for the axe to fall. (*Rises.*)

RULA: You know asking isn't any easier for me than it is for you. Accept me for what I am. Don't go. Don't leave me alone.

FRANK: I have to, for both of us.

RULA: You're just doing it for revenge!

FRANK: I asked you not to go, remember that? Begged you... But that's not what this is about.

RULA (*rising*): Go on then! Go on so I can get my rest, and get my grits together so I can get my hips out of here 'cause them people ain't going to pay their money to hear no crazy woman sing.

(FRANK *picks up suitcase.*)

I was born alone! So being alone don't phase me in the least, if that's what you think. I created myself, by myself. And I can take care of myself, by my damn self! I don't have to depend on anybody!

FRANK: Well, I do. That's what love is, baby. (*He moves to exit.*)

RULA (*snarling as she grabs him and violently turns him around to face her*): You wait just a goddamn minute! (*There is a momentary pause with the threat of real violence. Then she kisses him with a fierce, starving passion.*)

(FRANK *almost responds, but with an effort is able to restrain himself. RULA releases him. FRANK moves away. RULA gets herself together and moves into Nightclub.*)

FRANK (*from downstage, as* M.C.): Ladies and gentlemen, Miss Rula Payton-Dandridge!

(*Sound of applause. RULA smiles, acknowledging the applause as light fades on her.*)

FRANK: Every man has a woman that teaches him that he can love. The hell of it is he usually has to lose her to find that out. And once he knows it, the best that he can hope for is that the hurting will eventually turn into some kind of haunting...I still hear from her occasionally, a post card with the picture of some local point of interest from somewhere. I have women whose melody and memory are gone even before they are. In between I hang out in the PX, drink beer and tell war stories, just waiting for...

(*He can't think of what. Nor can he think of anything else to say. Small laugh. Exits as lights fade on the end of the play.*)

Tophat

A PLAY IN ONE ACT FOR MIME, ONE SPEAKER AND MUSICIAN

by PAUL CARTER HARRISON

Playwright/director Paul Carter Harrison is a New York native whose plays have been published and produced in Europe and around the United States. His early works (1962-65) include the one-act plays *Pavane For A Dead-Pan Minstrel, The Experimental Leader* and *Tophat*, which was the first of his plays produced by the Negro Ensemble Company in 1971. Subsequently, the NEC produced his play *The Great Macdaddy* (1974), for which he was presented an Obie Award, and *Abercrombie Apocalypse* (1982). Other significant works include his multi-media drama *The Death Of Boogie Woogie*, the musico-epic *Tabernacle*, for which he won an Audelco Award, and *Ameri/Cain Gothic*. Among his many directorial credits are included the conceptualization and direction of the original production of Melvin Van Peeble's *Ain't Supposed To Die A Natural Death*, prior to the Broadway production under the direction of Gilbert Moses, the direction of the Chelsea Theatre production of Aishah Rahman's *Lady Day: A Musical Tragedy* and the direction of the NEC posthumous production of Larry Neal's *In An Upstate Motel*. Major motion picture credits include the original screenplays of *Lord Shango* and *Youngblood*. He is the author of *The Drama of Nommo* and the editor of *Kuntu Drama,*,both published by Grove Press. The same company will publish Mr. Harrison's new anthology of playwrights of African descent. His most recent book is *Charles Stewarts' Jazz File*, a photo documentary. Mr. Harrison is a Contributing and Advisory Editor for *Callaloo Magazine* and a 1985-86 recipient of the Rockefeller Foundation Fellowship for American Playwrighting. He currently serves as Writer-in-Residence at Columbia College in Chicago, where he has developed his recent jazz-inspired operetta *Anchorman.*

SCENE: *One half of the stage signifies a ghetto "block"; the other half a "pocket park." Sounds of many vehicles in traffic. Lights come up, exposing a Black MUSICIAN framed in a rooming house setting. He is woodshedding. A garbage can in front of frame. A Black JUNKIE appears with brown shopping bag tucked under arms; he looks into garbage can, finds nothing, then anxiously advances to the edge of a taped white line (the street) and attempts to cross through the traffic over to the other side of the line where there is a park bench, a tree and a wire basket.*

The JUNKIE *makes several desperate attempts to cross the street (line). His anxious gestures indicate the frustration: he waves his hands furiously, puts one foot over the line, withdraws, thinks, makes several light halting efforts, hesitates, etc., takes out a handkerchief, waves it, thinks, wipes his brow, sits down on the edge of the line, and blows his nose violently. He begins to take off his shoes, one at a time, pouring sand out of each. His socks have enormous holes which expose his toes. Placing his shoes aside, he begins to search inside the inner band of his moldy hat, locates a match, places it between his teeth. He now begins to search inside of his shopping bag, from which he removes several items: a large, round alarm clock - the dials of which he adjusts to what he thinks is the correct time, and nodding the while; one roller skate which he observes, contemplates the traffic, then decides to put aside; a 45 rpm record which he zealously presses to his chest; knitting needles and wool; a large pepper mill; a small American flag which he waves vainly at the traffic. Finally he locates what he has been searching for: a crumpled package of cigarettes. He searches inside the package only to find it empty. Furiously, he throws the crumpled package across the line in front of the park bench. He observes his single match, throws it aside, replaces his hat onto his head, the articles back into the shopping bag, and places his head between his knees despondently. Suddenly, the traffic noises stop.*

Surprised, he looks up, searches up and down the street, stands, observes, quickly puts on shoes, takes up his shopping bag. Cautiously, he places one foot over the line, quickly withdraws it. Nothing happens. Hastily, he runs across the street (line). Safely on the other side, he turns and laughs at the traffic, which is now silent. He now begins to search the ground.

The MUSICIAN *continues to play as the* JUNKIE *searches and discovers a small cigarette butt. He places it in his mouth, puts down his shopping bag, removes his hat from head, and searches inner band for the match. Unhappily, he realizes that he threw it away on the other side of the street (line). He approaches the line, starts to walk across, having trepidly observed left and right, and traffic sounds erupt suddenly. Anxiously, the* JUNKIE *leaps back without crossing and waves his fist at the passing traffic, cigarette butt hanging from his mouth. He thinks for a second, turns around and begins a walking gesture, however, remaining in the same place (giving the impression of "walking" away). When traf-*

fic sounds fade, he turns and casually walks across the line, searches for the match, locates it, lights cigarette, then casually starts across the line once more. He is startled mid-stream by the roaring advance of cattle (sounds) stampeding down the street, which he eludes, balanced on the line, then pulling up the tape (street line) so that he might pass safely. Having rolled up the tape (like rolling up the sidewalks), he shoots it in the direction of the wire basket (If he hits it on the first attempt, he is delighted; if he misses, he picks up the tape and dunks it into the basket.)

Relieved, JUNKIE *begins to smoke his cigarette butt with exaggerated pleasure, ending in a nod.* MUSICIAN *ends with a raucous note as a* WOMAN's *voice is heard from behind the bush.*

WOMAN: I saw that...I saw you do it! We could have you arrested. I know we could...(*A middle-aged white or Black* WOMAN, *elegantly dressed in chiffon, comes out from behind the bush carrying a large purse and a sign that reads "KEEP OFF THE GRASS." Placing the sign on the ground, she reproaches the* JUNKIE.) You should know better. Or don't you know better? A public park is no place for that kind of thing. Don't you feel ashamed? (JUNKIE *doesn't respond. He is nodding.*) Look here, you. Don't pretend with me. I know what's right, and you'll never get away with it. Don't try to ignore me... (MUSICIAN *improvises throughout the* WOMAN's *verbal assault.*)... We could have you arrested, so don't pretend with me. I'm to be reckoned with...(JUNKIE *still unresponsive. Up from nod, he is confused.*)...I say, I'm to be reckoned with! Pick it up! Pick it up! (*With butt hanging from mouth, utter astonishment written on his face,* JUNKIE *picks up his shopping bag as if trying to protect his wordly possessions.*) Where's your sense of duty and responsibility? And right before my very eyes...(JUNKIE *looks around as if she had referred to someone else. He stands scratching his crotch.*)...Don't try to deny it! I saw you do it, and we won't tolerate it. Pick it up! There! It's over there! (*She points toward crumpled cigarette package.*) I've been watching you. I saw you when you came across the street. (JUNKIE *looks confused. He searches for the street line.*) You crossed against the light, didn't you? (JUNKIE *makes an agitated gesture as if about to respond.*) No! Don't deny it. It'll do you no good. I'm a witness... and a citizen, if you really want to know. (*Uncomfortable and impatient,* JUNKIE *starts to walk away.*) Don't walk away from me when I'm talking.

Stop! Stop! I'll scream for the police. (JUNKIE *stops in his tracks*.) I'll tell them you tried to rape me. (JUNKIE *gazes anxiously toward her*.) First you came up behind me and pinched my ass. I screamed. You ran away. That's how it always is in these times, and you can't deny it, right? (JUNKIE *recoils, frowns, shakes head disagreeably*.) You're a liar and your breath stinks, and then there's the business of my money which I fortunately hid in my bra...of course, an uncalculated risk in these times of famine and deprivation, you know. Intemperance...this being evident by my rudely dishevelled chiffon. Oh, look at me. Aren't you disgusted? (JUNKIE *nods his head with passive agreement*.) You damn well ought to be, my lovely "Vogue number" all torn to shreds...if you get the point! I'm a witness of one, but who will listen to your feeble excuses...you blunderer! (JUNKIE *stands bewildered and confused*.) Anyway, pick it up. Pick up that rubbish you threw over there. (JUNKIE *picks up the crumpled cigarette package under the watchful eye of the* WOMAN. *Slowly he shows it to her. She nods her head approvingly. He looks around for a place to deposit it, locates the wire basket, drops it in, pursuing the gesture with a nod*.) Good, well done. Now you're behaving civilized. But there, you're doing it again. Don't stand on the grass! Grass-don't-grow-on-trees, you know. Grass is a god-send, you know. (JUNKIE *appears disoriented*.) Look, perhaps you'd be better off sitting on the bench. That way you won't get into trouble. (JUNKIE *starts to say something*.) Don't answer back. Just do as you're told. The bench is for sitting. Grass is one of nature's simpler delights and must not be abused. Come on! If you behave, we might even let you stay. (JUNKIE *joins* WOMAN *on bench and begins to search through bag, as if preparing to sell her some article*.) Not too close, your breath stinks. Your body too. Besides, how do I know you don't really want to attack me? One can't be too sure. Familiarity, in case you haven't heard, breeds contempt...and lice! (JUNKIE *moves to end of bench*.) That's better.

(MUSICIAN *plays a riff as the* WOMAN *sits poised as if at a jazz club*. JUNKIE *removes large peppermill, the head of which he plays with, at times, as if it were a sax, attempting to demonstrate its versatility. He then pauses to take off his shoes. He begins to rub his feet and amuses himself by moving his toes which are exposed through his socks*. WOMAN *breaks mood of short musical interlude*.)

WOMAN: Did you feed the animals? (MUSICIAN *makes long squeel on instrument.* JUNKIE *is baffled.*) You mustn't feed the animals. And stop playing with yourself! I won't go on talking to you as long as you indulge in such obsenities. (JUNKIE, *puzzled, searches pants-fly.*) Look, if you insist on remaining exposed, we'll have you impounded! (JUNKIE *notices his exposed toes, quickly puts on his shoes.*) The parks are full of perverts these times. It's just not safe anymore. I told my husband so. It's just not safe. But then, about the animals, you didn't feed the animals, did you? (JUNKIE *shakes his head.*) Good! It's bad for their teeth. And their humanity. My husband told me, and he should know. If you like animals, then don't feed them. (JUNKIE *nods head.*) They become too dependent. And when you're not there, what then? But people are always careless, so inconsiderate. They simply, in fact, don't care. Only the animals care, in fact. Humanity notwithstanding, I prefer the primate gallery most of all...(JUNKIE *agrees while trying to draw her attention to peppermill.*)...they're most entertaining, so precocious, by far the best beast in the park. I told my husband so, but he's never interested. He's always so busy making money...taking care of plenty business...my husband, you see, is a true bag of gold.

(JUNKIE *becomes very amused.* MUSICIAN *still improvising.*)

Now, I don't have to lie to you. I don't even know you! My husband takes care so much business he never has time to come to the park. Still he knows all about teeth and what's good for animals. He's a birth control expert. He travels all over the world with his contraceptive toothpaste, and I come here for entertainment. He roams the great seas searching for cavities, but he never uses his product at home. Right now, he's in the Far East. He's going to clean-up-the-Yellow-in-the-Orient! (JUNKIE *and* WOMAN *laugh recklessly together.* MUSICIAN *riffs.* WOMAN *stops suddenly and reproaches the* JUNKIE.) Stop it! Stop it! (JUNKIE *stops abruptly and stares quizzically.*) You think it's funny, do you. Well I don't! What do you know about being left alone, to fall on your wits, to quaff and endure the many anomalies of nature...dogs fornicating, babies defacating...you're hopelessly without compassion. (JUNKIE *attempts to console her. Opens mouth.*) No excuses. I knew it all the time. Only the animals care because I care about them. They entertain me, and what do you do? Nothing! I am not amused. I swear by Sojourner Truth that my tears are not without provocation.

(JUNKIE *looks around nervously. Offers her his handkerchief in an effort to assuage her tears, afraid she might attract attention.*)

I was so peaceful before you came...the primates groping and fondling prettily their erected organs. Leave me, leave me alone. You're disturbing my peace you...you...Philistine!

(WOMAN *takes* JUNKIE's *handkerchief to wipe her eyes as he stands by anxiously trying to recover it. He finally snatches handkerchief apologetically and prepares to leave, tucking shopping bag under his arms.*)

WOMAN: Ah, that was very generous of you. How very refreshing it all was. You've helped me enormously to overcome a fearful setback in my afternoon amusement.

(JUNKIE *retreats;* MUSICIAN *honks;* WOMAN *squeels.*)

WOMAN: Wait! Don't go away. (JUNKIE *stops, looks around suspiciously and grips bag tighter.*) You can't go now, not when we're just getting acquainted. Come on, sit next to me. I'm convinced that you didn't mean to offend me. After all, I've confided in you matters that had been kept secret 400 years or more, for how much can one person bear alone?

(*Reluctantly,* JUNKIE *sits down and once again begins to search through his bag.* WOMAN *recoils from his body odor. She takes out perfume atomizer from her purse and gently sprays the back of her ears. Without warning, she vigorously sprays the* JUNKIE, *causing him to cough convulsively. She stops, smells the air, smiles benevolently at* JUNKIE.)

WOMAN: Don't you just love it? Just the thing to refresh Nature's essence...particularly if you're staying. Well, it is a public park, you know. I told my husband so. He's a real money-bag, but not at all entertaining. So, when I'm alone, I come to the park to see the primates...

(MUSICIAN *plays a long tremolo as* JUNKIE *yawns.*)

WOMAN: Suddenly, just suddenly, I'm hungry!

(JUNKIE *stares at* WOMAN, *then his bag. He begins a new search, this time removing from the bag an apple which he polishes on his scruffy coat.*)

WOMAN: Really, is this your best offer?

(JUNKIE *attempts to withdraw his offer.*)

WOMAN: No, no, don't be silly. History has proven it to be a crashing success...like pie-in-your-eye and all that shit. Let's have it!

(JUNKIE *stares blankly at her.*)

WOMAN: Well, have you nothing to say?

(*He begins to speak.*)

WOMAN: No! Better that some things are left unsaid. But wait, at least some wine. (WOMAN *reaches into her purse and pulls out a bottle of wine.*) Chateau Nuuf doo Pa-re!

(*As if demonstrating his merchandise for* WOMAN, *the* JUNKIE *goes over to wire basket, turns it upside down so that its base may be used as a table. He searches behind the bench and comes up with two long-stemmed wine glasses which he places on the table beside the apple and wine bottle. He now searches bag for the final touch article to dress the table: a candle stick and candle.* JUNKIE *is unable to find a match in the inner band of his hat. Thus,* WOMAN *gives him matches to light candle. As he lights candle he begins to nod while* WOMAN *pours wine. Jolting* JUNKIE *from nod with her elbow, the* WOMAN *postures herself elegantly.* JUNKIE *takes plate with both hands and offers* WOMAN *the first bite.* WOMAN *refuses first bite. Hesitantly,* JUNKIE *takes a modest sampling of apple. Again, he offers it to* WOMAN *who accepts and proceeds to devour the apple ravishly.* JUNKIE *observes curiously as he almost nods once more while looking at remains as* WOMAN *places the core on plate. She takes up her glass, gestures to* JUNKIE *to do the same. He does so with uncertainty. They touch glasses.*)

WOMAN: ...For Liberte...beaute...eh, Boot-tee, eh, what the hell, touche!

(*They drink.* MUSICIAN *plays a fast moving tune on low notes.* WOMAN *puts down her glass first, notices that the* JUNKIE's *face is glowing with enjoyment from the wine. She turns sour on him.*)

WOMAN: ...Now, just a minute, Jack. Don't think because we share the same table that we're going to be anymore intimate...I know your kind...my mind is clear, and I won't be intimidated...

(*Startled,* JUNKIE *puts his glass down on table slowly, confused.*)

WOMAN: ...It'll do you no good, you know...I'm a woman of sound judgement and impeccable character...though my thighs may look inviting, I won't be intimidated by your sleezy grin...I saw you winking out the corner of your red eye, rudely, I might add, down the crest of my sanforized breast...but we are the function and the rule, and we'll have none of it...

(JUNKIE *attempts to move away. She grabs him by the coat which comes off his shoulders. Desperately he rolls up sleeve of shirt, gestures as if tying a band around arm, and then gestures as if preparing to inject arm with a needle.*)

WOMAN: ...Now, as long as you promise not to take advantage, I'd be happy to withdraw my complaint and relax my defense of an otherwise indestructable dignity...just be civilized and all the rest of it...don't be presumptuous...so you promise...do you promise?...(JUNKIE *about to "inject" arm.*)...Oh, it's raining... (JUNKIE *looks confused.*)...how unlucky...I'll get all wet...do something quick...save my "Vogue-number"...do something...

(JUNKIE *stands, distracted from earlier action, and puts up an imaginary umbrella. He stands passively holding the umbrella as* WOMAN *snatches umbrella, causing* JUNKIE *to pursue in order to elude rain, and begins to clear "table" of wine and glasses, leaving* JUNKIE *to return "table" to its former place as a recepticle into which the apple core is placed.* MUSICIAN *plays monotonous tune on high register.*)

WOMAN: ...Oh, you've done it again...indeed, a clever prescription against what might have been certain disaster...You are kind, after all...in fact, almost...magical...there's nothing you can't do...I feel so indebted to you that fate would have no other course than I return a favor here or there where good faith permits it so...trick or treat!...there's nothing I love more than giving, naturally within the limits of my character and the endowed trust of my husband who, as you know, is a very rich man with few amusements, which makes my gifts to the underprivileged, trick or treat, an uncontestable necessity...Would you say this rain is out of season?

(JUNKIE *now sitting with* WOMAN *under umbrella, puts out his hand, looks up, shrugs his shoulder.*)

WOMAN: ...A modest opinion indeed. Humble are the underprivileged...you are one of those, aren't you?...but then, I'm a reasonable citizen, and I do believe that the "needy" should work... have you ever worked? (JUNKIE *grimaces.*)...I somehow detect a lack of ambition...you are, in fact, a worthless bum...shapeless and formless...(*She looks up from under the "umbrella."*)...It has stopped raining...you can put it away now...

(JUNKIE *closes "umbrella," reducing it to a smaller object which he shakes in his palms, open his hands and gestures as if he now has a "bird" on his finger, which he kisses and allows to fly away.*)

WOMAN: ...Still, I won't go back on my decision to help you, but first I must have the satisfaction of knowing that you're not just shiftless, roving, lice-ridden, derelict...though I'm not petty, you need work!

(JUNKIE *scrambles from the bench, picks up his shopping bag and begins to flee.* WOMAN *begins to scream.*)

WOMAN: He attacked me...he attacked me...help...help...my bra has fallen...help...

(JUNKIE *stops, looks at* WOMAN. *Reluctantly, he returns to bench.*)

WOMAN: ...That's better...remember, a civilized person never runs away from his responsibility...Now, what we need is a tool to occupy your hands...yes, a shovel will do...(*She searches garbage can for shovel, finds it.*)...Here you are, dig!...It will restore your confidence in society and society's faith in you...

(*Reluctantly,* JUNKIE *accepts the shovel, begins to dig near garbage can.* MUSICIAN *plays a blues riff as* WOMAN *presses her body next to his to establish the rhythm.*)

WOMAN: Uh-huh, now I know breaking new ground rules is difficult, but you will see, each stroke becomes easier...How marvelous it all is! and you might have thought it grim, but already I can see how really magnificent you are becoming...(*She feels* JUNKIE's *arms and shoulders. He continues to dig.*)...Who would have thought you should advance so rapidly...The best results come from solid hard labor...a necessary ritual, my husband would say, from which I benefit enormous entertainment...Uhmph! How wonderfully strong you are, not nearly as flabby as one should have thought...and a perfectly uncomparable grip on the handle...Notice, and I dare, how smooth your stroke has become... Umm-um-um!...suddenly, just suddenly, I fear I am being overtaken by what I'm certain will be a regrettable indignation to a once unblemished fidelity...but then, why pervert the essential vibrations of one's flesh... (MUSICIAN *squeels.*)...terrifying though it may be...we'll delay no longer or else one might fall victim to a guilty conscience...(*Agressively, she pulls the tree downward to floor, exposing a bed.*) Enough of this good service to the community... come prove

123

your worth to your benefactor...(WOMAN *embraces* JUNKIE *vigorously, leads him to the bed. He, now with a deadpan expression, continues the rhythm while hovering over woman. After a brief moment,* WOMAN *sits up, one hand to her breast, and announces in an exaggerated tone:*)...Enough, enough, good man...the hay must be let out to dry!...You are truly on your J-O-B, man!

(MUSICIAN *plays a squeeling note, then re-inspects his instrument.* JUNKIE *sits up on edge of bed, confused and slightly disturbed by the sudden change. Slowly, he returns to his shovel and begins digging.* WOMAN *orders her appearance, advances toward* JUNKIE.)

WOMAN: I dare say you match your weight in soil...you've proven beyond a doubt that you're worthy, and thus am I prepared to go further, for we mustn't discredit what is natural with the triteness of a seedy adventure, and since my husband is steeped in gold, I think it is now time to travel the world, don't you think?... For we are not without humility, we who are civilized, thus shall we simply straddle the route a bit further...let's say, till we reach the dry sands of Cameroun...or thereabouts...

(JUNKIE *doesn't respond, only continues digging.*)

WOMAN: ...but what other entertainment is there...not much to speak of these times...however, before we go, you'll need a new ensemble...you're reeking with piss! (*She reaches into garbage can and comes up with formal coat with tails and a new high crown top hat. She apprehends the* JUNKIE *by surprise, forces him out of his scruffy coat and into the new. She snatches off his cap as* JUNKIE *somberly observes his new accounterment with mixed feelings, then offers* JUNKIE *the top hat.*) Here...try on your luck...trick or treat!

(*Hesitantly, almost childishly,* JUNKIE *puts on the new hat. He smiles benignly.* WOMAN *inspects him and gestures a self-satisfied, mannered "gait."* MUSICIAN *plays series of minor key scales.*)

WOMAN: Hot damn!...You're stunning!!...in these times of travel, I'd say, if nothing better than the truth, a nose out of Ebony...my very own Top-hat!

(WOMAN *takes* JUNKIE *fondly by the arm as they strut over to the bench - however, not without her taking the shovel in tow, and he the shopping bag. They sit on bench. Lights change to blue.* MUSICIAN *plays a short interlude of scales as* JUNKIE *and* WOMAN *make continuous rolling motions of a boat.*)

WOMAN: Oh, Top-hat, I'm so happy today...We've traveled the full tour of ports, sixty-nine in all, and still no dry sands...you're a super navigator, I must say...

(JUNKIE *agrees by nodding his head. He holds clock up to his ears listening for a ticking sound - there is no sound. He listens intensely, turns the dials, listens.* MUSICIAN *plays the woodshed theme.*)

WOMAN: ...I can bear any distance, really, as long as you keep me entertained. As you know, entertainment in these times is hard to find...nutrition being what it is today...And speaking of gastrotory matters, Top-hat, I've noticed your indulgence lately has gone far beyond your needs, knowing very well that you must keep up your energy and the rest of it, but gorging yourself, indeed, may weaken your humility, which is all but slightly embarrassing, don't you think?

(JUNKIE, *listening to clock, nods head occasionally.*)

WOMAN: And don't play dumb with me, Top-hat...though a hard worker you may be, your excesses simply appall my sense of retribution...You must admit, one-half pound of caviar, creamed herring, half dozen bagels, a tray of baked apples, a bowl of coconut milk and brown rice, fresh salmon puree and garlic bread, seven varieties of goat cheese and a bottle of champagne is really a bit much for breakfast...

(JUNKIE *puts clock aside. As he listens to the* WOMAN, *his face changes slowly from being pleasant to revolted.*)

WOMAN: ...And lunch, could you call that a proper regimen... six monster artichokes, sour cream and mountain oysters, crab-stuffed eggplant...and that enormous pickled Porgy before that ghastly over-marinated pig-foot, followed by a half of watermelon...Top-hat, aren't you disgusted?

(JUNKIE *frowns, rolls, bends, squirms, indicating slight revulsion. Both move with rolling motion of boat.*)

WOMAN: ...If you're not, I certainly am, simply because the toilets haven't operated since dinner. Really, Top-hat, of all things, Pete Champagne and corn bread, smoked eel with vinegar and mustard sauce, sauted chitterlings, six helpings of collard greens, not to mention the two pounds of beef that went into your Fondue Bourguignonne with 36 varieties of hot sauce, and don't think I didn't notice that hideous side-order of home-fried potatoes under your chair...that's really nerve...but it's a good thing you drank a quart of buttermilk to wash down that Hashish cookie stuck in your throat...

(JUNKIE's *nausea reaches climax. He hangs his head over the side of the "rail" and regurgitates violently.*)

WOMAN: ...I only mention these things, dear Top-hat, because I do worry about your blood going bad and the rest of it, for the sake of entertainment. These are no habits for one whose appetite formerly ranged from fish-heads to very spare-ribs...I fear, oh how I really fear, that you will be overtaken with gout at a young age, and that is not amusing...you must agree...Top-hat...Top-hat, are you alright? (WOMAN *pulls* JUNKIE *up erect. He sits on bench appearing fragile.*) Now, so act sensibly, Top-hat, get yourself together - we're arriving at a new port, perhaps more exciting than the last. If we're lucky, and again, I must ask you, Top-hat, did you change your socks today?...(JUNKIE *nods head.*)...Top-hat, take off your shoes!

(*He takes off his shoes enthusiastically. He is wearing his original socks with the holes exposing toes. His expression changes to sadness, slightly embarrassed.*)

WOMAN: Top-hat, it's a shame 'fo God...Change your socks immediately...your fresh socks are in your foul sack.

(MUSICIAN *plays woodshed theme with great intensity.* JUNKIE *slowly reaches for his sack.* WOMAN *takes out her compact, opens it and views herself in the mirror.* JUNKIE *removes the old sock from one foot, places it aside and forces his foot into the new black sock.* WOMAN *searches in her kit and takes out a large powder-puff, dips it into her small compact filled with powder. She begins to smear her face all white.* JUNKIE *searches into the sack again and comes out with a striped sock. He examines it against the black sock on the other foot. Replacing it with the striped sock, he examines both socks, suspects something is odd about the matching. Again he searches the sack.* WOMAN *examines her face repeatedly, carefully, as she applies excessive amounts of powder on her face... under her chin, around her neck, behind her ears...*JUNKIE *takes out an argyle sock, examines it against the striped sock, removes the black sock, forces his foot into the argyle sock. Again he examines the pairing.* WOMAN *puts away her powder puff, her face smothered with powder. She places hand to her breast to adjust her bra cups.* JUNKIE *occasional-*

ly scratches the soles of his feet when thinking about what to do next. WOMAN takes out an eyebrow pencil from her kit. She wets it with her mouth, sticks point into ear of JUNKIE, who does not respond, examines her face in mirror. She draws thick, crude lines over her eyebrows. JUNKIE searches his sack, comes out with one plaid sock. He examines it against the argyle, takes off the striped sock and forces his foot into the plaid. He examines the combination of argyle/plaid. WOMAN, after being satisfies with her eyebrows, puts away her pencil and takes out false eyelashes. Meticulously, she secures them onto her eyes. JUNKIE appears slightly frustrated, searches into his sack and slowly takes out what apparently is the end of a white sock. As he slowly removes it from the sack, its length continues endlessly. He anxiously tugs at the extended length of sock until it is completely out of the sack. He examines the color and length of the sock against both socks. Uncertain, he searches into the sack again, comes out with a woman's garter belt. Embarrassed, he quickly replaces the garter belt into the sack. Holding the lengthy sock, uncertain what to do, he finally makes several turns with it around his neck, forms a bow- tie. WOMAN takes out a tube of bright red lipstick and smears her lips. She touches up her cheeks for a little color, completing her mask. JUNKIE searches around, locates his original socks, removes the argyle/plaid combination and restores his feet quickly into the original socks. Furtively, he puts on his shoes. WOMAN puts her lipstick away, puts a hand to her breast to adjust her bra cups, first one then the other, turns toward the JUNKIE who has picked up his clock and adjusted the dials. JUNKIE benignly, with futility, listens for a tick... MUSICIAN plays a squeeling note, ending the intense woodshedding wearily.)

WOMAN: Top-hat, oh Top-hat, the sea is leveling...we'll drop anchor near the coral reef...good thing we freshened up before entering the forest...a good thing, I always say, is a sweet thing forever... particularly when we getting into to the "rough of it."

(MUSICIAN plays improvisationally. They drink, place glasses on the tray held by the stage hand. Stage hand exits. Lights change to a green color. JUNKIE and WOMAN sit on bench, bouncing up and down. JUNKIE postures as the "wheel" of a car; WOMAN's head is reclined back against the "car" seat...bench...)

WOMAN: We're in the "rough" of it, dear Top-hat, just as I knew we would be, but for one blessing, the forest is so beautiful...don't you think so, Top-hat?...I don't mean to complain, but are we getting somewhere, Top-hat?...It's really so hot, yet I know this trip is necessary in these times...No wonder I am exhausted - as I told my husband who was there and I here, "We must go somewhere. Let's get over the hump of it"...to which he replied, "Brush your teeth three times a day and don't eat chocolate"...He couldn't bear the "rough," so we went nowhere...Passing between nowhere and somewhere is always exhausting, don't you think, Top-hat?...Top-hat, do I talk too much?...Don't despair, Top-hat, soon, yes, soon we will reach the summit and have enjoyed all that has passed... Come now, Top-hat, don't spare the gas...faster...faster...faster...oh, Top-hat, get down. No, stay up, up Top-hat. Get into high gear, Top-hat. Do it, Top-hat, faster...oh, oh, Top-hat, I can't anymore... the distance is too far, and it's no longer amusing...stop...stop... stop...this god-damn machine, Top-hat...I can't go any further... I've had enough...slow down...that's right...break it on down... good... easy now...ohhhhhh, what a relief...(JUNKIE *looks disappointed.*)... Now, don't take that tone of voice with me...it's quite clear this road shoulders more traffic than its years can support... We're not traveling a Super- Highway, you know...We'll go on later, indeed, I'm only human... Besides, I've got to "pee"...Now climb out while I go behind that tree...Here's your shovel...Keep your hands occupied while I recess, dear Top-hat...

(JUNKIE *reluctantly begins digging in the same hole as earlier. WOMAN comes out from behind tree holding a sign..."Comfort Station."*)

WOMAN: Now that the forest is properly watered, life can go on! (*She places the sign down, pointing in direction of tree.*) Good work, Top-hat!...I can see you've been painfully reliable in my absence... Keep up your strength and don't go soft on the job...Have you checked the fuel...Is everything lubricated?...We still have a long way to go around the world...(JUNKIE *continues digging.*)...But before we go further, I need some amusement...It's so desolate here, don't you agree, Top-hat...Don't you just loathe desolation... I want music...Oh, how I long for some gaiety...Top-hat, stop working and give me some attention...You haven't spoken to me all day...

(MUSICIAN *squeels, then inspects charts.* JUNKIE *stops work, thinks, goes to his sack, searches as* WOMAN *turns her back to him angri-*

ly. JUNKIE *takes out a 45 rpm record, offers it to* WOMAN. *She is delighted.*)

WOMAN: Oh, Top-hat, I knew you wouldn't let me down...your bag is so deep it's frightening...(WOMAN *sits on bench, places disc on her lap and slowly turns her finger around the surface.*) Now, Top-hat honey, give us a song!

(JUNKIE *postures and mimics the singing of the song "Nobody Wants You When You're Down and Out"...which is recorded offstage. He mimics two choruses while* WOMAN *swoons though words are often muddled due to his effort at providing an improvisational riff.*)

VOICE (*slow, classical paraphrasing in falsetto tone*):
Once I lived the life of a millionaire,
had no troubles had no cares;
But then one day I lost my luck,
found nobody to give me a luck.
'Cause, nobody wants you,
when you're down and out;
But if I get my hands
on a dollar again,
I'm going to squeeze it,
and squeeze it,
Till the Eagle grins.

Once upon a time,
I gained my wins;
Everybody came 'round
as my long lost friend;
But now my pockets empty,
beyond a doubt,
Can't find a sole,
to bail me out...
'Cause, nobody wants you
when you're down and out;
But if I get my hands
on a dollar again,
I'm going to squeeze it,
and squeeze it,
Till the Eagle grins.

(*End of the second chorus, recorded song stops as* MUSICIAN *takes up the melody.* JUNKIE *dances a "soft shoe"* WOMAN *presses the disc to her heart with delight.* JUNKIE *dances for two choruses, ending with a leap kick which sends him crashing to the floor.* JUNKIE *and* MUSICIAN *stop simultaneously,* MUSICIAN *tailing off in mid-chorus.*)

WOMAN (*as* JUNKIE *picks himself up off floor*): O.K....O.K.... that'll be enough for one breath, can't over do it, you know... Temperance is the answer to future enjoyment in these times, you must agree. But then, it's only my opinion which is a valued exercise and merits little discussion...my husband tells me...(*Offers* JUNKIE *the record.*)...Here, take this and don't lose it...we'll need it another day for inspiration...but today, we still have much mileage to make up...Shall we cross at the next bend?

(WOMAN *adjusts her bra cups.* JUNKIE, *satisfied with self, takes initiative, extends arm gallantly. They lock arms and begin a circumlocomotion, "camel walk" around park bench. Lights change gradually from green to yellow to white.* MUSICIAN *improvisationally interpolates speech.*)

WOMAN: Don't you just love strolling...It gets easy after a while, passing over hill and meadow, canyon and salt water...clay and moistened dunes...How remarkable if not otherwise fascinating the effortless leisure of our sojourn...We've been through so much together, dear Top-hat, much more than my imagination can allow, and I'll never be able to account for my behavior to my husband who, as you know, is very rich and has made all this possible in spite of the unfortunate truth that though our pleasures have been many, someday this must all come to an end, for how many new amusements can be uncovered in a short life committed to philanthropy?

(JUNKIE's *expression turns to sadness. He appears disgruntled, slightly forlorned, disturbed. He puffs and pouts. Suddenly, he stops. Aggressively, he unlocks his arm from* WOMAN. *Perspiring, he begins to make a protest.*)

WOMAN: ...Now, Top-hat, we'll have no scenes, threats nor slander...we don't care for that kind of thing, you know...You've had your dip in the "pot luck." You've got some nerve to be bitch-

130

ing...Really, Top-hat, you must know by now that the laws of nature are not without fault...

(JUNKIE *advances toward her plaintively.*)

WOMAN: No, don't come near me...This is the time for a very serious talk...After all, I'm still bound to my character, which, as you know, is impregnable, impeccable and, without a doubt, fair!...Now, what do you have to say for that...? (*He begins to speak.*)...Nothing! Besides, one can't be too safe in these times of wanton diseases and "turn-heel" dissertions, all without warning, indeed, just a question of time, and you know it, Top-hat...

(JUNKIE *attempts to speak again.* WOMAN *continues walking as she interrupts.* JUNKIE *drags along at her side plaintively, the effects of apparent withdrawal symptoms causing him much physical grief.*)

WOMAN: ...No, don't say another word...It'll only make things worse, further complicated, and I can't bear anything ugly. Believe me, Top-hat, it's best this way, in fact, simply...It used to be your charm, but I can see you've been spoiled...It'll do you no good to deny it...I've been watching you, Top-hat; you're thinking too much, and that's bad for any concrete understanding, for I sense your calculations have reduced our affair to the triteness of common adventure....Though I'm not priggish, I can't support your view since I had nothing to do with its conception...I was merely walking in the park observing the animals for entertainment when I witnessed your indiscretion and, being properly aroused to one's civic responsibility, I felt obliged to call your attention to the matter, when suddenly I was overcome with the depravity of your condition, worthless, shiftless and without occupation to engage your energies...

(JUNKIE *begins to appear heart-broken, his face anguished as if crying, panting, making spasmic movements as withdrawal seems to be overwhelming him.*)

WOMAN: Please, Top-hat, I can't bear my thoughts to be broken by theatrics...Can't you see I'm a victim of surprise?...After all, it was you who was so ruthless to me, laughing when you knew I was alone. And out of fear that you might attack me and further fester the wounds of my tragic disposition, I gave myself without a struggle...But then, no sacrifice is too great to avoid crude handling and rumors, which always miss the point...But you must admit, Top-hat, it all hasn't been without compensations...Think of what you've gained, Trick or Treat, Top-hat...now, Top-hat, do keep it gay!

(*The lights are now white.* MUSICIAN *plays with a greater sense of desperation, urgency, physically intense.* JUNKIE *has slowed the pace and finally sinks painfully to ground.*)

WOMAN: Top-hat, what's happening to you?...I'm afraid you're wilting in the noonday heat...May I peel you a grape?...Oh, where are we now?...There are no fruits to be had in these times, barring a few assorted prunes and very dry nuts...How dreary!...Top-hat, pull yourself together and do something quick...I'm afraid we're on the perimeter of a well-known disaster...Top-hat, are you thirsty? Would you submit to a drink?...Canteen!...Where is your canteen? (WOMAN *reaches into purse and removes wine bottle which she gives to* JUNKIE, *forcing its contents down his mouth. Revived, he staggers to his feet, begins mumbling inaudibly.*) Top-hat, dear, we have regrettably reached the desert...the most unhappy times of all, and still you have something to say...I shouldn't do it if I were you. No, I most certainly wouldn't...What good will it do us now...on these empty burning plains?...No, Top-hat, I'm not amused...Come on, Top-hat, keep on the pace, and if you insist on talking, please make yourself heard...Oh, but still yet there is a chance to avoid these strains of communication...by transistor...Good thing I never travel without it. (WOMAN *reaches in her purse and takes out a small transistor radio with coil attachment. She plugs the coil into her ear, listens attentively as* JUNKIE's *voice - recorded offstage - is now amplified.* JUNKIE, *stumbling in pursuit, falling to ground several times, staggering and losing contents of shopping bag which becomes scattered about in the process.* WOMAN *steps lightly.* JUNKIE *trudges heavily.* MUSICIAN *plays agonizingly.*)

WOMAN: Ah, this is much better, Top-hat. I'm suddenly in tune with your mumbling, or is it some impediment?...Yes, Top-hat, it's becoming clearer...a good thing too, for how much can one person bear alone...

VOICE (*rhythmic monotone*): Whoa Silver/Donner and Blitzen too/I ain't in step with you/stepping over your ass ain't worth a damn/steppin 'n' fetchin' anyhow/step lightly, almighty/don't stand on the grass/carry your own severed chain, no chance of us drowning/bare right bare left/walk two steps/stop/turn the other cheek, with no respite from A to Z when Z precedes A on yesterday's calendar/almighty, he said with a shit-eating grin-stop-fall on your face, - reverse your speed/on the third day he erected himself, she thought, just in time to reclaim what was dead now alive a millennium ago/still so many fences to climb/unannounced comes a man with few bridges to span or manholes to man save a good fart now and then when the unsuspecting alarm gives the signal to brand him on his left high/I put my ass in the wind... good looking out!...there's a cleft in the road with little resemblance to the last which filled my shoes with sand/almost tripped over a crummy lad-stone, almost/but shit, I was on the balance of life more than once or twice, so who can say what is...is not...inside out today or tomorrow being Good Friday and fish-heads so hard to get...

(WOMAN's *camel walk is becoming more sensually vigorous. JUNK-IE is staggering about as if being grinded into the ground by her movements.*)

WOMAN: Top-hat, shall we change the tune?

VOICE: I am man...

WOMAN: Chauvanist.

VOICE: And I am free/I know nothing of others' deeds than my own indignation in time we shall see what all have been seeking in me/I have no course but recourse I don't ask favours...get off my back god-dammit, I want out and nothing from nobody...

WOMAN (*fluid, sensual, powerful movement*): Think of your industry, dear Top-hat...

VOICE: One penny is as good as four pennies if you use your sense/I've traveled the full excursion of time and found one minute only worth the next which promised an end to the hecklers whom detained my advance with barbed-wired pubic hairs and mutual interest loans/a kick in the balls brings you quickly to a squat for a moment to review that you are or are not free to be man a taste which turns bitter then sour one chokes on free dreams with luck I may vomit/up again so fuck everybody/the road turns for me at the next crossroads...

WOMAN: For heavens' sake, Top-hat, do keep up your spirit... let's be gay!

VOICE: Black is the colour of the sky above day or night/an un-paved road brought me on a strange people where I was a beast be it man woman child or saint...it looked at me, I looked at it...we said nothing they said look up and I saw the beast again; it pissed on my neck; I spit at it but missed, still I don't know its name though I am disfigured for life and sought out to know why when I came upon an angel without doubt an angel wearing a Bowler hat sup-porting himself with an umbrella through the hole in his hand which was hardly noticed till he engaged the other hand to raise the hem of his Mackintosh to shit and think! sometimes stink/ I can make it, I know I can if I vault the next curve/my ass dragging in the wind I stepped on a flea and broke its spine in four places...

WOMAN (*intense, vigorous, movement*): How much longer must I bear these ingratitudes which betray all sense of graciousness though I knew in advance it would come to this...Oh, Top-hat, think of what trials I have suffered...Stop with your nonsense...I'm grow-ing impatient...

VOICE (JUNKIE *failing badly*): I am man and free/toe and heel on a Bull-shit tip and I want out...why toil on others soil, I want out/don't want to learn any tricks I've seen it all there's nothing new under my band-aside/what's the difference between treat or treatment gut bucket or rot gut? take a laxative and pull out the cork I ain't no fool/burns my ass to know I've been tricked it burns my ass to miss my signs and pass along the wrong foot-path to find suddenly I've got two pennies when I only need one/Damn, I must be losing my sense to throw in my hand with the sinking load...it's time to cough up my nerves find my compass or is it too late to retreat 'fore dawn/how many have seen me stumble and play the real fool, now that's being the fool and I ain't no fool, but backward ain't forward less you got time to turn around and I ain't got the time so I'm mad as a bitch/I have no course but recourse...

WOMAN: You're exhausting, Top-hat, I have no other opinion in these times...

VOICE (JUNKIE *crawling exhaustively on ground*): It ain't no fun to be hooked cause I am man and free but I'm turning jin at the next cross-road...yet soon, we will have crossed the desert and then... and then...yes, what then?...one coin could turn the trick but I'm tired I must be dying...looks like ashes on my laurels held out too far to reach...back up quick...quick, the path just slipped...

WOMAN: You must be suffering a sun-stroke, dear Top-hat... you were once so fertile...so much fun...now life with you is like sucking a dry pimple...I'll hear no more.

(WOMAN *pulls the plug out of her ear, turns off the transistor. MUSICIAN ends with a spasm of sound. JUNKIE collapses with exhaustion as lights return to normal. They are back at the "park scene." WOMAN looks around.*)

WOMAN: Thank god we made it...but I'm afraid, Top-hat, you were becoming a tiresome bore...of course, not unlike others before you...(*As* JUNKIE *lies exhausted on ground, she takes off his new coat and hat, places it back in trash, removes old garments and drops them at his side.*)...There's no better time than now to end this amusement...Sometimes I think my husband is right not to come to the park when all the amusements are the same in these times, just ambitious promises you must agree, Top-hat...I fear at moments my civic duty is a thankless task...But, what the hell...you may keep the hat as a momento but for one favour...(WOMAN *holds up hat before the distraught and exhausted* JUNKIE.)...a way to go home...

(JUNKIE *finds the roller skate that had emptied from his bag and offers it to her.*)

WOMAN: ...Would you mind terribly adjusting the straps?

(JUNKIE *obeys slowly. Anguished, he attempts a plea.*)

WOMAN: ...No, no, no, don't spoil my departure with solutions. I've heard enough, and I must say, I'm somewhat injured... At best, I can best advise you to continue your good labour...it'll win you other rewards than one small loss...(*The roller skate is fastened.* WOMAN *hands* JUNKIE *the top hat.*)...Never let it be said I betrayed the "needy" for myself. Good-bye, ballsy Top-hat. I trust you are properly rehabilitated.

(WOMAN *skates offstage.* JUNKIE, *confused, puts on top hat.* MUSICIAN *plays the woodshed theme. Standing on feet,* JUNKIE *discovers the shovel. Dejectedly,* JUNKIE *turns toward the sound of men working at construction which comes up slowly.* JUNKIE *looks at shovel suspiciously, disconcertingly. He then stares at the spot where he had been digging the hole.* MUSICIAN *plays as if sending out a warning. The sounds of hammering and drilling continue as* JUNKIE *begins to try his shovel, first slowly, hesitantly, then energetically. Suddenly, the sound of a warning voice... "Look out"... "Look out"...followed by the sound of falling bricks or gravel. JUNKIE slowly falls over his hole. The construction work sounds fade out. MUSICIAN is the only sound heard as lights dim on tree, then the JUNKIE, lastly the MUSICIAN playing theme in his room. CURTAIN.)*

Zora

by LAURENCE HOLDER

Laurence Holder is the author of the award-winning plays: *When The Chickens Came Home To Roost* and *Zora* which were presented in the heat of the summer of 1981, by Woodie King, Jr., Executive Producer of the New Federal Theatre. Mr. Holder has been produced with success by Rosetta LeNoire, Ellen Stewart and Hazel Bryant. Other notable plays of his are: *Man, Woman, Hot Fingers, Juba, Scott Joplin, Bird* and *Ole Nat King Cole.* He presently teaches at South Mountain Community College in Phoenix, Arizona.

CAST: ZORA NEALE HURSTON

SET: *Rocking chair in front of farm.*

TIME: *Present - the last day.*

LIGHTS: *Sunrise-Sunset.*

SCENE: ZORA NEALE HURSTON *sits pulling on her bags while waiting for the bus to show. She is full of pep and vinegar, but she also has a story about life that is worthwhile listening to.*

ZORA: Look at this place! Some old dumpy real Elsinore Hell. And look at me! Lord have mercy! I used to be something important, a somebody in the big time. Zora Neale Hurston. God! How did it all happen? (*Begins fishing through her bags while talking; she's looking for something.*) I been asking myself that question, and I ain't had the time to stop and answer it. And it ain't that I'm afraid none, either. No! Mama taught me how to grab the broom of anger and drive away the beast of fear, in our yard, by the pear tree, in Eatonville, Florida, the first Negro town to incorporate in America. Oh, I know what America was and what it is now. And I am definitely not afraid, but thinking about it does bring up a lump-up. (*Stops looking in bag and ruminates.*)

137

Maybe it all started when Mama died, when I was nine. Now I was definitely Mama's girl, and when Daddy went and married another woman who just couldn't get along with me, nor me with her, then I had to go and live with relatives, and they never understood me, so, of course, they mistreated me. But that didn't really bother me. I made my peace with the universe real quick and accepted the challenge of responsibility, so that when I was 14 years old, I joined a Gilbert and Sullivan traveling dramatic troupe, and between working as a maid, I had a little money, but what was more important I had myself a place to stay, not much of a home, but, still...it was a place. And it helped me go to night classes and get ready for college.

And suddenly, there I am, in Washington, D.C., the capital of the nation, and I am going to Howard University, the all cullud school. It was the mecca for all the really important black scholarship going on in the country. But when I show up, they start acting like they didn't know who I was. They just saw some sassy girl from the Florida basin, and they thought I was showing up for my first cotillion, but I had traveled, and even though I might have looked plain and ordinary, I was already a woman. I say a woman!

I met the great Alain Locke at Howard. He was a philosophy student getting ready to make a name for himself as the proponent of the New Negro, whatever that was supposed to be. Some niggers is mighty smart, you know, but they can't drive pigeons to roost, if you know what I mean. Oh, yes, I was sassy. Scarlet O'Hara didn't have a thing on Zora, honey. Not a thing!

At Howard I also met Herbert...Sheen. His father was a minister like mine, so we had a lot in common, although my Daddy, John Hurston, was also a lawgiver. He made up the laws for the first town, the first Negro town, to incorporate. yes! Me and Herbert had a lot in common, and being from the South just made it sweeter. Herbert was a medical student, and I was writing already. Herbert said he was on a mission. Well, I wasn't about to be outdone, so I was on a mission also. So, we went our separate ways for a moment. I mean I was on a mission. I had submitted some things to a literary magazine...the Opportunity literary contest and (*Fishes through bag and comes up with the story.*) won second prize for my story "Spunk." Honey, I just knew I was on my way to somewhere, though I still wasn't sure what I wanted to do, not yet anyway.

Anyway, winning the awards made it easier to be accepted into Barnard College on a scholarship. And since I had only finished two years at Howard, finishing school was a clear priority. But I must admit I had some trouble explaining some of the F's I had gotten. It is definitely hard studying for gym, if you know what I mean. But the awards started to make up my mind about some things including the fact that maybe writing was a way out.

Barnard turned out to be a new world for me. I met Franz Boas, a leading anthropologist, in 1925. He was liberal and wanted to study the Negro. Now, you might be wondering why I was interested in Anthro, but that was because it was the only way I could study the Negro. See, even in those days there were questions about whether the Negro had as large a brain as the Occidental. Boas and his colleagues wanted to find out about the correlation of intelligence and head size. When I heard that, I had to laugh. I mean, I knew all about the Negro, and since I was the only colored at Barnard, I got the bug to prove all I knew to the white man, so I accepted the assignment. But they soon made it clear to me that it wasn't enough to point out history to them, I've got to gather more information.

Well, they soon realized that this colored girl was for real because the first thing I did was go over to Harlem and start measuring skulls. Can you imagine this cullud girl standing on 125th street with a pair of calipers measuring the size of folks' heads? But the folk was all interested in this.

HEY! THE WHITE FOLKS SAY WE IS DUMB AND NOT EQUAL TO THEM 'CAUSE OUR HEADS IS SMALL AND OUR BRAINS IS TOO. SO COME ON UP HERE AND LET ME MEASURE YOUR BRAIN, HONEY. YES! AIN'T IT THE TRUTH! WHAT WILL THOSE PEOPLE THINK OF NEXT?

Yes! The colored folks was interested all right. They wanted to know the truth, and they weren't disappointed neither. Them niggers got big old heads...

Of course, that wasn't no proof about nothing. See, Papa, that's what I called Boas, had created a criteria of standards that told what a developed society was really like. He said it was based on how people responded. Well, natchally colored folks respond very differently. But Boas just couldn't see that even though he was feeling stupid about asking me about the possibility of a lower intellectual standard for the Negro people because I was burning them, burning them where they stood. Here I was, just a li'l ole country gal from the most rural part of the country, and I dint have no shame. You hear me! They knew I was extraordinary because I knew I was extraordinary. I must've mentioned that too, dint I? Well, you just never can say it enough to yourself. I mean, this ole mole ain't afraid of no coon shine. Yeah!

And it was the time of the Harlem Renaissance. I mean to tell you colored folks were soaring through the air like eagles. There was Claude (*McKay*), and Countee (*Cullen*), and Langston (*Hughes*), and Wallace (*Thurman*), DuBois, Garvey, Ethel Waters. I knew them all, and we were all thriving, growing, finding out all about ourselves, on all levels. And all that energy ain't never been matched. Oh, I know what America was and what it is now.

We were grand and used to strut, honey. I was probably the original Darktown Strutter. And the white folks was having a hard time trying to prove that we was inferior and all. And not only were we intelligent, we were beautiful. Langston and Wallace were two incredibly handsome stallions. Pretty, pretty men! And the three of us used to strut. We would walk right into a rent party or some of them white folks' gatherings and just knock them dead. And nothing started until I started telling some of my patented porch lies. "Tell 'em a story 'bout something, Zora." Shucks! I had me enough stories to last a lifetime.

SEE, THERE WAS THIS SLAVE WHO HAD A REPUTA-
TION FOR KEEPING OUT OF WORK BECAUSE HE
COULD OUTWIT ALL HIS MASTERS. AND BECAUSE
OF THAT HE WAS ALWAYS BEING SOLD. WELL, ONE
DAY HIS NEW MASTER CALLS HIM OVER AND SAYS
TO HIM: "YOU GONNA PICK UP 400 POUNDS OF COT-
TON TODAY OR I'MA SHOOT YOU. I KNOW ALL ABOUT
YOU AND YOUR TRICKS." WELL, THIS SLAVE'S MOUTH
JUST FALLS OFF, BUT HE SIDLES UP TO THE MASTER
AND LOOKS HIM DEAD IN THE EYE AND SAYS
TO HIM: "IF'N I MAKE YOU LAUGH, YOU'LL LET

ME OFF, WON'T YOU?" THE MASTER LOOKS HIM
BACK, DEAD IN THE EYE, AND SAYS: "IF'N YOU
MAKE ME LAUGH, I'M GIVE YOU YOUR FREEDOM.
" NOW, THIS MASTER WAS NOT KNOWN TO LAUGH,
EVEN IN BED, BUT THE SLAVE SAYS, RIGHT BACK TO
HIM, "BOSS, YOU SURE ARE A FINE-LOOKING YOUNG
MAN. " THE BOSS SAYS: "SORRY, I CAN'T SAY THE
SAME THING ABOUT YOU." AND THE SLAVE SAYS:
"OH, YES YOU CAN, IF YOU TOLD A LIE AS BIG AS THE
ONE I JUST TOLD YOU." WELL, THE BOSS JUST COULDN'T
CONTAIN HIMSELF, AND HE BUSTS OUT LAUGHING,
AND THAT OLD DARKY HAD HIS FREEDOM THAT
NIGHT.

Oh, it was a good time. Langston, Wallace and me put together
an anthology of our work. Langston had his poems, and I had my
poems and my award-winning stories, and Wallace was just the
grandest editor anybody ever did have. And even without money
or too much recognition, we gave the world "FIRE." It was a good
time because everything was happening everywhere.

SKIRT BY SKIRT ON EVERY FLIRT. THEY'RE GETTING
HIGHER AND HIGHER. DAY BY DAY IN EVERY WAY,
THERE IS MORE TO ADMIRE. SOCK BY SOCK AND
KNEE BY KNEE, THE MORE THEY SHOW THE MORE
WE SEE. THE SKIRT RUN UP, THE SOCK RUN DOWN,
JINGLING BELLS RUN ROUND AND ROUND. OH,
WEEK BY WEEK AND DAY BY DAY, LET'S HOPE
THINGS KEEP ON THIS WAY. LET'S KNEEL RIGHT
DOWN AND PRAY.

It was the Jazz Age. We were exotic and beautiful. And me and
Langston quickly realized that. Langston, the Father of the Weary
Blues. Anyway, we realized that Eatonville had a whole lot of poten-
tial to it. Our folktales had been with us without any corruption.
And me and him wanted to do a Broadway show, a collaboration.
We were going to call it *Mule Bone*. Just him and me. He had just
the right touch with some of those ideas. A real genius.

141

(*Her mood changes upon reflecting about Langston. She is saddened and angered by her recollections.*)

But he dint have no right going off and dragging in one of his "truffles" on the deal; just because he's feeling good about something don't mean he goes around and gets some woman involved in our project without even discussing it with me. The project was mine too. And she was just a typist, not even no creator. I was the one who had gone to Alligatorville and collected the folklore. Most of the damn thing was mine. Now, why in the hell does he want to go and do that to me? Get some little woman involved I mean, I was the one who laid over the pit of snakes for three days, buck naked. And he knows his name is important to the project. He does. And I keep telling him that it is too. Shucks! I'm the one selling his poetry book down there to all the railroad workers, and they are loving it. He's getting national exposure, and I'm doing it for him. Anyway, you see the point. We got two egos and no money, and then me and him have the most godawful fight. From being friends and all to being non-speaking enemies. I mean, that hurt me to my heart. Dammit, Langston! Dammit!

Of course, the real trouble with the whole thing is that we ain't got no money, and we had to deal with the humiliation and frustration of a patron. Yeah, in those days if you had talent, you could get a patron. And me and Langston, we had the same one. Mrs. Rufus Osgood Mason, III. Wealthy, arthritic, and a bitch on wheels. I mean, I had to kiss much ass to get anything, and she wanted every conceivable kind of control on you. Not just your work, which is bad enough, but she had to control how you acted, and talked, and dressed, and walked. And she insisted on being called "Godmother."

ZORA, I WANT ALL OF YOUR MATERIAL THAT YOU COLLECT SENT DIRECTLY TO ME ON PARK AVENUE, DEAR. YOU DON'T SEEM READY TO ME YET, AND I DON'T WANT YOU TO MISUSE IT.

Now what can "misuse it" mean, huh? I'll tell you. It means I can't make no money from it, that's what it means. So, me and Langston are running around trying to keep the Broadway ideas away from her because if she finds out, the two of us will have to find another patron. It was horrible. So, I tommed. That's right. I tommed, and that simply was not being done in this New Negro, uncolored era. And it ate me up inside. Ate him up too. Langston was always getting sick, and I was a wreck. Papa Boas wants an anthology, and Godmother wants the same thing, but neither of them can know that I'm working with the other one because one'll cut off the money, and the other will cut off my scholarship, and that'll be the end of my schoolin'. So you damned right. I tommed. And that left me and Langston, both of us sick and dreamin' about the big time...but still no money, so our project never did come off, but it wasn't because we dint try. We just let those people in on all our thoughts. We believed what they were saying about us. We were brilliant and all, but what we hadn't perceived was that they didn't believe it. And anyway, as soon as things start to get nice for the Negro is when they have their damned depression. We start to strut, and then they take away the sidewalk, so there's no place to walk.

(*Reaches into bag and takes out a cigarette and begins smoking with flair and style.*)

I was starting to get uppity anyway. I smoked. And it wasn't proper for a black woman to do that. Nowadays they can choke themselves to death, but when I was coming through, everything a woman did was a threat to a man. Oh, I know what America was and what it is now. One day I wanted a fag, and Wallace lights up one for me, and suddenly who do I see in my face? That's right. Herbert. Now, me and him has been engaged for a long time now, and he's come to collect his woman. And here's his woman puffing away on the devil weed. Poor Herbert. He didn't know it was unlucky to pick up a worn glove, but he wants me. And it really is something for a woman to be wanted in the face of all her denials. It pleases her. It pleased me, but it dint make me no better disposed to him. But here I am getting married to someone who wants to take me to Cincinnati. Cincinnati? Give me a break, Herbie.

GIVE ME A BREAK, HERBIE. WHY DON'T YOU
LOOK AT ME AND SEE THAT I'M NOT THE SAME
YOUNG GIRL YOU THINK I AM. I HAVE CHANGED,
HERBERT. I REALLY HAVE. I'M GONNA GIVE YOU
A HARD TIME. I AM. NO DEAR! I AM NOT GOING

TO GET UP EVERY MORNING AND FIX YOUR EGGS.
I AM NOT EVEN GOING TO STAY IN BED AND FIX
YOUR EGGS, EVERY MORNING. NO DEAR? THAT
DOESN'T MATTER? I AM DEFINITELY NOT GOING TO
GIVE YOU SIX KIDS. I KNOW IT'S ROMANTIC. JUST
YOU AND ME AND ALL THOSE CRUMBCRUSHERS
IN YOUR MIND. BUT IT JUST AIN'T ME, HERB. YOU
STILL DON'T CARE? HERBERT, IF YOU REALLY
DON'T CARE, I DON'T EITHER. I'M JUST FLATTERED.

Herbert knows how to dance, and he's a piano player. I sometimes have visions of coming home from a hard day and having him play the piano to soothe the savage beast in me. And if that didn't do it, we could always dance, and if that couldn't, then he could sing a lullaby. but those visions wasn't Herbert's. And all the time this is going down, I'm deep into my Bohemian life. I'm wearing my headrags, and my dresses don't know who Dior is, and I'm selling hot dogs on the corners just to make ends meet, and I'm eating them things too, and they ain't doing a thing good for my gut, which seems to really go off on me about once a year now.

So I marry Herbert during one of my impromptu trips to nowhere, and he seems dumb about me not wanting to go off to Cincinnati with him. He's surprised and hurt, and it takes me about four months to console him and send him on his way. And I know I'm going to miss him because he's a Southern boy and he knows how to sing and dance and make love. Shaw nuff and nuff said.

So my first real marriage is over. It's like all the men, all the real men in my life have a hard time with Zora. They can't get Zora into the box, so they have to get away from her. I guess I understand it, from my Father, to Langston, and now Herbert. The real problem is that I'm a single woman at heart, a colored woman daring to be an artist. Out of the home. Out of the kitchen. Out of what you had to call a typical man's view. I was just too much for them. For all of them.

So I went right back down South to finish my collecting. I had been down before to interview one Cudjo Lewis who had been the last survivor of the last slave ship. He had only been a slave for five years when the war had freed him, and Papa Boas thought that he might know some of the African rites and all like that, but when I had been down there, he had pretended he dint know nothing, and made me feel like a fool. Well, live and learn I always say. No matter how big in the shoe you get, you still got to walk, and I guessed I hadn't really approached him the right way. And then again, I thought that maybe Cudjo had gotten like a lot of folks had. They came to America and grabbed a hold of Christianity and did their best to forget about Africa. But when I got to ole Cudjo this time, I opened him up like a clam. And he just loved talking to me this time. Must have been the way I looked. It's amazing what a little confidence can do for you. So I was down South and collected some of the finest folklore that has ever been collected.

And I comes back and I writes it up, and lo and behold Godmother can't get the damned thing published. Now I don't have to go nowhere and slave and worry myself sick, or sleep over no pit of snakes like some barbecue chicken, and then write like a dog in the night, and then not get nothing published. And old Papa sure ain't saying a word to me either. Maybe it was the way it was written. Maybe it ain't scientific enough, or maybe they don't like the way I portray my people. Big, bad, and independent.

Anyway, I'm just sitting around one morning staring and staring at the Hudson River when a friend comes by and asks me if I got some fiction because she's got someone interested in Negro fiction. Fiction! I look at her and then I open my drawer, and out tumbles *Jonah's Gourd Vine*. She starts reading it and stumbles out of the house sayin': "This is it, Zora. This is it."

Anyway, if I was confused about what I was going to do with my life, I sure ain't no more, especially when they tell me that if *Jonah* ain't published, then there's no way I'm gettin' my Anthropology work published. Well, I want to die, but Fiction? Shucks! I could write about Eatonville forever. That's home. So I gets out of the trap at last. No more Franz Boas and his world of schizophrenic scholasticism. And no more Godmother. And all it costs me is some time and a couple of bouts with the gut sickness, and the friendship of a genius. But *Jonah* is the first major piece published before my anthro work: *Mules And Men...*

Well, I move into the big time, honey. Had me a car, nice clothes, and plenty of shoes and all the lotharios I can handle. And I am trying to get an authentic musical on Broadway. I seen all of them monstrosities on Broadway too, you know. The actors were fine and all like that. I mean, they were all talented, but the work wasn't true, and mine was because it's based on all my studies. Well, the show only gets to Broadway once, and the critics love it, but the Broadway producers don't. They got monsters on the mind: *Green Pastures, Emperor Jones, Porgie and Bess*. And all the new Negroes shy away too. What a shame. They are all so caught up in integration that they have forgotten what they are trying to integrate. My people got a mystique, a performance ethic. We adorn things, make it our own. You don't take no genius and sell out for no cheap suit.

And all the Negroes took exception to my saying it too. I'll bet you can't find anyone saying anything too tough these days. It takes a special person, and in those days I was the only one saying anything. I mean, I was rich, had clothes, status, two books in the stores, and a good-looking man, Albert Price, III. Just too good-looking for words. And just what was he doing when he ran into me, the Prime Mover? Anything I told him to. And he did everything too. I deserved some of his sweet light after all I'd been through. So we set up housekeeping and made it legal. I knowed he was younger than me, but so what? I was in love with him, and he dint have no expectations of me; he just wanted what I had to give him. But when he dint want to come down South with me, I was hurt, but I immortalized his ass in my next book. They say it was my best book, my best novel. I sure know it was something special. Come from the heart. *Their Eyes Were Watching God*.

Even today people come up to me and they ask me: "How come Janie Mae could be so cruel to her second husband, the one that had gotten her the house and was the Mayor, while he was on his death bed?" (*Chuckles knowingly.*) Because that son of a bitch sold out for a cheap suit. He threw away the genius, the story telling and dancing and the natural spontaneity. You can't put spirit into no closet. Spirit got to go where the light is, where the joy be. And I was famous. Again. More famous than ever before.

The whites loved...*Eyes*...for all the wrong reasons, but my colored contemporaries, as usual, tore it to pieces. For one, that Richard Wright reviewed it and he complained about the minstrel image he thought I was perpetuating. Galls! But the worst review was from my old friend, Alain Locke, the New Negro? He said that the folklore took away from the book. He said it distracted him from the fiction. I wrote a scathing attack rebuttal to *Opportunity* magazine, and I told him a thing or two. Firstly I told him his review was dishonest and that he didn't know a thing about Negroes and that he had never written or produced a thing he could call his own. He had set himself up like some kind of High Priest of Literature, but he didn't know his ass from his elbow. Of course they didn't publish the damn thing.

But people got more adventuresome with me and asked me to review other people's books. One of them was Richard Wright's. And it was my turn. Git out the kitchen if'n you can't stand the steam. But that was a mistake on everybody's part. I should have left well enough alone, but breeches loves a coat tail, and I couldn't resist the challenge.

I never had written anything directly political, and everyone felt I was avoiding the whole racial drama. But I wasn't. I just wasn't using their rhetoric. Wright and all the others were using the rhetoric of reaction to what the white man was talking about, but there was no Negro rhetoric. There was nothing positive anywhere except my books. I was bypassing the melodrama that whites were advocating and I was creating another set of patterns, and it's too damned bad they weren't picked up on too.

I mean, I just wouldn't want to invite Richard Wright or his sad people to my house for dinner, so why in the hell would I want to read about them. And that's the way I wrote the review. You should have seen the fireworks display. You would have thought I had single-handedly assassinated the President. Here was the book that was going to be the Pulitzer Prize winner, and all the world was ready to believe that Wright's picture of Negroes in Negroland was the existing picture, and it wasn't. Where were my people in all of that? It was a false picture. Don't no one I know wake up in the morning thinking about killing whitey, and he be mentally all right. If you think like that, you ain't got a mind. And there are a helluva lot of minds out there. But I wondered why all the others just sat around quiet and let Wright's picture be a majority picture of the Negro for the rest of the world. I wonder who let it get that way and why it still is the picture that's favored.

I had sent an application to the Guggenheim Foundation for a renewal of a fellowship to research voodoo in Haiti and Jamaica. So when I get it, I leave and take me a Panama Steamer to Port- au-

Prince...but dealing with conjure is dangerous sport. And I get ill, suddenly, mysteriously. I thought I was going to die and I just knew that someone was telling me to stop studying all that stuff. You know, they chop up the horse hair real fine and put it in your food and kill your ass. They can poison you with spiders and insects. And I ain't no fool and I'm half dead anyway, so I get the hell on out of there and come back and write up the whole damned thing and get it published; it's called *Tell My Horse*. Maybe it didn't do all that well at the cash register, but I didn't have time to feel bad. Uh uh. Too busy! Dealing with the Federal Writers Project. I was the editor of the Florida division. Taught too. At North Carolina College for Negroes. Well, it was a job here and a conflict there. And all the time I'm moving with these jobs I'm writing all the time like a fool. Finished the book, though, and called it *Moses: Man of the Mountain*. And as sure as my name is Zora, the white folks love it. It's exotic, different. I mean, I told the world that Moses was an African, an Egyptian. Freud knew it. Anyway, you'd think I'd try to bring the whole fabric of the church to the ground because the Negroes tore it up. Alain Locke again. I know he doesn't like me because of all that craziness with Langston. I couldn't trust him. I couldn't trust any of them. And then this sweet, young thing I've been carrying around me has turned my stomach sour, and he is leaving a bitter taste in my mouth. I got to get out of here. He's cavorting all over town, getting drunk, refusing to work, just carrying on, spending my money? He is a damned gallstone. Well, I fix his ass right quick and file for a divorce. And, would you believe it, this Negro wants to countersue. That's right. Denying all my allegations by saying that I promised him an income until he finished school, and to top the whole thing off, as if that wasn't insane enough, the nigger says I practiced hoodoo on him, so I have to withdraw the suit. I had to before this stupid shit ruin everything I've been working on, which seems to be slippin' and slidin' every which way but (*Points up with finger.*) No matter!

I'm Zora Neale Hurston, the woman who's jumped the broom, so there's nothing to jumpin' the sun.

I leave New Negroland and I get together some productions of a musical I call *Great Day*. It's really a smarter version of *Mule Bone*, but I can't use that name. It was really a good show. A critical success but a financial disaster, but something was going out of the fabric of Negroes. They were starting to get militant. They weren't interested in Negroes anymore, where they came from and where they were going. No, they were becoming Americans. And that was sad. I wrote an article for a magazine called "Crazy For This Democracy." I should have known that the winds of life had shifted. Black people really believed they would get this thing called integration. That the people who were dying would not die in vain. And that should have been the rule, but once again, the people were selling out. I say to hell with it! My back is broad. Let me personally and privately be responsible for my survival or failure to survive in this man's land. I want no double standards of measurements. If I am a skunk, then I mean to stink up the place, and if I'm a walking rosebud, I'll do that too. I am a conscious being, all complaints and pleas of the pressure groups, inside and outside the race, to the contrary. I'll jump up and support this democracy as soon as all the Jim Crow laws have been repealed. When they are all gone, I'll support America. But I'm not selling out for any cheap suit. I've seen some of the people looking at white man's institutions and then joining up and then they can't stand them. From the greatest to the smallest. Who can say that communism has not used Paul Robeson or Richard Wright? Well, they can never use me, baby, because my ass is just too smart for them. I used my head, and I can see above the clouds to the stars...

So I go to Florida to finish my next book. And I finally get *Dust Tracks On The Road* published. It's going to be a series of autobiographical volumes of which this is merely the first. I figure I owe myself a treat and so I decide to take my houseboat up the coastline to New York. Yes, honey, the houseboat. And since *Dust Tracks* did all right at commerce street, it even won an award from the *Saturday Review* for a thousand appreciated bucks, for contributions to foster and improve race relations. I was in demand, speaking engagements everywhere. And I wrote a gang of articles for major magazines like *American Mercury, Time, Reader's Digest, Saturday Evening Post* and I'm sure I'm forgetting some.

It's 1949. I've had five major books published and I'm still worried about money, ever so dependent, all the time, and ever so tired now, all talked out, all played out, and it's Christmas. If there had been a solid gold bear under the tree, I could not have gotten out of bed to get it. That's how sick I was. Gall bladder and colon. Ain't that too much. And old Lippincott, my publisher, he won't let me write about upper crust Negroes. My God, I've got to put some distance between me and all this. One minute I'm hot to trot, and the next everything has gone off, but Zora is going to write about any damned thing she wants to, including crossover stories.

That's right. I can write crossover stories too. I know who I am, and Lippincott and all the rest can go to hell. Find me another publisher and write about white folks too. And that's just what I did. *Seraph On The Suwanee*. Published in 1948. God! It didn't too well do, if you know what I mean. My God! They've missed every little point the way they are wont to when they don't want to hear the truth. Men resent artists, women artists, and there just aren't that many of us out here. And besides, there's the issue of the scandal. Yes, the scandal I mean, they made out like I was some kind of a sex pervert or something, and that just isn't true.

But they hit me with a morals charge. (*Laughter.*) Sodomy. I was accused of sodomizing a ten-year-old boy. Sodomy! Now everyone asks themselves how in the hell can a woman be accused of that and they don't come up with an answer. Everything comes up empty. Trumped charges. The day the incident is supposed to have taken place I wasn't even in town. But that makes no difference to the black newspapers because they hear about the story and they owe it to their readers to print the facts. The lousy facts they never even started to collect. And the white papers don't have to do a thing. The black ones did it all. And by the time the thing was over, I was wasted. The Assistant D.A. then was Frank Hogan, and he investigated an discovered that the mother had a grudge against me and that the ten-year-old boy had a history of emotional problems. But who would let someone come into their neighborhood to plug a book or anything if they were thinking the person was a criminal? Who the hell would think that way? Who? I don't know anyone who thinks that way. I don't. I was innocent. The charges were dropped.

It never came up to trial, but it was too late. They had finally gotten their maverick bitch into the corral this time. And she didn't have a thing to say. It was all she could do to put her head on sack of potatoes and go on off back to sleep.

So I came back home to Florida and set up this place. Through the trial and all I lost what few friends I did have, what with living on them for support and all. I sold an article now and then, but nothing like the thunder I used to strike with. I even made a fuss about some election irregularities, but it was plain to see. My career was going nowheres. And with it not going anywhere I got a chance to take my mind off the rigor of individual expression as the sole authority upon which you move through life. I can still tell a story though. "Tell them a story, Zora." I will.

NOW THERE WAS THIS MAN WHO ALWAYS LIKED TO GO FISHING ON THE SABBATH. NOBODY COULD REALLY TALK HIM OUT OF IT EITHER. HE JUST WENT. WELL, ON THIS PARTICULAR SABBATH HE WAS FISHING WHEN HE SPIED A HUGE CATFISH UNDER THE LILY PODS. SO HE BAITED HIS HOOK AND TOSSED HIS LINE AT THE CATFISH. WELL, THAT OLD FISH LOOKED AT THE LINE AND THEN DECIDED IT WOULD EAT THE BAIT AT THE END OF THE HOOK. SO IT GRABBED A HOLD AND PULLED. IT PULLED SO HARD THE MAN FELL INTO THE WATER AND GOT PULLED DOWN. WHEN HE CAME UP FOR AIR, HE SAID: "TELL MY -" WHUMP! HE WAS PULLED DOWN. HE CAME UP A SECOND TIME AND SAID: "TELL MY WIFE -" WHUMP! HE WAS PULLED DOWN A SECOND TIME. WHEN HE CAME UP FOR THE THIRD TIME, HE WAS SPUTTERING AND STAMMERING FOR BREATH. HE SAID: "TELL MY WIFE TO FEAR GOD AND CAT-FISH." WHUMP! HE WAS PULLED DOWN AGAIN AND NEVER DID COME UP.

No one could figure out who he was talking to. I guess it's the same with me. People must come by here and hear me talking, and they must wonder about me. But it don't bother me none. Not anymore. You see, I have fought with the entire system and I'd guess I'd have to call it a draw. But I sure do feel whipped. But even though I'm alone, I ain't lonely. Get that! You know a dog is sick when the fleas leave, but I still got my memories. And remember something, you don't lose a thing by not looking like me. I was a pear tree before I could remember. And being a pear tree means you don't have time to crack under the strain of life's silly jokes. I was always Zora, you know.

END

Parting

by NUBIA KAI

Nubia Kai is a poet/novelist/playwright living in Detroit. Her work has been published in the *Journal Of Black Poetry, Obsidian, Black Scholar, Black World, Solid Ground, Thedamu, Wayne Review, Compages, Quilt, Promenade, Nostalgia Into The Present: An Anthology Of Writings From Detroit* and several other publications. She has been awarded two McCree Theatre Awards, two Michigan Council For The Arts Creative Writing Grants for drama and fiction and the National Endowment For The Arts award for poetry. Her play, *Parting* was first produced by Woodie King, Jr. at the New Federal Theatre in New York, July-August, 1983.

CHARACTERS:

SUDAN JAMAL KOUYA - *About twenty-nine, tall, lean, attractive poet/artist/street warrior.*

SHERRIE CLARINGTON - *A beautiful woman about twenty-three; compassionate, sensitive.*

ACT I

Scene I

(*Lights come on to a living room setting with a kitchen setting in the background of a small apartment. Apartment is decorated with revolutionary art, posters, African art, statues, many many books stacked on milkcrate bookshelves. Suitcases stand by the front door, dishes are stacked in boxes on the cupboard in the kitchen, the record player and records are packed up in the middle of the room giving the appearance that someone is moving. SUDAN stares around the room amazed, then turns and stares at SHERRIE.*)

SUDAN: What dah fuck is goin' on? (SHERRIE *turns away from him silent and disturbed.*) Sherrie? You hear me talkin' to you?

SHERRIE: I told you already.

SUDAN (*angry*): Told me what? You runnin' out the theatre like somebody crazy. Think ah know what you was talkin' 'bout? Baby, ah was tryin' tah keep your ass calmed down. What if the pigs had come? You know I coulda blowed my parole and had to go back to that hole over some stupid shit? Is dhat what you want?! Hunh?! (*Soft but stern.*) Don't ever do that again. I'll kill a niggah, man or woman 'fo' I let 'em send me off to jail. Okay?

And if it's one thing ah can't stand, that's a bitch gettin' loud on me out in public, and it really ain't like you to git this upset and emotional and shit! I don't know what your problem is, but ah sho' wish you git it together. (SHERRIE *is silent, depressed, almost in tears. She stands looking out the window with her arms folded.*) What's the deal with the bags, and this? (*He glances around the room, swallows the lump in his throat.*) You, ah, movin' the furniture around?

SHERRIE (*she turns and faces him*): I'm leavin' you.

SUDAN (*his heart snaps, but he tries to assume a cool air*): What else is new?

SHERRIE: I'm serious, babee.

SUDAN (*harsh*): I'm serious too.

SHERRIE: Please, don't make it difficult.

SUDAN: I ain't makin' nothin' difficult, yet.

SHERRIE: Yet.

SUDAN: Not yet. You the one talkin' about breakin' up the home.

SHERRIE: A home. You call this a home? You ain't never even here.

SUDAN: Eey, do we have to go over that again?

SHERRIE: No. We don't never have tah go over it again.

SUDAN: Which is 'spose to mean what?

SHERRIE: Jus' what I said.

SUDAN (*softly, trying to allure her*): Come here.

SHERRIE: No.

SUDAN: You never disobeyed me before.

SHERRIE: I'm on my own now.

SUDAN: Ha, ha, ha. (*Sarcastic.*) You on your own now. Sound like one of them women's liberation broads. A nation is nothing without the family.

SHERRIE: We're not a family. We're a far...

SUDAN: Shut up! Who you think you talkin' to?!

154

SHERRIE: That's the problem. I can't talk to you. I jus' gotta listen to you while you talk. I can't say shit.

SUDAN: So they done got to you now with that counter-revolutionary feminist bull.

SHERRIE: Look, I'm talkin' 'bout me and you and nobody else in the whole world but me and you and what we bin goin' through. And I can't take no more of it.

SUDAN: May I ask why?

SHERRIE (*slowly, deliberately*): I'm very unhappy and very lonely with you.

SUDAN: That's not what you told me the other night.

SHERRIE: I didn't say I had stopped loving you 'cause I haven't.

SUDAN: Well then, whatchu talkin' about?

SHERRIE: I'm talkin' about it's over and I'm gone.

SUDAN: Why?

SHERRIE: Shouldn't it be obvious?

SUDAN: If it was, woman, ah wouldn't be askin' you.

SHERRIE: Ye-ah. And if it was obvious to you maybe you wouldn't have treated me the way you did.

SUDAN: Wait a minute. Wait a minute. What dah fuck you mean? Treated you how?!

SHERRIE (*in pain*): Oh God, if I have to explain to you...

SUDAN: Ah wanna know whatchu talkin' about!

SHERRIE: I'm talkin' about I ain't treated like a good bag o' shit around here and I'm...

SUDAN (*cutting*): Ain't dat a bitch! How you think you 'spose to be treated? You think I'mo take off my robe and lay it in the mud for you to walk on?

SHERRIE: What would be wrong with that?

SUDAN: She-eet. We ain't in England, babee, with King Arthur and his masons. This is twentieth century America and black folks is dyin' everyday for nothin'. That's what's wrong with you now. You believe in the Hollywood version of everything. 'Specially when it come to love. You think love is bringin' a broad candy and flowers when a cat starvin' damn near half to death himself.

SHERRIE (*very serious*): That's not true. I believed in you more than I believed in myself. I haven't asked you for anything, not even the things I should have.

SUDAN: Well don't start. Ain't nothin' changed. The weather's still cold outside and it's gettin' colder. And you ain't makin' it easier for me with all this complainin'!

SHERRIE (*perturbed*): You asked me why I was...

SUDAN (*furious*): I'm listenin'! I'm listenin'!!

SHERRIE (*depressed, head lowered*): You're not listenin'. You jus' raging at me.

SUDAN (*looks shocked, stares at her for a minute, then ambles around the room; softer*): I'm listenin'.

SHERRIE: Remember, night before last, after we had made love and you told...

SUDAN (*snaps at her*): To hell with the lecture, get to the point!

SHERRIE (*upset*): Every time I try and tell you you cut me off. I don't think you...

SUDAN (*sharp*): Go ahead. But git to the point.

SHERRIE: I'm trying.

SUDAN: Try harder!

SHERRIE (*extremely nervous*): Remember...remember the other night...

SUDAN: Sherrie! Unpack your bags and go to the bedroom.

SHERRIE (*very serious, firm but soft*): No.

SUDAN: I haven't given you permission to leave.

SHERRIE (*gently*): I don't need your permission to leave.

SUDAN (*cynical*): Ye-ah. You on your own now. Well, you damn sho' is, baby, cause you ain't leavin' me. You fired! I'm puttin' you out!

SHERRIE: You puttin' me out?

SUDAN: Damn right. You don't like it here, git the fuck out! Dhat's all you had to say in the first place. Simple. You don't like it, git out! Fact, ah want you out. If a woman ain't happy with me ah ask her to leave. Ain't treatin' you right, well, you sho' in the shit don't have to stay! There's plenty more where you come from and plenty more where you goin'!

SHERRIE (*in tears and wiping them from her face*): You won't even hear me. You won't...

SUDAN (*harsh, bitter*): Git out! Gon' on, git out!! (*He moves towards her agressively, as though he is going to force her out. She turns away from him abruptly, bends over and cries into her hands. He stops.*) Shut up! Jus' shut up and git out! (*He walks away, disgusted and ir-*

ritated, to the other side of the room. SHERRIE *continues to cry.*) Look, dhat shit is gittin' on my nerves. Why don't you go in the bathroom, take a shower or somethin'. (*Pause.*) Go in the bathroom! Go ahead! (*Points in the direction of the bathroom. She walks across stage, exits offstage to bathroom. He watches her leave stage, turns back mumbling.*) Ah ain't listenin' to all that snivelin'.

(*He goes to closet, takes out a pack of Kools and a cigarette lighter from his jacket pocket, lights cigarette, smokes nervously, goes to kitchen area behind the livingroom, takes a bottle of wine from the bottom of the cabinet, takes a glass from the cupboard and pours a drink. He drinks the wine down, starts to pour another drink, then puts the glass in the sink and drinks straight from the bottle; he smokes, walks towards the bathroom with bottle in hand. She comes out, staring at the bottle.* SUDAN *looks at the bottle..*)

Surprised? Has bin a long time hasn't it? See whatchu got me doin' to myself? I see you bin hittin' the bottle quite a bit when I'm out. (*Cuts his eyes at her.*) Bin smokin' up all the weed, too.

SHERRIE (*shrugging her shoulders*): Gotta do somethin'.

SUDAN: Seem like you could find something better to do then git high all day. Ah asked you to type those poems up for me. I see you ain't done that.

SHERRIE: You lent the typewriter to Ali.

SUDAN (*takes a swig of wine*): Ah told you to git it back from Ali. Thought you had it by now.

SHERRIE (*walks across the room*): Wow. I forgot to tell you. I completely forgot. I had shoved it back so far in my mind 'cause ah didn't know how...

SUDAN: Git to the point!

SHERRIE: Ali don't have it. He pawned it for some dope.

SUDAN (*surprised*): He told you that?

SHERRIE: Kali told me first, then he told me himself. He said he was sorry and that he'd git it back soon as he got paid.

SUDAN (*angry*) : Then he goin' git some more dope.

SHERRIE: He said he'd git it back.

SUDAN: She-eet. I'm hip to dem niggahs with joneses, baby. They don't be playin'. They steal from they own mama 'cause they can't help it. (*Pause. He walks around the room pacing the floor.*) Ain't dhat a bitch, done pawned my muthafuckin' typewriter for some shit!! Stupid niggah! (*Turns to her.*) Don't see how you forgot some-thin' like that. Ah don't know what's on your mind.

SHERRIE: There's bin a lot on my mind, lately.

SUDAN (*muttering, intensely angry*): Ah oughtta off that mutha-fuckin' junkie callin' himself Allah. Stupid ass junkie! He must think I'm a gotdamn punk. He's sorry, he's gon' git it back, hunh? He gotdamn straight he gone git it back, and I want it back tomor-row or I'mo take it outta his ass! (*He takes a swig of wine.*)

I wanna git those poems in before the deadline. And you, you so high you can't remember somethin' as important as that. Smokin' up all the weed. You smoke more weed than I do. And ah notice you all the time gotta get high before we git down. You go grab you a joint for you to grab my joint. (*Viciously.*) I don't like that.

SHERRIE: You don't have to worry about that...

SUDAN (*hot, angry*): I ain't worried about it!! There's plenty of good pussy in the world! (*He takes a long swig of the wine and finishes it off, then he turns and hurls the empty bottle against the back cabinet or wall. SHERRIE ducks down. The glass shatters and falls on the kitch-en floor.*) GO ON!! GIT OUT!! GIT OUT!!! DON'T BRING YOUR BLACK ASS BACK!

(*SHERRIE is quiet and very depressed. She takes her jacket from the couch and puts it on over her sweater. SUDAN turns away from her, hands in his blue jeans, extremely agitated.*)

SUDAN: Wait a minute! (*SUDAN glances at boxes of dishes stack-ed next to the cupboard.*) Before you go ah want you to unpack these dishes, put the record player and the jams back and leave those suitcases.

SHERRIE (*surprised, but speaking very softly*): But...these are mine.

SUDAN (*ill-tempered*): How you figure they yours? Everything in mah house belongs to me...<u>including you</u>. And you ain't got my permission to leave! And you ain't leavin' till you unpack this stuff. You ain't takin' none of mah shit outta here! Where you think you goin' with the box? My main inspiration is music; my poems come from the rhythm of the music. You gon' cut off my soul. Hell naw. You ain't takin' the box. And the dishes, they stayin' here. Whatchu think I'm 'spose to eat out of?

SHERRIE: Look, you can keep everything if that's the way you feel, but just let me take my suitcases. My mother and father got those for me when ah graduated from high school. Ah wanna...

SUDAN (*lights up a cigarette*): They mine now. (*He tosses his head back arrogantly.*) Everything in mah house is mine...including you. And you ain't got my permission to leave! And you ain't takin' the suitcases 'cause ah gotta go to New York next week, and I'm gon' need 'em.

SHERRIE: But they're not yours.

SUDAN: We made an agreement, remember? Everything in the house belonged to me.

SHERRIE: But not a gift that my parents gave...

SUDAN: Everything! We said everything! Everything is every-thing, ain't it?!

SHERRIE (*getting loud*): You jus' bein' honory. Jus' plain honory!

SUDAN: I'm goin' to New York next week and I need the suit-cases.

SHERRIE: You need both of them? Can't you let me take one of them?

SUDAN: Yeh, I need both of them. I use the small one to keep my carving and etching tools in.

SHERRIE: So I'm 'spose to take my clothes outta here in paper bags?

SUDAN: You lucky I'm lettin' you take your clothes. Whole lot-ta dudes burn up a bitch's clothes when she walk out on him!

SHERRIE: Dudes that don't have they heads wrapped too tight.

SUDAN (*contemptuous*): You tryin' to say ah ain't got mine wrapped too tight?

SHERRIE: If you think burning up my clothes can be justified, then yes.

SUDAN: You simple bitch.

SHERRIE (*taking her purse from beside the couch*): I'm leavin'.

SUDAN (*fiercely*): You ain't goin' nowhere till you put the rec-ord player back and the dishes and leave those suitcases!!

SHERRIE (*she starts crying*): Jus' let me go, Sudan...Let me go in peace, okay. I don't want no trouble. I don't wanna fight you.

SUDAN: Ain't nobody gotta fight. Ah ain't gon' hurt you. Jus' do what ah told you to do.

(SHERRIE *moves the record player back against the wall on a stand, puts the records back.* SUDAN *goes to a closet, takes his jacket out and brings out two joints from his jacket pocket. He lights one while* SHER-RIE, *still crying, puts up the dishes.*)

SUDAN (*agitated, taking quick drags from the joint*): I'd wish you'd stop that cryin'. (*Pause.*) Say, whatchu cryin' for, jus' 'cause ah told you to put dhat stuff up?

SHERRIE (*sobbing, leans over against the cabinet*): Dah...the w-whole thing...

SUDAN (*coldly*): When you git finished you can leave. Ain't nobody holdin' you here.

SHERRIE (*angry, crying*): You holding me here now!

SUDAN (*cuts his eyes at her*): Ah gotta mind to do more than that. (*He takes a long drag from the joint.*)

SHERRIE (*slamming a dish into the cupboard*): Look, if you not gon' let me leave withou a bunchu hassle, then what am I doin' this for?

SUDAN: 'Cause ah told you to do it.

SHERRIE (*turns away fretfully and continues putting up dishes*): Sudan, I want the suitcases.

SUDAN: Ah don't wanna hear no more about those suitcases.

SHERRIE: You selfish. You so selfish you stink!

SUDAN: Fuck you.

SHERRIE: Hey, I'm ready tah go.

SUDAN: Soon as you put up the dishes.

SHERRIE (*very nervous and frustrated*): Ah wanna go now. Ah wanna go right now. Please be kind enough to put the dishes up later. Jus' let me leave now.

SUDAN: All you gotta do is put up the dishes!!

SHERRIE (*shouting*): I wanna leave now! You got no right to keep me here!!

SUDAN (*belligerent*): Damn, if you don't stop shouting at me, woman!

SHERRIE (*loud*): I'm leavin'!! (*She starts to walk to the couch to get her purse. He blocks her path.*)

SUDAN (*holds joint out to her*): Why don't chu smoke a joint?

SHERRIE (*softly*): No...Thank you. (*She steps back from him, walks around the room avoiding him while trying to get to her purse.*)

SUDAN (*following her around the room with his eyes*): You never refused any before.

SHERRIE: I'm not in the mood for any.

SUDAN (*lights a joint, then throws the matches down angrily*): Naw, you only in the mood when we git ready to fuck! Well come on, baby, you might as well smoke some.

SHERRIE (*she stares at him solemnly*): Ah don't wanna do that.

SUDAN: Ah ain't asked you what you wanted to do. You ain't asked me nothin'! You jus' git up and pull out like ah wasn't shit! Like I ain't doin' the best ah can for you, like we wasn't a family!

SHERRIE: I thought a minute ago you was puttin' me out.

SUDAN (*arrogant*): I am puttin' you out!

SHERRIE: Oh, you puttin' me out for leavin', hunh? (*She picks up her purse, heads for the door.*)

SUDAN: Where you goin'? (*He rushes to the door and stands in front of it.*) You gon' walk through these arms and legs? You ain't put up the dishes yet. (*Takes a long drag from the joint.*) And furthermore...I wanna fuck.

SHERRIE: I don't.

SUDAN: 'Cause you don't don't mean you won't! Ha, ha, ha.

SHERRIE (*distraught*): You're even worse than I thought.

SUDAN(*alarmed,insulted*):Whatdahfuckisthat'sposeto mean?! Hunh? (*He moves towards her with his fist gnarled.*)

SHERRIE (*calm*): Jus' what I said.

SUDAN (*he backs against door and stares at her wide-eyed and furious*): I don't know what your problem is but you ain't goin' no mutha-fuckin' where! You hear that! (*Points at her.*) YOU AIN'T GOIN' NO MUTHAFUCKIN' WHERE!! SO SIT YOUR ASS DOWN!!

SHERRIE (*meekly*): I thought you wanted me to leave.

SUDAN (*shouting*): Ah don't wantchu to leave! You know damn well ah don't!

SHERRIE: You didn't say that.

SUDAN (*embarrassed, but loud*): I'm sayin' it now! That's what you wanted to hear? I'm sayin' it! I don't wantchu to leave, Sherrie!! I don't wantchu to leave!! (*He breaks down and starts to cry, but he is embarrassed and tries desperately to compose himself.*) Ah don't wantchu to leave. What else can I say.

SHERRIE: You could have told me.

SUDAN: I'm tellin' you now. Ah don't wantchu to leave. (*Pause.*) Please stay.

SHERRIE (*gloomy*): I can't.

SUDAN: Sit down. We can talk about it.

SHERRIE: We've tried that.

SUDAN: We can try again. (*Sincere, apologetic.*) I'm ready to try again. I don't wantchu to go.

SHERRIE (*wearily*): Not now, please not now. You're hyper and I'm hy...

SUDAN: Hyper? Me? You the one cryin' and gittin' upset.

SHERRIE: 'Cause you wouldn't let me talk to you.

SUDAN: You got the floor now.

SHERRIE: If I got the floor, then let me pass.

SUDAN (*abrupt, determined*): No. Ah wanna talk to you first! Take off your jacket; you makin' me hot.

SHERRIE: I'm not takin' off my jacket.

SUDAN: Aww c'mon, don't make me have to hurt you.

SHERRIE: You're tryin' to force me here against...

SUDAN: I'm not. Ah jus' wanna talk to you, and you wanna run out on me.

SHERRIE: If dhat's all ah was doin' I could've done that a long time ago.

SUDAN: Take off your jacket, Sherrie. (*He grabs her behind the neck and snatches off her jacket. She struggles. He pushes her, hurls the jacket to the floor and backs against the front door.*) You ain't goin' no muthafuckin' where! Ah got the key to the inside, ya know. (*He pulls a key from his blue jean pocket, locks the door, then puts the key back into his pocket.*)

SHERRIE (*pleading*): Let me go, please, let me go.

SUDAN: No. Ah wanna talk to you.

SHERRIE: Not now.

SUDAN: Yes now.

SHERRIE (*breathing hard, crying*): Let me go, Su...!!

SUDAN (*hypertensive, raging*): I AIN'T LETTING YOU GO SO QUIT ASKING ME!!! (*He goes to her and grabs her by the shoulders; she wrenches herself away and moves around the room away from him. He catches her from behind and rips the back of her blouse. She turns, strikes him in the face and they start to fight. She fights him as hard as she can; he hits her twice, the second time landing her on the floor by the couch. He kneels on her arms that are pinned against the floor and grips his hands tight around her throat. He chokes her, squeezes harder, then gradually lightens his grip as the telephone rings. As though the sound of the telephone makes him realize what he's doing, he releases her, then breaks down and rests his hands on her shoulders, shaking and sobbing while she lies motionless on the floor.)*

SUDAN *(crying)*: Please don't go. Please don't...don't...don't...

(She stirs, raises her knee, turns her head slightly to the side, gasping for breath. He kisses her neck, then rests his head against her neck, sobbing. Lights.)

Scene II

(A little later. SUDAN stands in the kitchen gulping down a glass of water. He is still hypersensitive, but his demeanor now is sorrowful, remorseful. He hangs his head dismally while pacing the kitchen floor. SHERRIE exits from bathroom, stage right, onto the stage. She wears a different blouse and face is slightly swollen on the left side. They stare at each other for a minute.)

SUDAN *(ashamed)*: You okay?

SHERRIE *(softly)*: I'm okay. I jus' wanna go now.

(He walks over to her, gazes at her face and touches the swollen spot. She jumps back.)

SUDAN: Does that hurt?

SHERRIE: A little.

SUDAN *(slow, remorseful)*: I'm sorry.

SHERRIE: I know.

(He cups her face and gently kisses her forehead, the swollen side of her face. She tenses up and pulls away. He pulls her by the hands.)

SUDAN *(pleadingly)*: Don't pull away from me, please, baby. *(He pulls her to him, kisses her hard and passionately on the lips. She tenses up again and pulls away. He catches her by the hands.)* Why you pullin' away from me?

SHERRIE: I don't feel like it right now.

(He lets go of her hands. She moves away from him into the kitchen area.)

SUDAN: You don't even want me to touch you. Mah woman don't want me to touch her.

SHERRIE: Not right now.

SUDAN: It's an expression, a way of sayin' I'm sorry. *(Tears in eyes.)* Don't you understand...my need to hold you right now.

SHERRIE: Can you understand my need <u>not</u> to be held?

SUDAN (*hands in his pockets, he turns away brooding, then walks into the kitchen*): You want a glass of water?

(*She nods her head. He reaches in the cupboard for a glass, takes a pitcher of water from the refrigerator and pours her a glass. He hands it to her; she drinks.*)

SHERRIE: Woo-o, it's cold.

SUDAN (*boyishly*): You're cold, Sherrie.

SHERRIE: You're a little boy of never never land.

SUDAN (*half-smiling*): Ah know, baby, but you cold, cold Sherrie wine. Get a man drunk, outta his mind, then leave him sick and slobberin' in his shit. That's what you do to a cat. (*He walks away into the living room, sits on the couch and lights up a cigarette.*) I don't wantchu to go.

SHERRIE: I don't wanna go either, but ah ain't got no choice.

SUDAN: You do have a choice. You can stay. You don't have tah go.

SHERRIE: You didn't leave me a choice. When I tried to talk to you before, you ignored me jus' like you did this time. I've waited four years for things to get better, but they just get worse.

SUDAN (*embarrassed, humiliated*): I'm listenin'. I'm ready to listen now. Whada you want me tah do, baby? You want me to git a job?

SHERRIE: Nothing. Nothing.

SUDAN: Aww c'mon, give a cat a break.

SHERRIE: I am gon' give you a break. We can both get a break.

SUDAN (*shaking his head miserably*): No, baby, no. Why you doin' this to me?

SHERRIE: Why did you do what you did to me?

SUDAN (*very sad*): Ah lost my temper. Ah jus' didn't want you tah go.

SHERRIE: I mean the whole time. The whole four years, it's bin the same thing.

SUDAN: What's bin the same thing?

SHERRIE (*expressive*): I'm still supporting you. I mean I don't mind it if that's what has to be done, but after three years?

SUDAN (*irritated*): That ain't no big thing. That ain't no long time. Some of the brothers on the continent and in Asia be separated from they families for lo-ong periods. I means years, baby, especially when they in combat. Women gotta fend for themselves. (*He rises from the couch and starts pacing the floor.*)

The ol' brothers down South, sometimes took 'em years to git work. Sisters had to clean the cracker's house or sleep in the cracker's bed to git food on the table. Fact, mah daddy got laid off during the Depression, and my mama did daywork for 'bout five years. Course, mah ol' man worked though; he got odd jobs here and there, but for five years mah mama got the steady income in the family.

It didn't cause no problems with them; I mean, she didn't git all uppity and think she was gon' run the household jus' 'cause she made most of the money. Course, mah ol' man woulda put his foot up her ass if she did.

But he didn't mind workin'. Nigger worked his ass off and acted like he loved it. Thought he was the John Henry of Ford Mo. Company. He be braggin' about how they use to come out to the factory the night before it opened and stand in line. Can you imagine, niggers linin' up ten, eleven o'clock at night and waitin' all night 'til six o'clock when the doors open, and dhat still don't mean you gon' get hired. He did that every night for five months till he got re-hired in '36 and brag about it! See, workin' for Mr. Ford was a prestigious thing back then, but it ain't about shit to me 'cept slavery.

I guess I didn't inherit that John Henry mentality from him. I say crush the muthafuckin' railroads and the monsters who own it.

SHERRIE: We're not in a situation like that.

SUDAN: How is it different? Ah mean, how is it any really different than it was a hundred years back. We ain't got no more now than we had then. Fact, we got less.

SHERRIE: The form is different. That's what's different. Not the oppression, but the form it takes. But the circumstances you laid out - what's happenin' in other parts of the world or forty somethin' years ago don't fit these. You ain't in no armed combat; you like to go around pretending you are, but you're not.

SUDAN: So that's the way you feel...about what I'm doing. (*Heated.*) No, I don't have guns, but I got poems. (*He goes to closet, takes out typed copies of poems and slaps them down on a table.*) And I'm workin' on a play now. And I might get a commission to do

165

some engraving work for this cat in New York. Those are the strongest weapons I got right now, and ah gotta use 'em. If you gimme a chance. It's better than bustin' mah ass building their empire. Ah ain't bustin' mah ass in no factory. (*Looks up at her.*) Ah mean, ah might if that's all I could do to take care of us. Seem like to me niggers deserve better than that, though.

SHERRIE: I agree...since I'm bustin' mah ass in a factory. (*She walks away from him disgustedly. He looks startled, then embarrassed.*)

SUDAN (*abashed*): Ah don't want you doin' that either...you know that.

SHERRIE: But it's tolerable when I do it.

SUDAN: Whatchu want? You want me to get a job? Okay! I'll get a job. If the engraving deal don't go through, I'll look for a job when I come back, and...and then I can take care of you like it's 'spose to be.

SHERRIE: You don't have to do any of that now, not for me. You had all the time in the world. You watched me git up and go to that bakery every morning, workin' overtime, wouldn't even come pick me up when I got switched to afternoons when the car was right here. That's how much you cared about me bustin' mah ass. You didn't even care whether ah got home safe or not. (*Loud.*) The only nights you came to get me was when I got my paycheck. That's what you cared about - the money. You too good to bust your ass while you pimp off of me.

SUDAN (*infuriated, intense, he crashes his fist against a lamp table*): GOTDAMIT, THAT'S A LIE!! (*He moves swiftly around the room away from her.*) If I was pimpin' off of you, your ass would be out on the streets hoein'. So don't use that term...

SHERRIE: The form is different, that's all. It's the same thing. (*Pause.*) You wanna hear more?

SUDAN: Not really.

SHERRIE: I thought you were ready to talk.

SUDAN: Well ah done heard it! I'm a low down niggah who treats you like a dog or a bag o' shit or whatever you said. That's all you sayin', baby.

SHERRIE: Is that what I'm sayin'? I should take that back, then. You don't treat me like a dog or a bag o' shit. That's an understatement. You treat me worse. With a bag o' shit you flush it out, you flush it down the toilet and git rid of it. You won't even give me the privilege of walkin' outta here. And a dog? If you treated me half as good as you treated Babe, I wouldn't be leavin' now. You don't holler at him like you do me. And when he's tired and at your feet, you at least pat him on the head and tell him he's a good dog. You take him for walks. I don't git that kind of courtesy. And you cuddle him and play with him and smile at him. All you wanna do is ram it in me.

SUDAN (*upset, but trying to be calm*): Ah don't wanna hear no more.

SHERRIE: There is more, you know...a whole lot more. Like your women. They haven't stopped callin' the house. If you got to have your other women, you could respect me enough to tell them not to call here all kinda hours of the night.

SUDAN (*frustrated*): Aww c'mon, that ain't got shit to do with me. I didn't give those broads, ah mean sisters, our phone number. Brenda took it from the register. And Mkati, well we was workin' together. Me and Brenda was too; we was acting in the same theatre company. Most of the time they called it was about business.

SHERRIE: At two o'clock in the mornin'?

SUDAN: Alright, that wasn't all they called about. But ah ain't had nothin' to do with it. Ah was jus' workin' with the sisters. And it's some lonely women out here, baby. They be on a dude like he's goin' outta style. I told 'em not to call here no more. Look, we can get the phone number changed. Okay? But you know sisters gonna be callin' here for other things 'cause I work with sisters, and I like workin' with sisters.

SHERRIE: What kinda work was you doin' when I came in that night and you and Brenda was kissin'?

SUDAN (*apologetic*): We was actin' together. We was rehearsin' over here. That was part of the script.

SHERRIE: You were rehearsing in the bedroom?

SUDAN (*in a weak voice*): It was a bedroom scene.

SHERRIE: You really expect me to believe that?

SUDAN: You can believe it or not.

SHERRIE (*amused*): Ha, ha, ha, that's even funny.

SUDAN: The kinds of things I do, ah don't need no jealous woman. We never could git along if every time I acted with a sister or drew a nude model, you think ah got a thang goin'.

167

SHERRIE (*firm, determined*): Les be serious. Les be truthful and honest with each other. You're making excuses for everything, and that shit has played out. You know you been goin' with those sisters. It takes so much more away from you when you lie.

SUDAN (*depressed, embarrassed*): They were lonely women. Had been lookin' and searchin' for years for a man to tell 'em they were beautiful...beautiful Black women. Ah tried to keep my distance, but they kept after me. (*Loud.*) They begged me to <u>love</u> them!

SHERRIE: And you couldn't refuse.

SUDAN (*dismally*): I wish I had of. Ah really do.

SHERRIE (*half-smiling*): You in a world of trouble, aren't you, babee?

SUDAN (*looks up at her surprised*): Whada you mean?

SHERRIE: When things get hot you leave town. Jus' got back from California, now you goin' to New York. Don't play innocent. They called here all while you were in California, pissed off, threatening to kill each other. I'm surprised they didn't threaten to kill me, 'cept it was like ah wasn't even there. The bullets was flyin' back and forth, and I wasn't even there. Guess they jus' see me as your submissive little woman that justs puts up with all your shit and never says anything. Evidently that's the impression you gave them.

SUDAN: I see I gave them the wrong impression.

SHERRIE: Ah want some respect. If I can't get it here, I'll go somewhere else. (*Pause.*) One of the sisters said she was gonna kill you...Mkati? Said she had her black belt in karate and knew how to deal a dude a death blow.

SUDAN (*smirking*): She ain't lyin' about that either. (*Muttering.*) Stupid broad.

SHERRIE: You left jus' in time so I could be left here and have to hear that and not you. I don't wanna be in the middle of it.

SUDAN (*suspicious*): What else did they tell you?

SHERRIE: Oh, a whole lotta things. Between the two of them ah could almost figure out your whole chess game, except that certain parts didn't fit, and I know they're other players in it.

SUDAN: She-eet. If you think I got more women then you and them two, you crazy. That's your imagination.

SHERRIE: You been makin' trips to New York quite a bit. Ah got a feelin' there's a woman there.

SUDAN: Why ah gotta have a woman everywhere ah go? When I go outta town, that's a chance for me to be to myself; ah git a chance to really think and work.

SHERRIE: Ahh, but I bin watchin' you and I bin seein' where your inspiration come from. You don't write no poems or paint no pictures less it's a woman by your side blowin' in your ear. You have a woman everywhere you go 'cause that's the way you are.

(SUDAN *paces slowly back and forth in the room; he is nervous and peeved.*)

There is a woman there, isn't it?

SUDAN (*stops and turns to her*): No.

SHERRIE: There is, isn't it?

SUDAN: No, Sherrie, it's not.

SHERRIE (*firmly*): There is, isn't it?

SUDAN (*shouting*): Ah said it ain't!!!

SHERRIE (*disturbed but soft-spoken*): Ah wanna know the truth.

SUDAN (*loud*): Ah'm tellin' you the truth!!

(SHERRIE *turns away repulsed. There is a long pause.* SUDAN *continues to pace the floor; he stops.*)

Okay, okay. Ah don't know how you found out about it, but I got involved with a woman there. It wasn't planned. Ah sho' didn't go there lookin' for one. But you're right, I need love to create by. Y'all so beautiful, ah can't help myself.

SHERRIE: You can take love, Sudan, but you can't give it.

SUDAN: I'm still learnin'. Give me a chance. (*He turns away and starts to cry, all the while trying hard to suppress his tears as he leans against the sofa.*) Fix me some tea...please. This wine has made me sick to my stomach. (*He frowns, places his hands on his stomach.*)

SHERRIE: What kind do you want?

SUDAN: Any kind. No, no, give me some sage.

(SHERRIE *takes a kettle from the cupboard, runs water in it and puts it on the stove. She lights the burner, takes a cup and saucer from the cupboard. She turns to him staring, sympathetically, as though feeling the pain of his tears.*)

SUDAN (*humiliated*): Whatchu starin' at?

SHERRIE: At you. I've never seen you cry.

SUDAN: Is that what you wanted to see?

SHERRIE: No.

SUDAN: What more do you need? Aren't my tears enough to tell you how I feel?

SHERRIE: They don't tell me anything is gonna change.

SUDAN (*wide-eyed, approaching her*): But they are! Look, who knows, maybe one day our people'll have to practice polygamy to survive, like the brothers be sayin'. But me, ah don't want no parts of it. I only want one woman, and that's you. (*Pause.*) Maybe I have been neglecting you. But...but ah'm sorry. I'll make it up to you. Look, we can get married. That's what you wanted. (*Smiling.*) Ah'll marry you.

(SHERRIE *blushes, then laughs.*)

SUDAN (*aggravated, angry*): What's so funny?! Shut up, damit! Shut up, ah said!

SHERRIE (*still laughing*): After all these years. (*Stops laughing.*) You think that's what I wanted? I thought we were <u>already</u> married.

SUDAN: I mean we can really get married. We can go downtown, git a license.

SHERRIE (*surprised*): Is that what marriage is to you? Does the piece of paper really make the difference? Whose authority is it that you really respect - the state's authority? - the white man's? Ah thought our commitment to each other was the real marriage. You sound like you doin' me some kind of favor.

SUDAN (*sits on the couch, wringing his hands, embittered and angry; mumbling*): You won't git no more offers, that's for sho'!

SHERRIE: Then it was a favor. Well, no thank you. (*Pause.*) I think your tea is ready. (SHERRIE *pours the tea leaves into the boiling water, then stirs it around with a spoon. She takes a strainer from the cupboard, puts it over the cup and pours the boiling water through the strainer. She waits.*) You want honey in it.?

SUDAN (*head hanging*): Yeh.

(*She takes a large jar of honey from the cupboard, pours it into the cup and stirs it. She brings the tea to him, setting it on the cocktail table in front of the couch. He grabs her hand and starts kissing it, then presses his cheek against it. Whispers.*)

Sherrie...Sherrie...(*He pulls her by her buttocks and presses his head to her stomach. Breathy.*) Sherrie...

(*She is uneasy and pulls away from him, but her love begins to show painfully on her face.*)

SUDAN (*sad*): You don't even want me to touch you. How you think that makes me feel?

SHERRIE: What does it do? Does it do something to your ego?

SUDAN: It goes far deeper than that. Ah shouldn't have to tell you. If I've hurt you, then you know what it feels like to be hurt. (*He sips his tea from the spoon.*)

SHERRIE: Ah gotta go now.

SUDAN: Do you really have to go? Ah mean, do you have to go somewhere right now?

SHERRIE: I'm 'spose to catch the ten-thirty bus.

SUDAN: Where you goin'?

SHERRIE: To Dayton, to stay with my cousin.

SUDAN: Who, Letta?

SHERRIE: Yeh. She think she might be able to get me a job at the new independent school she works at.

SUDAN: I wish you luck, but I hate for you to go like this.

SHERRIE: Will you please open the door? (*Pause.*) I'm gonna miss my bus.

SUDAN: So miss it.

SHERRIE (*getting upset*): Do we have to go through this again?

SUDAN: Why don't you call Letta and tell her you're not comin'?

SHERRIE: 'Cause I am comin'.

SUDAN (*stern*): Not tonight you ain't.

SHERRIE (*fiery*): Whatchu gonna do? You gon' beat me and choke me...?

SUDAN: I'll do whatever I have to do. I'd rather see you dead then to see you walk outta here.

(SHERRIE *starts to cry.*)

Stop cryin', baby. Everything gon' be alright, you'll see.

SHERRIE (*shaking her head*): I'm not stayin'. You can't...

SUDAN (*hot-tempered, loud*): BUT YOU CAN'T GO!! (*Passionate.*) You can't just take four years and walk out the door with it, like it wasn't nothin'. That's four years of my life you takin' outta here... jus' like that! (*Pops his finger.*)

(SHERRIE *tries to open the door.*)

The door is locked. (*He sits on the couch drinking his tea. She turns to him silent, inwardly fuming.*)

Why don't you take off your jacket and come sit down?

SHERRIE: You bastard. (SHERRIE *goes over to window, stares out of window crying with her back to* SUDAN. *He goes to her, embraces her from behind, enfolding his arms completely around her, kisses her neck and cheek.*)

SUDAN (*whispers*): Don't go...don't go...baby...

(*She turns around. They stare at each other; her love for him is shown through her expressions. They embrace passionately, kiss. Curtain.*)

END OF ACT I

ACT II

Scene I

(*Later that night. The couch in the living room has been converted into a bed. They lie in bed together kissing and caressing one another passionately. The sheet and blanket cover them to the shoulders. A colored light and lamp make the room dim but visible enough so that the couple can be seen clearly.*)

SUDAN (*drawing his lips away, still enfolding her*): Mah beautiful woman...(*Pause.*)...Baby...

(*They kiss, stare lovingly at each other, kiss again.*)

You feel so good to me, baby. Gotdamn, you feel so-o good. It gits better and better don't it? (*Pause.*)...Don't it, Sherrie?

(*She blushes and buries her head in his chest coyly. He slaps her on the behind.*)

Don't it, baby?

(*She tosses her head back and laughs. He joins in.*)

I like to watch you laugh. Laugh some more. (*He tickles her.*)

SHERRIE (*laughing*): Quit it...Ha, ha, ha, ha...stop Sudan...(*She slaps his hand.*)

SUDAN: Never, baby...never...(*He tickles her again. She laughs. They embrace and kiss.*) Don't never go away from me. I need you. I love you...(*Pause. He faces audience with his arm around her.*) Guess ah gotta start showin' it more. (*He pinches her chin.*) Hunh?

SHERRIE: Yeh, besides jus' in the bed, ya know.

SUDAN (*shamefaced*): Ye-ah. (*He gazes at her lovingly, bends and kisses her cheek.*) If I treated you as good as I do in the bed, everything would be alright. Ah'm startin' to understand that. Ah mean, it's takin' me ah long time, but ah'm startin' to understand.

SHERRIE: Are you, Sudan?

SUDAN: Yeh, I think I am.

SHERRIE (*gazing at the covers*): Ah was thinkin' about it while we were making love.

SUDAN: What?

SHERRIE: If you really understood, or if we were jus' making love and it would be the same ol' shit when we got up.

SUDAN: That's what you were thinkin'?

SHERRIE: Yes. I was worryin' about whether or not I was makin' a mistake. That's why it took me so long to come.

SUDAN: You think this is a mistake? (*He puts his hands around her head and kisses her.*) How can what we feel for each other be a mistake?

SHERRIE: How long will it last?

SUDAN (*soft, expressive, full of passion*): Forever...forever...(*He showers kisses over her face while he talks.*) Even if you die, or go away, I'll love the memories of you. Ah'll love you forever...Ah don't have no reason to stop...

You're so beautiful, nothing seems to change you, no matter what dah hell is happenin' in the world, you're always you...even when you're angry you're beautiful...even when you're sad, but I like you best when you're laughing...That's how I see you. You're a beautiful work of art. You're a masterpiece of creation, something ah couldn't begin to compete with. That's why I could never paint you, but you inspire everything I do that's creative. If it's any beauty in it, it's your beauty.

SHERRIE: It's your beauty too. Those things are coming out of you.

SUDAN: You think so?

SHERRIE: I know it. I see and know the beauty in you. That's why I've waited so long hoping and praying you would change.

SUDAN: I'm gon' change, baby. I mean, I'mo start treatin' you better 'cause you deserve it. Nah, I ain't kissin' no broad's...I mean sister's ass, but I'm gon' be good to you like a true man is 'spose to be.

SHERRIE: It'll all take time; it won't happen overnight.

SUDAN: Oh yeah, yeh, baby, it's gonna take time. That's why I say gimme more time.

(SHERRIE *starts crying.*)

SUDAN (*caressing her neck*): We can. Why you cryin'?

SHERRIE (*wiping her tears*): Ah don't know...

SUDAN: Ah hope it's from joy.

SHERRIE: It's from both, Sudan, joy and hurt.

SUDAN: Hurt, why?

SHERRIE (*with anguish*): 'Cause...'cause...(*She cries.*)...it could of been so beautiful; it could have been heaven, and ah wanted it to be so bad...'cause it was there, it was there, but it didn't go nowhere, like we jus' fell outta the sky and died.

SUDAN: It can still be whatever you want it to be.

SHERRIE: Not by myself, it can't.

SUDAN: You ain't by yourself. You got a man here who's crazy about you, even if ah do still got a little nigger in me and I go off my rocker now and then. Eey, it's a trip dealin' with these devils everyday.

SHERRIE (*frustrated*): The problem's more than a little nigger; it's a whole lot in you. Hell, in most of us. But it's serious, and I know I can't live like this anymore.

SUDAN (*removes his arms from around her and turns away annoyed; bitterly*): So ah got a lotta niggah in me, hunh?

SHERRIE: Three, four years ain't gon' change what's happened in the last four hundred years. I'm starting to see that more and more now.

SUDAN: Niggah can't never change?

SHERRIE: Ah didn't say that. You so sensitive. You take what I say as insult when it's not. Ah'm looking at you and feelin' you and tellin' you what I see. Ain't we 'spose to be mirrors for each other? I see you. You see me. But ah can't talk to you...not even after I give in to you...

SUDAN: You gave in to what you felt, not me.

SHERRIE: But what I feel doesn't change anything, not even you.

SUDAN: Ah wantchu, woman. Ah can't afford to lose you. You the most valuable thing ah got. I'll do what ah have to do to keep you. Ah jus' won't have no woman dominating me.

SHERRIE: It ain't even about that. Why does that bother you so much?

SUDAN: 'Cause it ain't s'pose to be like that.

SHERRIE: It ain't about neither one of us dominatin' the other, that's what I think. I can't see bein' treated like an eight-year-old when I'm a grown woman, and that's what it's like when somebody's dominating you. You can't be yourself, whatever that is, not when you can't breathe.

SUDAN (*grimacing*): You gon' choke me to death, baby.

SHERRIE (*looking at him hard before speaking*): If that's the way you feel, Sudan, then there's no point in foolin' ourselves. (*She pulls the covers back, exposing her long, thin-strapped nightgown and starts to get out of bed.*)

SUDAN (*rises, pulls her by the arm; alarmed*): Where you goin'? What did ah say?

SHERRIE (*disturbed*): Damn, you can't be that blind...or that deaf that you don't hear your own words.

SUDAN: You know what, baby, evidently I am 'cause ah wouldn't be sayin' nothin' to make you leave me.

SHERRIE: But you jus' did.

SUDAN: Whatever ah said, ah take it back.

SHERRIE: But you can't take it back. And if you don't know what you said, how do you know what to take back? You'll jus' say it again.

SUDAN: Then ah won't say nothin'. (*He pulls her down aggressively on the bed and kisses her. She resists. He takes her arms and holds them.*) Don't fight me...Don't...(*He kisses her face.*) Jus' love me like you bin doin'.

SHERRIE: My love is being wasted.

SUDAN (*pulls away from her, startled*): Is that possible? To waste love?

SHERRIE: You wasted it; you threw it away.

SUDAN: Not threw it away. I didn't see it; that's why it shot past me. Not till you was walkin' out the door did it hit me. And, baby, it hit me. It hit me like a bomb. Now you know why I went to pieces. Ever had a bomb dropped on your head? I have. And the only reason I'm alive to tell it now is 'cause you stayed...(*Pause.*)...Sherrie...

(*He pushes his head under the covers and kisses her breasts, then he pulls up and kisses her. She squeezes him. They roll over in bed so that she lies on top of him. They smile.*)

Now, ah know what ah got. The real wine...a gem. I knew it all the time. I jus' forgot.

SHERRIE: I forgot too.

SUDAN (*tenderly*): Thanks for remindin' me.

SHERRIE (*smiling, glowing*): Don't mention it. Gotta do that. (*She rubs her nose against his, grinning. He tickles her and they roll over so that they lie beside each other.*)

SUDAN: Love you, woman. (*Pause.*) Love me?

SHERRIE (*passionate*): Too much.

SUDAN: Don't say "too much." How can you love me too much?

SHERRIE: Ah don't know. Or maybe it's that I don't love myself enough. (*Pause.*) Ah wonder sometimes, is it that Black women need love so much that they'll accept it anyway they get it... even in its worse form?

SUDAN (*raises up on his elbow and stares at her*): That's what you think you gotta accept?

SHERRIE: That's what I've accepted. And you brainwashed me into thinkin' I should. Why should I be a slave? Everything living wants to be free and loved completely.

SUDAN (*sorrowful*): Maybe it's me who's been brainwashed.

SHERRIE: You have been. We've all been brainwashed. Black people, white people, Indians, men, women, children. I bet it ain't many people in the world that don't go through that.

SUDAN (*lovingly*): Ah gottta gem. Any fool can see that you deserve better. (*Pause.*) I wish I was able to give it to you.

SHERRIE: Love don't come for no price. It's free.

SUDAN: Ain't nothin' else free to go along with it. Like you say, how long can you love a niggah, that can't put food in your mouth?

SHERRIE: That's not exactly what ah said. It's not so much the money or comfort you can give me, it don't cost nothin' to be kind and considerate.

SUDAN (*slowly*): You're right, it doesn't. It's the simple things that I seem to miss.

SHERRIE: That's what ah was tryin' to say when ah said we wasn't a family...

SUDAN: I know, at first ah thought you meant somethin' else.

SHERRIE: What?

SUDAN: It don't matter now.

SHERRIE: Was it about us losin' the baby?

SUDAN (*distressed*): Ah said it don't matter.

SHERRIE: It does matter. I believe you still hate yourself for that. (*Pause.*) I wish you wouldn't.

SUDAN (*guilty, twisting the covers*): Ah don't wanna talk about it no more.

SHERRIE: Somethin' ain't right.

SUDAN: The whole gotdamn world ain't right!

SHERRIE: Somethin' ain't right in your world.

SUDAN (*stern, bitter, he raises up*): You right, babee, it's jus' as fucked up as the world out here, and I'm gettin' sick of the whole muthafuckin' shit!! (SUDAN *gets out of bed wearing shorts.*) You hungry? Can I get you something from the kitchen?

SHERRIE (*shakes head*): No.

(*He goes to the kitchen, switches on the light, takes a bottle of orange juice from the refrigerator, drinks. Returns to bed looking depressed.*) What's wrong?

SUDAN (*cold*): Nothin'.

SHERRIE (*runs her hand up and down his back; gently*): Why are you ashamed to talk about things that be pressin' you?

SUDAN: I'm not ashamed.

SHERRIE: Afraid?

SUDAN (*annoyed*): Afraid of what? What do I have to be afraid of? You know how many times I had whiteboys and bloods pointing guns to my head?

SHERRIE: You not afraid to fight, but it's like you afraid of your own feelings. It don't seem like you have to wear your manhood on your chest if you secure about it.

SUDAN: You tryin' to say I'm not a man?

SHERRIE: I think you have a lot of growing to do as a man. I really do. I don't mean to hurt your feelings by sayin' that.

SUDAN: So that's how you feel? No wonder you packed your shit up to split.

SHERRIE: I said you had alot of growing to do.

SUDAN: What about you?

SHERRIE: I have too. That's the problem. I can't grow with you. You won't let me.

SUDAN (*bitter*): What's the deal? You wanna be a star? You wanna grow taller than me?

SHERRIE: Does that bother you? Would it matter whether I did or not?

SUDAN (*admittedly*): You probably already have.

SHERRIE: Come again?

SUDAN: You heard me. You think I don't admire you?

SHERRIE: No, I didn't think you did at all. Sometimes I felt like you hated me.

SUDAN (*genuine*): Whatever you felt, I never hated you. I might have resented you, but I never hated you.

SHERRIE: Why would you resent me?

SUDAN (*slow, reflective*): I don't know. Why does anybody resent anybody else?

SHERRIE: Insecurity.

SUDAN: See why I need you? (*He raises himself fully on the bed, puts his arm around her and kisses the side of her forehead.*) I love you. I'mo try and show you. (*Caresses her.*)

SHERRIE: What? By making love to me?

SUDAN: That and a whole lot more. (*He kisses her. She yields, hugging him close as he leans on top of her. Lights.*)

Scene II

(*Early afternoon of the following day. The couple tumbles under the covers, displaying intense and passionate lovemaking, i.e. kisses, embraces, etc. Lights.*)

Scene III

(*Second night. Bed scene. There's a red light in the lamp by the bed. They lay quietly in each others' arms, embrace and kiss. Lights.*)

Scene IV

(Later next afternoon. He sits up in bed shirtless and smoking a ciga-rette. She exits from bathroom, wearing blue jeans and a sweater.)

SUDAN (*smiles*): Lookin' good in them tight pants, 'cept ah don't want every nigger lookin' at yo' ass. Ain't you got somethin' else you can wear?

SHERRIE: They're not that tight.

SUDAN: The hell they ain't.

SHERRIE: They're not any tighter than your pants.

SUDAN: Look, I'm a dude. Yeh, ah know, the way women are these days, how they come on a dude right out front about goin' to bed with no ifs, ands or buts. But, still, I don't attract the kind of at-tention you would. At least, ah don't think. 'Course, I had a young sister approach me the other day while ah was walkin' down the street. She jus' came up to me and said, "Hey, babee, you sho' got a hip walk. Bet you got a hip ride; bet you could ride me all day and all night." Ah jus' kept on steppin'. I ignored her. But there's cats out there too, jus' as bad.

SHERRIE (*annoyed*): Now you tellin' me what to wear again.

SUDAN: Go 'head, wear what you wanna wear. Ah gotta come outta that, tellin' you everything.

SHERRIE: I'm gonna have to go get something to eat.

SUDAN: Yeah, okay. You need some money?

SHERRIE: Um-hum.

(SUDAN gets up, puts on the bottom to his pajamas and goes to the closet. Takes a wallet from his blue-jean pocket. She walks over to him. He hands her ten dollars.)

SUDAN: Think that'll be enough?

SHERRIE: It should be. I'm jus' gonna get somethin' for today. *(Pause.)* I need the key to git out.

SUDAN (*nervous*): Look, ah, why don't I wash up and I'll go to the store. Ah gotta go by that way anyway.

SHERRIE (*smiles*): What's the matter, you don't trust me?

SUDAN: Naw, it ain't that. Like ah say, ah gotta go by Joes' pad for a minute, so I might as well save you a trip.

SHERRIE: Joe lives a little ways from the store.

SUDAN: It's goin' in the same direction.

SHERRIE (*smiling*): Am I being held a prisoner here?

SUDAN (*laughs*): Okay, baby, I give up. I don't have no reason not to trust you. I know you a person of your word. (*He reaches in the front pocket of his blue jeans and pulls out the key.*) You gon' come back?

SHERRIE: I'll be back. (*Smiles.*) You don't have to pace the floor till I come back.

SUDAN (*hands her the key; smiles*): Ah'm gon' lie back down and daydream about you. (*He gets in bed. She unlocks the door.*)

SHERRIE: See you in a minute.

(*She exits. He picks up a* Black World *magazine from the lamp table and thumbs through it. SHERRIE yells.*)

SUCKER!!!

(*SUDAN throws down the magazine, leaps out of bed, storms to the door and opens it, flinging it wide open. She stands by the wall next to the door. He dashes out into the hall.*)

BOO!!

(*He jumps, turns around, faces her, hands on his hips, angry but silent. She doubles over laughing.*)

SUDAN: Git your ass in there.

(*SHERRIE, still twisted with laughter, enters the apartment. He follows her and shuts the door.*)

SHERRIE (*grinning*): Ah was jus' playin' with you.

SUDAN (*embarrassed*): I wish you wouldn't play like that.

SHERRIE: Cmon, where's your sense of humor? Ah was jus' playin' with you, but I was also checkin' you out, seein' where your head was at. (*Laughs.*) Ah-haa, so you was comin' to drag me by my hair back to bed.

SUDAN: Stop fuckin' with me.

SHERRIE (*embraces him from behind, grinning, rests her head on his back*): You a poor sport. (*He turns around. They kiss. He smiles. They both laugh.*) Ah'm hungry. And ah know you are. I'm goin' to the store...for real. (*Smiles.*)

(*They walk together to the door. He opens it for her. She exits. He reaches out his arm and pulls her head gently through the open door. They kiss.*)

She exits. He closes the door and walks in the bathroom, exits. The lights are dim. He sits on the bed. Blackout on him. Spotlight is on SUDAN and SHERRIE in a flashback scene in the kitchen. SUDAN storms into the apartment, crying, enraged. SHERRIE is eight months pregnant, cooking on the stove.)

SHERRIE *(alarmed)*: What is it?! What's the matter?! *(Wipes her hands on her apron or dress, goes over to him, touches his arm. He shoves her away.)*

SUDAN *(contemptuously)*: Jus' leave me alone, gotdamit!! All you muthafuckas leave me alone!!

SHERRIE *(perturbed)*: Don't take it out on me, whatever...

SUDAN: Fuck you! Fuck you! Fuck you, and yo' mama too!

SHERRIE *(calm)*: What's the matter, Sudan?

SUDAN *(angry)*: What ain't the matter?! That's what you should be asking me! What ain't the gotdamn matter?! *(He snatches off his beret and throws it on the floor. SHERRIE stares at him.)* Whatchu lookin' at?

SHERRIE *(quietly, resolute)*: Nothing.

(SUDAN moves towards her and backhands her across the face. She screams, clasps her jaw and falls against the sink.)

SUDAN: Don't you tell me I ain't nothin'. Think a Black man don't hear enough of that shit everyday, gotta come home to it too, bullshit. Not in mah gotdamn house. Pregnant or not, I'll kick the muthafucka out, don't make me no difference. Ah ain't so sure I want no kids, no way! *(Bitter, hurt.)* What dah fuck we need more kids to raise in a place like this!? Hunh?! Genocide. That's what it is, genocide! 'For it even git here! What schools he gon' go to? Whose store he gon' shop at?! What's he got to look forward to? A job at Fords or bein' some middle class lackey, or a fag, or a junkie?! So who needs 'em?! *(Loud.)* How can we save them when we can't save ourselves!!! *(Turns away from her, grips his stomach as though in extreme pain, turns back. Wide-eyed, numb.)* They got J.B.

SHERRIE *(surprised)*: Who?

SUDAN: They killed him; he's dead.

SHERRIE: Who?

SUDAN: The pigs. The gotdamn pigs, who you think?

SHERRIE: When?

SUDAN: Today. This mornin'. He was set up.

SHERRIE *(hurt)*: No-oo...

SUDAN (*cut eyes at her*): Yes, baby, yes. Blew his brains out. I saw him. (*Voice trails off as he ambles around the kitchen.*) I saw him... (Pause.) And guess who was the hacket man, the fink! (*Suspicious.*) Or do you need to guess?

SHERRIE: Who?

SUDAN: Mr. Cool, the supercool revolutionary himself - Les Williams.

SHERRIE (*shocked*): Les?

SUDAN (*bitter*): Yes, Les. The leader, the muthafuckin' leader is a agent, was workin' for the Man all the time...and we workin' for this lackey like fools, thought he was our brother.

SHERRIE: Les? A pig?

SUDAN: He's more than that, he's a helluva actor! He sho' had me fooled. He set J.B. up, and I'mo take his head off when I see him! Yo ex-lover.

SHERRIE: I only went out with him a few times.

SUDAN: How ah know you tellin' the truth? All ah know is when I met chu, you was seein' him. Right?

SHERRIE: I never really went with him, though. I knew less about him than you...

SUDAN: Aww, shut up! You was his lady. Did you go to bed with him?

SHERRIE: Would it make any difference if I had? We been together almost two years now. Does that matter?

SUDAN (*fierce*): It matters to me. When you lay down with pigs you smell like 'em. How ah know you ain't a pig like him?! (*Walks over to her, chokes her. She tries to get away. He shoves her against the sink and tightens his grip around her throat.*)

SHERRIE (*gasping, struggling*): Please...please stop...

SUDAN: How ah know you ain't a pig?! Are you?! Tell me, are you!!?

SHERRIE (*gasping*): No-o.

SUDAN (*half-crazed*): You lyin'!! You jus' livin' here so you can spy on me! Ain't chu?! (*Chokes harder, then suddenly lets go, knocks her down with his fist. She screams. He kicks her several times in the back and the stomach. She moans, groans, then lets out shrieking wails as the curtain closes.*)

END OF ACT II

ACT III

Scene I

(The bed is folded back into the couch. SUDAN *is dressed in blue jeans, dashiki. He sits on the couch, lights a cigarette. His mood is somber.* SHERRIE *unlocks the door and enters with a grocery bag.)*

SHERRIE *(smiles):* I'm back.

SUDAN: What took you so long? I thought you weren't coming back.

SHERRIE: Ran into a few old friends. Remember Mickey?

SUDAN: Real short brother, with a big 'fro?

SHERRIE: Yeh, I saw him, and we talked for awhile. Then I ran into Malika on the way back.

SUDAN: How's she doin'?

SHERRIE: Fine. She had the twins with her. She's almost through with law school. She's glad of that. *(She sets the bag down on the kitchen table, takes off her jacket, hangs it in the closet, starts unpacking the groceries.)*

SUDAN: I forgot to tell you to get some more wine.

SHERRIE: I musta read your thoughts 'cause I bought some.

SUDAN: Right on. Pour me a glass.

(She takes two glasses from the cabinet, pours both of them half-full, goes to him carrying the two glasses of wine, hands him one and sits beside him.)

A toast. *(Holds up his glass.)* To a new day. For a whole lifetime.

(Click glasses. SHERRIE *sips her wine while* SUDAN *gulps the wine down, then stares solemnly into the empty glass.)*

SHERRIE: What's wrong?

SUDAN: Nothing. What makes you think anything is wrong?

SHERRIE: You sure not as cheerful as when I left.

SUDAN: Sorry, sorry, but I don't feel like bein' Step 'n' Fetchit today.

SHERRIE: That's not what I meant.

SUDAN *(sensing her hurt):* Hey, hey, *(Puts his arm around her, kisses her cheek.)* baby, I'm sorry.

SHERRIE: What's on your mind?

SUDAN: Nothin'...and everything. Does that make any sense to you? No. Ah know it doesn't. Stop tryin' to figure me out 'cause you'll never do it. I can't figure my own self out. (*He rises, goes to kitchen, pours another glass of wine. Holds up glass.*) Here's to unsolved riddles.

SHERRIE: I don't know about you, but I wanna solve mine.

SUDAN: Then solve yours, but keep your nose outta mine, 'less you wanna hear some ugly shit. (*Gulps down the glass of wine, then pours another glass.*) Well, what you so quiet about now? Guess you don't wanna hear what's on mah mind after all? Maybe that's the problem - you can't accept the bad with the good. Everything ain't gon' be rosy like wine. (*Laughs, drinks some wine. Pause.*) Ah feel like I'm all alone on a battle ground, and mah enemy's closin' in on me. I can feel his breath on my neck. Ever feel like that?

SHERRIE (*looks up at him sadly*): Yes.

SUDAN (*paces the floor, loud*): Damn, Sherrie, whatchu wanna hear - 'bout how rotten I feel? Why I can't stand to look at myself in the mirror anymore?!

SHERRIE: I know. I've watched you. I died with you a long time ago. You're not even the same person I knew.

SUDAN: Maybe you never knew me.

SHERRIE: Maybe I didn't. I jus' thought ah did. I believed in what I saw.

SUDAN (*angry*): And what did you see, hunh? Tell me, baby, what did you see? (*Rushes to her.*) A hero? Another superstar? A Malcolm? A Christ? Whatchu lookin' for, baby, don't exist. I'm human; I got faults; I ain't perfect.

SHERRIE: You just said you'd rather die like Malcolm then...

SUDAN (*embarrassed*): I would rather die like Malcolm, but...

SHERRIE: But you can't live like him.

SUDAN: Dammit, is that what you want?

SHERRIE: I want what I saw. A man, a brave and beautiful man. (*She takes his hand, enfolds him around the waist and presses her head against his stomach.*) Calm down, you ain't on no enemy territory here.

SUDAN (*passionate*): Whatchu doin' to me?

SHERRIE: Makin' you mellow like wine.

SUDAN (*pulls away blushing; takes a cold jar of water from the refrigerator, pours a glass*): We ain't turned on no music in a few days. But, then that ain't surprising, is it?

SHERRIE: See, you said you couldn't do without your music.

SUDAN (*slowly*): That's jus' 'cause we bin the music. (*Gazes at her lovingly.*) Hey, I'mo turn on the music. That okay?

SHERRIE: Fine.

(SUDAN *goes to record player, takes an album from the open book - case beneath it. Plays a fast popular tune, starts moving, rocking into a popular dance.*)

SUDAN: C'mon and dance with me.

(*She rises and dances over to him. He turns up the record player, and they dance with intense energy for a few minutes. Then a loud consistent knocking is heard from the floor upstairs.*)

SUDAN (*raging, furious, shaking his fist at the ceiling*): Fuck you, ol' skinny, dry-ass cracker! If you don't like the music, then move out, muthafucka! Move your white butt out! I'll play mah jams loud as I want! (*He goes over, turns up the record player full force. The knocking on the ceiling is louder, faster.*) Go tah hell!! Go back to hell where you came from, devil!!!

SHERRIE (*hands pressed over ears, shouts*) Stop it!! Stop it! Please, cut that thing down!

SUDAN (*raging at man upstairs*): Yo' mama!! And her withered hole, cocksucker!! Come on down here so I can take off your head!

SHERRIE: SUDAN, PLEASE!!! (*She goes past him, turns the record player down to a minimum. He continues to rant and rave.*)

SUDAN (*turns to SHERRIE*): What's this honkie doin' livin' in the building anyway? We should have burnt him out when you first moved here. Turn the record back on. I wanna dance some more. I wanna sing and shout, and ah don't give a fuck who don't like it.

SHERRIE (*upset*): Look, we can't do that. There's other people in this building; we gotta respect them.

SUDAN: Shit, the only one that complains all the time is that whitey!

SHERRIE: Be cool before he calls the police.

SUDAN: Let 'm call the police. Let 'm call the gotdamn police. Ah got somethin' for them too! Ah got somethin' for all of 'em!!

SHERRIE (*pleading*): Please, please...

SUDAN: To hell with you. That's all you Black women have ever done - contain a Black man, 'specially when he's ready to fight. Soon as he's ready to cut a honkie's throat, she come with those phony platitudes about Christian ethics and purity, turnin' the other cheek, while her man watches the whiteboy fuck her in the ass - like she love it!

SHERRIE: That's a lie.

SUDAN: The hell it is. You and your misdirected ideas of love, you bin holdin' us back for the last 400 years, and before that, long before we even came to this country!

SHERRIE: You bin holdin' us back, too. Truth is we bin holdin' each other back, haven't we?

SUDAN: Ah said what ah said and I meant it! Y'all bin holdin' us back.

SHERRIE: Why? Why is the blame always put on the Black woman? I don't understand it. Why is all the responsibility put on us like we the saviors of the world or something?

SUDAN (*slow, contemplative*): Maybe you are, jus' that...Mother of the universe, Queen of the planet. (*Laughs.*)

SHERRIE: Is that funny? So it was a joke to you all the time, while I was blindly believing you.

SUDAN (*serious*): It's no joke. I was jus' laughin' 'cause I'm startin' to git drunk. (*Pours another glass of wine, drinks.*) Hey, (*Glances at small amount of wine left in the bottle.*) You gon' have to go back and git some more wine.

(*She looks hard at him.*)

Never mind. I'll git it.

SHERRIE: There's another bottle in the bag.

SUDAN: Why didn't you say that 'stead of lookin' at me like you crazy. (*He finishes the glass of wine, drinks the rest out of the bottle, throws the empty bottle in the trash and stretches his arms.*) Now I'm ready to do it some more.

SHERRIE: I thought you were hungry?

SUDAN (*walks to her, pulls her around the waist*): I am hungry - for you.

SHERRIE (*uneasy, pulls away*): I'm hungry for some food.

(*She goes into the kitchen. He stands, disgusted, hand on hip.*)

SUDAN (*throwing up his hand*): Well, ah ain't gon' force you. It's plenty more where that come from. Ah sho' ain't got to beg for it!

SHERRIE: I got the stuff to make some chili; don't you want some?

SUDAN: What ah want taste a whole lot better than some damn chili.

SHERRIE (*irritated*): Look, we bin doin' it day and night for two days. Let's take a break. Besides, I'm tired.

SUDAN: What you tired of? You bin in bed for the last two days.

SHERRIE: That's what ah mean, I'm tired of it.

SUDAN: Tired?!

SHERRIE: Yes, don't you ever git tired?

SUDAN (*laughs, then serious*): Naw. See, I come from Africa. (*Mimics an ape grinning, showing all his teeth, beating his chest.*) 99% animal and 1% homosapien. Didn't they ever teach you how much niggers love to fuck in your human relations class?

(SHERRIE *finishes unpacking the groceries, takes out a pot, puts ground beef in pot.* SUDAN *comes behind her, rubs her buttocks.*)

SHERRIE: I dont' feel like it right now.

SUDAN (*turning away from her angrily*): C'mon, you know how it upsets me when ah can't git none.

SHERRIE (*angry*): Well, it's about time you grew up. Why don't you stop actin' like a little boy?!

SUDAN: A little boy? You know what little boys do? (*Heads in direction of bathroom.*) They go in the bathroom and they jack off!

(*He turns the volume on the record player full blast. The knocking begins immediately from upstairs. She rushes over, turns down the volume.*)

SHERRIE (*hot*): If you jack off, you can jack off from now on!

(*She goes to the closet, grabs her jacket.* SUDAN *comes out of the bathroom.*)

SUDAN (*serious, calm*): Be serious. Look, ah'm jus' goin' in there to pee, that's all. Put the jacket back. Les not keep goin' in circles. I gotta pee, that's all. Might even take a cold shower; it might cool me off some.

SHERRIE (*hurt*): Why do you say things like that? Don't you know your words hurt me more than your fists?

(SUDAN *steps back into the bathroom, slams the door. Lights.*)

Scene II

(*An hour later, they sit together at the kitchen table eating chili, wheat crackers, salad. Two candles are lit in the center of the table. Jazz music is played very softly in the background. They sit perpendicular to each other holding hands across the table.*)

SUDAN (*pensive, sad*): My moods change like the colors of the sunrise, don't they?

SHERRIE: You read my thoughts well.

SUDAN (*gazing at candles*): Somethin' about candlelight, (*Smiles.*) even when the sun is shining...the way it flickers, like it's reachin', searchin' for more light and your mind and your spirit search with it...Yah know what ah mean?

SHERRIE: Um-hum.

SUDAN: Look how they flicker towards one another like there's magnets between them. (*Raises her hand up to his lips, kisses it.*) The dinner is outta sight. Have I forgot to tell you lately how bad you can burn?

(*They smile. He kisses her hand again.*)

That shower sho' cooled me off. I imagined I was in the Congo, and it was raining softly on my naked body while I bathed in the river. I was waiting for you, the woman I dreamed of since my youth. (*They smile. He eats a handful of salad, pours a glass of wine, drinks.*) We been through some deep shit together, haven't we?

SHERRIE: Yeh, and I'll never forget it. I've learned so much from you, I could never regret any of it.

SUDAN: I'm kinda nervous, though. I noticed your bags are still sitting by the door. When you gonna unpack them?

SHERRIE: Soon. Soon as I get a chance.

SUDAN: Did you call Letta, tell her you weren't coming?

SHERRIE (*uneasy*): Uh, no, no I didn't. I should have.

SUDAN: She'll get the message since you didn't show. (*Pause.*) Why don't you play Miles Davis, "Sketches Of Spain?" I haven't heard that in a long time.

(*She gets up, goes to record player, puts on "Sketches Of Spain." Music is up 60 seconds, then turned down low under voices.*)

Yeh, Miles hit it on the nose. That the kind of music make a person reveal their mysteries.

SHERRIE: What is it that you keep so secret?

SUDAN: The simple things. My need for peace and love and beauty...the things you bring into my life. The music, the food, your presence...What more could a cat ask for?

SHERRIE (*jokingly*): What was comin' outta that shower, thorezine?

SUDAN: Me and my thoughts. Ever told you 'bout when I was a little boy, I was in the boy scouts, and we used to go campin' a lot. I started having this dream almost every night. We was out campin' and I got away from the group and ran off by myself. I was running up a hill and when I reached the top I ran right into some quicksand. Every time I tried to take a step I sunk deeper and deeper. So I stopped and looked up, and there was a bright light over my head, and then I heard a voice say, "Be still, be still and your body will lift you out of it." And it kept sayin' it, and I was lookin' around tryin' to hear where it was comin' from and then I would wake up. I ended up quittin' the boy scouts 'cause I was scared I was really gonna run into some quicksand. I still have that dream sometimes.

SHERRIE: What do you think it means?

SUDAN (*slowly*): Being still. Being. Just being. Bein' at one with myself and nature. Like now. Bein' still...that's the only way I can survive. (*Pause.*) 'Cept it ain't that simple. I'm still sinkin' in the quicksand. Every time I try and take a step, I go down deeper and deeper. (*Intense.*) What am I doing wrong?! (*Rises, paces the floor.*) I don't understand how everything went haywire. Everybody went crazy! Niggahs killin' each other! Brothers! Brothers! Mah gotdamn brothers - scared, weak, diseased-minded muthafuckas, scared of their own shadows.

We had the beast by his throat. All we had to do was squeeze. But we ran when he blinked his baby blue eye. We should have been free! We could have been a long time ago if it wasn't for our own fear! These split-head, white cock-suckin' ego-maniacs! Revolutionary frauds! Clowns! I'mo write a cartoon series on the revolutionaries of the sixties. (*Laughs.*) If some capitalist ain't already done it!

SHERRIE: Why don't you sit down? Your food is getting cold.

SUDAN (*cutting*) Don't tell me what to do! (*Points finger at her.*) See there, you bein' domineering already.

SHERRIE: It was just a suggestion, like that dream. You're not being still. I see you sinkin' further in the quicksand.

SUDAN (*boyish, pouting*): You don't see nothin'. If I hadn't told you the dream, you wouldn't know nothin' about it. (*Pause.*) Did you hear what I said? Was you even listenin'? You beg me to talk to you, then you tell me to sit down and be quiet. I'm not your little boy. I don't care how much of a boy you think I am. I got my pride.

SHERRIE: The pride in a man don't count when his head is cold.

SUDAN (*hateful*): Shut up! Shut up your fat mouth - hoe!

SHERRIE (*reserved*): You said that purposely just to...

SUDAN: Just to hurt you. (*Evil.*) Yes, just to hurt you.

SHERRIE: It didn't work this time.

(*He goes into the bathroom, slams the door. She eats, cries quietly, wipes her face with a napkin, rises, goes to record player and plays Stanley Clarke's "Children Of Forever." He exits from bathroom, stands near the bathroom door.*)

SUDAN: Why you playin' that song?

SHERRIE: I just put on a record.

SUDAN: Why did you put on that record?

SHERRIE: I just wanted to hear some music so I grabbed the first album I saw. If you wanna hear something else I'll take it off.

SUDAN: Please take it off. (*Pause.*) It's funny how I get subtle reminders from you about children. I know you wanna have them. Or do you wanna have any? Maybe that's why you haven't got pregnant in awhile? Maybe you don't wanna get pregnant by me? Is that what it is?

SHERRIE (*slow, soft*): You're still full of guilt about the baby dyin'. That's the hell you live in. You never stopped hating yourself 'cause I never hated you for it.

SUDAN (*sad, remorseful*): It had got so far outta hand. You should have left a long time ago. (*Sits on sofa.*) Before it happened. You should have left then. At least I wouldn't of had to look at your empty belly. (*Pause.*) But you stayed. You stayed. Didn't you know I would see her in you, that my payback was wakin' up and facing you every morning?

SHERRIE: It was a mistake then. I should have left you alone, instead of tryin' to be a lifesaver. I couldn't save my own life, let alone yours. I didn't know my presence made you feel like that. I stayed 'cause I felt you needed me then more than ever before.

SUDAN (*confused, stretches out, puts his head on her lap*): Maybe I did. I don't know.

SHERRIE: No, you didn't need me then. And you don't need me now.

SUDAN: I'm not complainin'. I'm glad you stayed. Parting is the worst part. Who knows, I might have sunk all the way in the mud and never come out if you hadn't stayed and loved me. (*Pause.*) I still see our little girl, ya know. I see that tiny body floating around me everywhere. I've put blinders on my eyes so I wouldn't see. (*Cries.*)

SHERRIE (*pensive*): And I put blinders on mine so I wouldn't see. But now I see; I see it all now. There're so many ways you can destroy a man. I've done more harm to you then good by letting you do anything you please, not demanding respect from you... You don't respect yourself anymore. I don't respect myself. (*Stern.*) All of us, yeah, all of us Black sisters thinkin' we makin' you stronger by being your footstools. We're ruinin' you. We're turning you into mama's boys ego-maniacs, tyrants. Don't you see what's happened to so many of us who took that position? We cease to be human, let alone Black, 'cause it's gotta be a balance, a give and take on both sides or it won't work. We've done more harm to you than if we had taken a knife and cut off your dicks. 'Cause we cut your souls off when we cut ourselves off. (*Lights.*)

Scene III

(*Early the next morning.* SUDAN *is asleep in bed.* SHERRIE *is in the bathroom. Telephone rings. He wakes up, stretches, puts on blue jeans hanging over the lamp table.*)

SUDAN: Okay...okay...(*Ambles to the phone.* SHERRIE *exits from bathroom.* SUDAN *glances at her.*) I got it. (*On telephone.*) Yeh. (*Eyes look surprised.*) Who? Ah think you got the wrong number. (*Hangs up phone.*) You up early.

SHERRIE: I never really went back to sleep.

(*Telephone rings. He answers.*)

SUDAN: Yeh. (*Pause.*) Who is this? Look, you got the wrong number, understand? So don't call here no more, git the message!

SHERRIE: Who is it?

SUDAN: Some cat lookin' for a Millie. That ain't you, is it?

(SHERRIE *walks to the closet, puts on her jacket.* SUDAN *is alarmed but feigns composure.*)

Goin' to the store? (*He goes to the sink, runs water.*)

SHERRIE: I'm leaving now. I won't be back except to get some more of my things. But I'll be in Dayton for awhile, so I won't really need them.

SUDAN (*with back to her, pounds his fist against the sink, cuts off water, turns to her; vicious*): Why you connivin' bi...

SHERRIE: Why don't you say it...?

SUDAN: Bitch.

SHERRIE: So ends my legacy with you. The wife of a dog can't be nothin' but a bitch.

SUDAN (*laughs*): That was mean...And the last three days, what about the last three days? Did they mean anything? Was it a game?! (*Storms around the room.*) Ohh, oohh, I'm hip to you. You was jivin' me all the time! Makin' me believe you was gon' stay!

SHERRIE: It was your game, not mine. You thought you could fuck your way out of it, and you los'.

(*Phone rings.*)

SUDAN (*picks up receiver*): Hello. Yeh, yeh. (*Nervous.*) Dig, don't call here no more, hear? I don't care! (*Lowers voice, turns away to conceal conversation from* SHERRIE.) Look, look, ah'll talk to you some other time, not now. No. No! Jus' cool down. Hell naw! You can't prove it. Look, if you don't want it...

(*She picks up suitcases.*)

(*On phone.*) Dig, hey wait. (*Covers phone.*) Sherrie, wait a minute, I'll be off in a second. (*On phone.*) Goodbye. (*Slams down phone.*)

SHERRIE: Was that Brenda? I forgot to tell you, she told me about the baby.

SUDAN (*shocked, mad*): That's a lie! That's a damn, funky lie! It ain't none of mah baby. She tryin' tah pin dhat shit on me when every dude in the company done had a piece of her. So she can shove that shit! And ah don't 'preciate her tellin' you dhat. Can't you see it's a trick jus' to make you jealous and mad at me, so you would leave me. Then she could have me.

SHERRIE: It doesn't matter. I'm leaving anyway. (*She turns to the door.*)

SUDAN (*desperate*): But...but you can't go! (*Rushes to the door, pushes his hand against it.*) How could you walk outta here after what we've bin through jus' in the last three days?

SHERRIE: Easy. I've made up my mind. What have we bin through the past three days but circles, circles leading to nowhere. Nothing changes overnight. And you need to be alone.

SUDAN: Let me be the one to decide that.

SHERRIE: Not at my expense. You gotta plenty of women. There'll be...

SUDAN: But they ain't you.

SHERRIE: Would you open the door?

SUDAN (*hand still on door*): No! No! You can't leave.

SHERRIE: We goin' in circles again, but this time I'll fight you to the death. Sooner or later I'm gittin' outta here, and you know it.

(SUDAN *slowly removes his hand from the door, walks sadly to the kitchen chair, sits, hanging his head. She opens the door, picks up suitcases, walks partially through the door, turns to SUDAN.*)

SHERRIE (*softly*): I'll call you.

(*She exits, closes door. He sits solemnly at the table, then cries. Rises, restraining his tears, gets wine from cupboard, pours a glass, drinks. Stands in the middle of the floor, cries. CURTAIN.*)

The Box

A ONE ACT

by DANIEL W. OWENS

Playwright Dan Owens was born, raised and educated in Malden Massachusetts. He graduated from the University of Massachusetts at Boston with a B.A. in English, attended the Yale School of Drama and received his M.Ed. from the Harvard Graduate School of Education. Mr. Owens' plays have been produced by The New Federal Theater, The Frederick Douglass Creative Arts Center, The Negro Ensemble Company, The Afro-American Studio Theater, The Theater of Universal Images and The Richard Allen Center for Culture and The Arts. He was twice a participant in the Eugene O'Neill National Playwrights Conference and also the recipient of a Rockefeller Grant for Playwrighting.

CHARACTERS:

DAVID - *A young black man in his early twenties, intelligent, intellectual, philosophical; from a middle class background.*
CHRIS - *A young black woman in her early twenties, strong but feminine, been around and has seen both sides of life.*
LONNIE - *A young black man in his early twenties, strong, fiery, quick to act, been on the corner most of his life.*
OLE MAN - *Grizzly, wiry, ancient black man.*
VOICE - *actually the slavemaster.*

Scene One

(The scene opens with three characters DAVID, CHRIS and LON-NIE seated in a dimly lit box. They are just awakening. In the opposite corner from them is a ragged, grey-haired old man seated, humming to himself. The rest of the stage is completely dark.)

LONNIE *(rising slowly)*: What the hell is this place?
CHRIS *(stretching)*: No windows...doors...bars...<u>Damn</u>!

195

DAVID: A box.

LONNIE: A box?

DAVID: Could be some sort of jail or something...Huh...Maybe even hell.

CHRIS: Why not heaven?...You hear that hummin'...Look at that ole man in the corner...Hey ole man...

DAVID: He seems to be in a trance...just keeps on humming...He sure is ragged.

CHRIS: He sure looks old...Don't look like much passed him by.

LONNIE: I'm so hep.

DAVID: If we don't find a way out of here, a lots is going to pass us by.

LONNIE: Don't seem to be a way out...<u>But</u>...they got us in here. Maybe the ole man knows.

CHRIS: If he did he still wouldn' be here.

LONNIE: How you know how long he been here?

DAVID: Which brings up an interesting point...How long have we been here?

CHRIS: Last thing I remember was a...a Tuesday night comin' home from the State...I had jus' saw "Interlude" 'fore it left.

LONNIE: Hey...I was there that night...BUT...but the last night I remember was that Friday 'cause my buddy had a birthday party.

DAVID: What was the date?

LONNIE: April 7.

DAVID: That makes your date April 4.

LONNIE: What about you?

DAVID: Well, I had just come from school for semester break... So that makes it around April 15.

CHRIS: Then what's today?

DAVID: Who knows...

CHRIS: Ya know, we don't even know each other's name...I'm Chris James.

DAVID: David Stoningham.

LONNIE: Lonnie Chapman.

DAVID: We don't know each other...We didn't grow up in the same neighborhood...

LONNIE: How you know?

DAVID: Just guessing.

LONNIE: Sheeet...I come from 103rd street 'n damn proud of it.

196

CHRIS: I'm from Milburn Ave.

DAVID: I live on Hastings Terrace.

LONNIE: Lucky you.

DAVID: Well anyway...Those first two things being right, we have practically nothing in common...relatives...friends...social circles.

LONNIE: Nothing but our color.

DAVID: So.

LONNIE: So...Maybe this is the big round up.

DAVID: Oh...Shit...Come on, will ya.

CHRIS: Goin' on what both you said, sounds to me like a whitey doing it.

DAVID: What makes you say that?

CHRIS: One...we all niggers...Two...we don't know each other or have anything in common...Three...what nigger you know could do such an outside thing?

DAVID: Pretty strong case you have there.

LONNIE: How 'bout the ole man's case?

DAVID: Forget the ole man for now...We better start thinkin' of answers to questions like where, when, why, 'n how.

CHRIS: Ya know, I jus' thought of somtin'.

LONNIE: Like what?

CHRIS: Well, I can't remember the last time I ate or slept.

DAVID: So.

CHRIS: So, I ain't hungry...Are you?

DAVID: Come to think of it...NO.

LONNIE: Listen...I ain't tired or hungry either...I can't remember the last time I slept 'cept for when I woke up in here.

DAVID: That means somebody has been feeding us and putting us to sleep.

CHRIS: 'n we don't know who...Ain't this a bitch.

LONNIE: Someone's keepin' us alive, but for what...To be like that ole man?

CHRIS: Don't knock him...He's managed to survive.

DAVID: To be what?

CHRIS: Alive.

DAVID: Carrots are alive.

CHRIS: So are snakes.

LONNIE: Hey...Hey...Slow down...Both of you.

DAVID: I apologize.

CHRIS: Sheeeet.

LONNIE: Hey listen...Either of you a revolutionary or somtin'?

CHRIS: Not hardly.

DAVID: Not a bad idea.

LONNIE: What?

DAVID: That maybe one of us has something or is something that someone wants.

LONNIE: You never answered.

DAVID: Me..Heh...Heh...No not me...But staying on the same train of thought, what does one of us have that someone might want...One of us or all us...Money...Power...Information?

CHRIS: Sheeeet...I got so much money I'm a month behind on my rent 'n two months back on my car...Hell...All the power I got is between my legs...And the only information I got is how to blow a good thing.

LONNIE: Hell...I ain't even got enough money to put down on a car...No power 'cept I can drink more wine than anyone else on my block...But I do have some information.

DAVID: Yeah...Go ahead.

LONNIE: Well, I know how...how to get dumped on every day of your life.

DAVID: Sounds like we all are a bunch of losers.

CHRIS: Losers...Shit...You ain't said a damn thing yet.

DAVID: For money I got bank loans on a college education that don't mean shit...Power...Yeah, power I got...token president of the student government...As for information...I can tell you what teachers to take for easy marks...

LONNIE: I expected a little mor'n that.

DAVID: Hmph...So did my parents...Well anyway...

LONNIE: Maybe we should shake up the ole man a little bit... Least ways if he don't talk he might change that damn tune.

CHRIS: He's so pitiful.

LONNIE: Pitiful hell...He doesn't seem to be worried 'bout what's happenin'...I wonda if he even knows we're here...Maybe I should make him aware of the fact.

CHRIS: Hey, wait a minute...Are you crazy?

LONNIE: Maybe.

CHRIS: What harm that ole man done us?

DAVID: She's right...Why hurt him unless he becomes a real threat?

LONNIE: Hell...This is damn stupid jus' standin' aroun' talkin' shit 'n doin' nothin'.

DAVID: Well, what do you want us to do?

LONNIE: Tear this place apart.

DAVID: With what - our bare hands...Damn...You felt those walls...Hard and cold...Bare hands won't mean shit against them.

CHRIS: So we jus' wait...Wait for...

DAVID: Hey, remember the old man.

CHRIS: Look here, nigger...this ain't no time to get sarcastic.

LONNIE: They can't keep us in here for long...No tables... chairs...beds...toilets...not even a pail, dammit.

DAVID: Look how long we been here now...Close to two weeks for you two.

CHRIS: Might not have always been here.

DAVID: Right you are.

VOICE: In a moment all of you will be dead.

(*Silence.*)

LONNIE: Who the fuck said that...Jesus Christ...What's happenin'?

CHRIS: Are we goin' mad...Is this a nuthouse?

DAVID: Possible on both counts.

LONNIE: How you so cool 'n collected...You know somtin' nigger?

DAVID: Not more than you.

CHRIS: Oh god, this has to be a joke...Some kind of weird joke. Oh god, let it be a joke...let it be a joke.

LONNIE: Joke shit...this ain't no joke...Ole man...Ole man...Who said it, dammit...Who said it, ole man...Who?

CHRIS: Why you askin' him, Lonnie?

LONNIE: 'Cause he ain't the least bit bothered 'bout anything... the voice...this box...us...He must know somtin'...That damn hummin'...Stop it, ole man...Stop it.

CHRIS: Hey, it's gettin' darker...The lights...the lights.

DAVID: Quick...Grab hands:..Hold tight...Hurry...Hurry.

LONNIE: We all togetha.

DAVID: Yeah.

CHRIS: Yeah...But what about the ole man?

LONNIE: Fuck him...He don't care 'bout us.

CHRIS: But he's jus'...

DAVID: Ssssssh...listen.

LONNIE: Explosions.

DAVID: And their getting closer.

CHRIS: Hold me...hold me.

(*Each successive explosion gets louder and louder 'til it seems the next one will be right on top of the box.*)

CHRIS: Help us...Someone help us...Please help us.

Scene Two

(*The box is completely dark and still. Above on either side is a platform, on one seated on a stool - audience right - is the OLE MAN bathed in a strobe light. On the other platform is LONNIE in a loin cloth, with chains on his wrist and ankles. He is bathed in swirling multicolored light. The sounds of a milling crowd and a cracking whip can be heard. Suddenly a VOICE.*)

VOICE: Alright, ladies 'n gentlemen, step right up...a little closer please...that's it...that's it...we gonna begin biddin' on this here young buck.

LONNIE: Biddin'...What the hell he mean biddin'...Take these chains off, ya hear...Take 'em off.

VOICE: We have here a fine young specimen...Make your choice, ladies 'n gentlemen...a possible field hand...a possible stud...what's your desire...Now, if it's a field hand ya want, look at those shoulders... those forearms...look at that neck ladies 'n gentlemen...But, if it's a breeder you desire, this one here is pure stud material...Look at those flanks...that chest...For any of you who desire, I'll be mor 'n happy to raise that flap a little so that ya can look at his credentials.

LONNIE: What the hell's goin' on...I ain't no slave...I ain't gonna be anyone's slave...Not now...Not ever...What he talkin' 'bout... Gotta get away...Gotta run...Can't...Chains...Can't...Help...Somebody help...Help me...

OLE MAN: Five hundred dollars massa pay for me. Said I was the mos' 'pensive black he evah buy. Gave him five healthy young 'uns I did. First year I was here...Five...Then...Then somtin' hap-

pened...I couldn' give him no mo'...First massa thought it was da
woman...so he switch me aroun'...still nothin' happen...massa even
buy a new woman...still nothin'...Finally massa sent me out in da
fields...say I no mo' good...Put me out dere ta pick...Out in da fields
wif evil ole Jess Harper, da overseer...He whip ya if ya look at him
wrong...Saw him whip many a hand...near killed two...He make
me wanna run away...Make me wanna take off into da swamps...
Take my chances wif dem snakes 'stead of Jess...Sure wish I coulda kept on givin' massa dem chillun...But den maybe betta I
stop...maybe betta I stop.

VOICE: This boy is bound to triple your investment, ladies 'n
gentlemen...Whether pickin' or studdin', you can't lose. Look at
him...Such a marvelous specimen...no scars...no bruises...good
teeth...clear eyes...What am I bid...Do I hear 50...50...55...55...60...
60...65...70...75...75...80...80...85...

LONNIE: You all betta believe me...I ain't no slave...I ain't no
animal...that shit don't work no more...them days are over...Lis-
ten...Hear me...If this is a joke...I ain't laughin'. Stop...Stop.

VOICE: 150...150...155...160...165...165...170...170...170... Ladies 'n
gentlemen, this here neegra is guaranteed to be broken...If he get
ornry, jus' give him a taste of the whip...he'll jump back in line...
Do I hear 175...175...180...185...185...Do I hear 190...190...200...200...

LONNIE: Okay...Okay, it's a joke...Ha, ha, ha, ha, see I'm laughin-
in'...I'm laughin...Let me go...Please let me go.

VOICE: 235...235...240...245...Do I hear 250...250...Do I hear
255...250 ...250...Goin' once...twice...Sold...for 250 dollars to Mr.
Henry Chapman of Chapman Hills, Virginia.

LONNIE: I ain't goin'...I ain't...I'll fight him...I'll kick...bite...spit...
I won't work...I ain't goin'...I'll kill myself...That's what I'll do...I'll
kill myself...I ain't goin'...I ain't...I ain't...

Scene Three

(*Lights out on platforms. Lights come up slowly in the box.* LONNIE
is lying on the floor trembling. The OLE MAN *is back in his corner humming.*)

LONNIE: I ain't...I ain't...(*Continues to mumble.*)
CHRIS: Lonnie...Lonnie.

DAVID: Lonnie, snap out of it...Lonnie...Lonnie, let me help you up...That's it...easy...Let's walk around...Lean on me.

CHRIS: What happened, Lonnie...What happened...Ole man, you were gone, too...what happened...Talk, dammit...Talk. Where'd you go...Ole man, say somtin'...Say somtin', ole man...Dammit... Stop that hummin'

LONNIE: Tried to sell me...sell me...Tried to sell me as a slave... Tried to sell me for 250 dollars...I ain't goin'...I ain't...

DAVID: Who tried to sell you...Who...

LONNIE: A voice.

DAVID: What voice...Where?

LONNIE: A voice...chains...whips...people...a cracker...a cracker voice...Tried to sell me to stud.

DAVID: How'd you know it was a cracker...You see him?

LONNIE: His voice...Heard his voice.

DAVID: Did you see him?

LONNIE: His voice...his voice.

CHRIS: Ease up David...Can't you see he's shook up?

DAVID: Better shook up than dead.

CHRIS: Bastid.

DAVID: Been called worse.

CHRIS: Don't doubt it...But let him set down.

DAVID: Okay...Okay...Sit down Lonnie...Easy now...Easy... Chris...Look.

CHRIS: What?

DAVID: His wrist...Chain marks.

CHRIS: What's happenin' David...What's happenin'...Is this a dream...a nightmare...Is it hell...What is it...What's goin' on...I'm scared...scared to death...

DAVID: Death...Dead.

CHRIS: Come on David, stop it...First I wake up here with two strange guys...then that ole man...stop hummin' ole man...stop it... I'll shut you up...I'LL shut you up.

DAVID: Chris...Chris...come back here...Chris...easy honey... easy.

CHRIS: 'N...'n the explosions...Now this with Lonnie...Are we goin' crazy...Are we...Could this...this really be hell...David...David.

DAVID: Easy Chris...Easy...Come on, sit down...lean on me... Here, let me hold you...Remember how when you went to the show

202

and saw a horror movie...Remember...and when the real scary part came on, you closed your eyes 'til it was over...Well... let's try that now...close your eyes and pray...pray it's a horror movie.

CHRIS: Oh David, I wish it was that easy...I wish it was...David, let's talk...Let's talk 'n never stop talkin'.

DAVID: Okay...Tell ya what, I'll sit between you 'n Lonnie 'n we'll lock arms.

CHRIS: The ole man too?

DAVID: Sure...Ole man...Ole man, you wanna talk...Ole man, come closer...Sit with us.

CHRIS: Never mind...How's Lonnie?

DAVID: Lonnie...Lonnie, how you feel?

LONNIE: Huh...Okay...Okay, I guess...Jus' had to get my head togetha...Hell, I thought I was worth mor'n 250 dollars.

CHRIS: Glad he can joke 'bout it.

DAVID: Better to joke than to worry.

CHRIS: Maybe you're right...But I've always been a worrier, even though it never did much good...Maybe 'cause I worried 'bout things 'stead of tryin' to change them.

LONNIE: Heh...Heh...I never worried 'bout a thing...Take life as it comes...Roll with the punches.

DAVID: What about low blows?

LONNIE: Them too.

DAVID: Not me...I had to try to change things...Could never let anything stand the way it was...Had to try and change it...Couldn' let well enough alone.

CHRIS: So we've noticed.

DAVID: Huh?

CHRIS: Nothin'...(*Lets out a groan.*)...The lights...It's happenin' again.

DAVID: Hang on tight...everyone hang on tight.

CHRIS: What good will that do? We'll jus' be put asleep again.

LONNIE: The noise...the noise sounds like...

DAVID: Machine gun fire.

(*It gets progressively louder as the box gets darker.*)

CHRIS: Hold me...Hold me...Don't let me go...Hold me please...

Scene Four

(*This time the* OLE MAN *is seated on the platform at audience left.* CHRIS *is chained and in a tattered dress, she on audience right. The lighting is the* OLE MAN *in the strobe light and* CHRIS *in swirling multicolored light. The stage is completely dark except for the platforms.*)

VOICE: Ladies 'n gentlemen, I must say I'm pleased to be able to put on the block this next one...A beautiful black is this one...skin like black velvet...teeth like ivory...eyes like a cat...No bad luck here tho...She carries herself like a jungle princess...I've been told there's royalty in her blood...Look at those shoulders, strong, straight... Those young, firm breasts...Look at those hips...those thighs...many a hidden pleasure, no doubt...A handmaiden or servant girl...No field hand, this one...Possible a breeder though...Inspect her ladies 'n gentlemen...But be careful, she bites.

CHRIS: I'll do more'n bite...Claw out their filthy eyes...Touch me 'n I'll spit on your heads...Buy me 'n I'll slice your throats at night when you sleep...I won't be a servant girl for anybody...How can I get out of here...How...These chains...these damn chains.

VOICE: Ladies 'n gentlemen for such a magnificent animal I must start the biddin' at 150 dollars...Do I hear 150...160...160... 170...180...180...190 ...200...210...210...220...230...

OLE MAN: Me 'n Mary woulda been married most part of two years now if massa hadn' sold her 'n li'l Pal to that Louisiana gimmin. Li'l Pal was cute as a button...Big brown eyes, nappy head, he nevah cried, always coo'in' 'n smilin'. Look jus' like me, he did. He be walkin' 'bout now, I guess. Met Mary two christmas ago, I did, when massa brought her down to dee shed, said she was too mean to be in dee house. Said he couldn' break her lessn she got some hard work in da fields. She sure was beautiful. First time I saw her, said to myself gonna make her mine. Sure 'nough, for a whole year 'n den some she was mine. When da crops started to fail, massa had to sell some of his hands to make ends meet. He sold Mary 'n Li'l Pal. Said to massa to sell me too. Massa said no. Thought I'd kill myself...Sure did love Mary...Tought I'd kill massa...Sure 'nough wanted to...Nevah see Mary 'n li'l Pal no mo'...Sure did love li'l Pal...Jus' might kill massa yet...

VOICE: 270...280...280...290...290...290...Ladies 'n gentlemen, if I can't get mor'n 300 dollars for this, I'll be sorely disappointed...If anything, 300 dollars is dirt cheap...Do I hear 300...300...310...320...

CHRIS: Touch me 'n I'll scream...I'll puke all over ya...Leave me alone...Let me go...Let me go...Please...Please...David...Lonnie...Help me...Help me...(*She falls to her knees whimpering.*)

VOICE: 350...360...370...If ya breed her, ya triple your investment. I'm willin' to bet she can suck two 'n be carryin' a third...Do I hear 380... 380...390...

CHRIS: David...David...I'll close my eyes, David...I'll close my eyes 'n it'll go away...No more voices...I'll close my eyes...my ears... can't put my hands over my ears...I can't...I'll close my ears...David, I'm tryin' ...I'm tryin'.

VOICE: 400...400...Do I hear 410...400...400...Goin' once...twice... Sold...to Mr. William James of Council Bluffs, Virginia.

CHRIS: I'll close my eyes 'n my ears...I can't hear...I can't see...It'll go away...Help me...Help me please someone...Help me.

Scene Five

(*Lights out on platforms. Lights come up slowly in the box. The* OLE MAN *is back in the corner humming.* CHRIS *is on the floor seated next to* DAVID *crying, shaking.*)

DAVID: Oh god...Lonnie look at her...What'll we do...Chris honey...Chris...Easy...easy.

CHRIS: It didn't work...David, it didn't work (*She starts to beat on him and collapses in his arms trembling, weeping.*)...David you lied...you lied...It didn't work...Hold me...Hold me...Hold me...

DAVID: I got you honey...I got you.

LONNIE: Dammit...No water...No blankets...Nothing to give her or wrap her in...What the hell is this place...Who's doin' this... Who...Where the hell are you...Show yourself...You bastids...No good mothafuckas...Show yourselves...Where are you...Who are you...Ole man, you gonna talk if I have to rip out your tongue 'n put it back in myself...Talk ole man...talk or I'll kill you ole man...I'll kill you...Talk...Dammit...Talk.

DAVID: No use screaming at him...If he did know, he'd be out of here by now.

LONNIE: What makes you so sure...You're so damn brave 'n cocky...Wait 'til your turn...Wait 'til you go out...You don't know how it feels...the fear...the loneliness. Hearin' strange voices...voices talkin' 'bout ya like ya a animal or like ya not even there...You're so damn sure of yourself...What makes you so sure 'bout anythin'...How you know...Huh...How you know? Jus' maybe you one of them...maybe you 'n the ole man togetha...Huh...That it...You 'n the ole man...Maybe you don't·go out there.

DAVID: Don't talk crazy.

LONNIE: It wouldn' be so crazy if ya don't go out there...Maybe I ought to split your head 'fore I work on the ole man...How's that?

DAVID: Look, you're falling into their trap.

LONNIE: What trap?

DAVID: Division...Suspicion...Confusion...Hate...

LONNIE: Maybe I'm fallin' into your trap.

DAVID: Come off it, will you.

LONNIE: Come off it hell...I'll come on it...Come on your head...

CHRIS (*faintly*): Lonnie...Lonnie.

LONNIE: Yes, Chris...Yes.

CHRIS: Lonnie, don't fight with David...We gotta stick togetha... Don't fight with him Lonnie, please.

LONNIE: Okay, Chris...Okay.

DAVID: We all sure we don't have something they want?

LONNIE: Why ya ask that again?

DAVID: Because I can't see any logical reason why someone would do this.

CHRIS (*almost back to normal*): Why does it have to be logical... Nothin' 'bout this set-up is logical...A word like logical doesn't exist here.

DAVID: Maybe so...Maybe we ought to stop thinking like we usually do.

LONNIE: Jus' think 'bout survivin'.

CHRIS: Yeah...Maybe that's how that ole man made it.

DAVID: But we can't.

CHRIS: Why not?

LONNIE: Yeah...Why not?

DAVID: What's left then?

LONNIE: Our lives.

DAVID: But what happens to us?

CHRIS: What happens to us if we don't?

DAVID: Survival of the fittest.

LONNIE: Come off it, nigger...No one said that.

DAVID: That's what it amounts to in the long run.

CHRIS: Look here David...We don't need no philosophical argument 'bout survival...Noooo good.

DAVID: Can't you both see someone or something is trying to break...crush our spirits...destroy us as human beings?

LONNIE: Bullshit...But look here, nigger, if they are, then damn, they sure as hell got us in the right place to do it.

DAVID: But that's just it...We can't let them divide and conquer...We can't let them destroy us.

CHRIS: Why?

DAVID: 'Cause...'Cause.

CHRIS: Dammit, nigger, where the fuck you been all your life... Maybe you never had to think 'bout life 'n death 'fore 'cept in a classroom...Maybe you don't know how to survive...Maybe Lonnie was right...You ain't been out there yet...In here you think you're dead...Out there you wish it...You haven't been stripped of everything real...human...That voice hasn't talked 'bout you like you were a prize bull...You haven't heard those faceless voices...the crackin' whip...David, right now in this hell you're pretty secure, dammit...Wait 'til you're out there 'n you feel your soul 'n mind shatter into a million little jagged pieces...Whether this a game...a joke...or some fucked up experiment I don't know...<u>But</u>...I do know that I gotta get out of here...I gotta escape, 'n to escape I gotta survive...

DAVID: Okay...Okay, maybe you're right.

CHRIS: <u>Maybe</u>.

LONNIE (*coughs violently*): Hey...What's that?

(*The lights dim in the box.*)

DAVID: Some (*Coughing.*) kind of gas.

(*All three pass out. The box becomes black.*)

Scene Six

(OLE MAN is on the platform at audience right, same lighting. DAVID is standing on a block chained, in loin cloth, the same lighting effect for him as for the other two.)

DAVID: Hey...Hey...I'm here you bastards...I'm ready for you...I don't believe a damn thing you say...Hear me...So go on and bid... Go on with your game...your joke...Come on motherfuckers...Play with me.

VOICE: What do ya think Henry...should I geld him?

DAVID: What?

VOICE: Should I geld him or let him get by with a good lashin'... I know...I know we usually geld his kind, but he's such a damn good breeder...I'll lose two...three thousand dollars.

DAVID: What the hell's going on...Wait one fucking minute... What you mean geld...What lash...I ain't being castrated...I ain't being whipped.

VOICE: I sent for Doc Langley, but I sure as hell hate to do it... Rather give him fifty lashes.

DAVID: Where's the auction...Where's the auction...What do I hear bid...Somebody bid.

VOICE: Ole Doc will be throwin' in the heap near three hundred dollars...I can't do it Henry.

DAVID: Do I hear 100...100...50...25...Do I hear 25...Somebody bid...Bid.

VOICE: I know we supposed to set examples 'n all that...but...

OLE MAN: Massa took me 'n uncle Joel to a public whippin' yes'day. Saw massa Hughes lay on 50 lashes cross his boy Thompson...Heard tell they caught Thompson peekin' at massa Hughes wife one mornin' when she was a dressin'...Massa Hughes sure 'nough laid that whip, like to kill poor ole Thompson. Like to scare de devil outta me. Hehehe, one time I peeked up young missy's dress when she was standin' on the step ladder in de library. Lucky fo' me no one saw. Last month massa Harris geld his boy James fo' touchin' mistress Harris' leg when he helped her into her coach. She said he rubbed her thigh. Mo' likely she wanted him to 'n he wouldn'. Me, I stay clear away from massa's wife 'n his girl chillun. I don't need no mo' trouble than I got...Don't need no mo' trouble than I got.

VOICE: Look Henry, any other nigra 'n I wouldn' hesitate...You know that.

DAVID: Whatever I did I'm sorry...I'm sorry, you hear...Please don't whip...don't cut me...I'm sorry...

VOICE: Doc just pulled up...Guess I gotta decide.

DAVID: Listen...Listen to me, please...No need to go this far... Ain't no need...Just ain't no need.

VOICE: Doc, got me a nigra here that needs your expertise...

DAVID: No please...Please no...Please.

Scene Seven

(*Lights out on the platforms. Lights come up slowly in the box.* DAVID *standing quite shaken,* CHRIS *and* LONNIE *standing around him. The* OLE MAN *is back in his corner humming.*)

DAVID: Don't do it...Don't...I'm sorry...I'm sorry...Got to live...be whole...survival...survival...

CHRIS: Lonnie, grab him, hold him...Come on David, sit down with us.

LONNIE: Guess he knows now...He won't be so high soundin' now...

CHRIS: He had to come through it, I guess...No way around it.

DAVID: Wanted to cut me...Wanted to cut me off.

CHRIS: What's he sayin'...Cut him off?

DAVID: Nevah looked at her...never touched her...Whip...Don't cut me off...Please...Please.

LONNIE: He didn't go through the auction...I wonda what happened...David...David...I don't care what you say, Chris...I think it's time one of us shook up that ole man...He must know somtin'... Every time one of us goes, he goes...When we come back, he comes back.

CHRIS: But he jus' an ole man...He don't look like he can do any harm.

LONNIE: Maybe not...But he must know what's goin' on. (*He walks over to the* OLE MAN.)

CHRIS: Don't hurt him Lonnie...Don't hurt him.

LONNIE: Ole man...Ole man...Stop hummin' ole man...Start talkin'...Ole Man, I don't want to hurt you...Don't make me hurt you...Ole man, I know you know somtin'. (*He starts to reach down.*)

CHRIS: Lonnie...Don't.

LONNIE: Chris, our life might depend on this ole man...If you don't care...I do...He lived his life...I'm still young...Either he starts talkin' or I'm gonna start walkin'...all over him...Ole man.

CHRIS: David...David...Stop Lonnie, David...David.

DAVID: Don't touch me, please...Please...Please don't touch me.

(LONNIE *pulls the* OLE MAN *up and slams him against the wall.* CHRIS *screams.*)

LONNIE: Ole man...I'll break every one of your fingers, then your arms, then your legs...Less...less you start talkin'...Talk ole man...Talk.

CHRIS: Stop Lonnie...Stop...Oh god...Someone stop him...

DAVID: Why didn't they bid...Why didn't they bid...?

(CHRIS *jumps up, runs over to* LONNIE, *and tries to restrain him. He tries to shake her off.*)

LONNIE: Stop it Chris...Get away from me...This ole man knows somtin' 'n I'm gonna find out what.

CHRIS: Lonnie, it ain't gonna do no good...It jus' ain't.

LONNIE: How the hell we gonna find out, less'n I try?

CHRIS: Ole man, please, please...Say somtin'...Help us ole man...Please help us...Ole man, he'll hurt you...I don't wanna see you hurt...Ole man, say somtin' please.

DAVID: Chris...Lonnie...Chris.

(CHRIS*and*LONNIE*turn to him.* LONNIE*releases the* OLE MAN. CHRIS *and* LONNIE *walk over to* DAVID.)

CHRIS: David...David, you okay?

LONNIE: Hey, how you feelin'?

DAVID: They were gonna castrate me.

LONNIE: Wow.

CHRIS: No auction for you, huh?

(*Just as* CHRIS *speaks, a door silently opens in the back of the box near the* OLE MAN's *corner. He slips out unheard, unseen.*)

CHRIS: Hey...No hummin'.

(*They all turn.*)

LONNIE: What the fuck...He's gone...that sneaky ole bastid disappeared.

DAVID: But where...How?

LONNIE: Let's start searchin' this place again...They got us in 'n out...the ole man jus' disappeared. There's got to be a door somewhere.

DAVID: Gotta be...gotta be...

CHRIS: How'd they do it...How...What the hell is gonna happen... What the hell is gonna happen?

(*Lights drop suddenly in the box. Sounds of confusion and fear. Suddenly silence. Still no lights, then the humming of the* OLE MAN.)

VOICE: The slave insurrection was broken up today ladies 'n gimmin 'n the ringleaders hung by the neck 'til dead. The leaders a black girl called Chris, from Council Bluffs, and two black boys, one called Lonnie, from Chapman Hills, and the other a unknown nigga called David, and all their devil-inspired like won't be a threat to us kind, peaceful folk of Virginia any longer.

CURTAIN

Mary Goldstein And The Author

(PART ONE: A TRILOGY FOR THE BLACK FAMILY)

by OYAMO (Charles F. Gordon)

Oyamo holds an MFA in playwrighting from the Yale School of Drama. He is a member of New Dramatists, and he has written over twenty plays, including: *The Resurrection of Lady Lester, The Juice Problem, Blue Journey, The Last Party, The Thieves, The Lovers* and a musical entitled *Distraughter and the Great Panda Scanda*. Oyamo has been the recipient of Rockefeller, Guggenheim, CAPS, NEA and NYSFA grants, and a McKnight Fellowship for residency at the Playwrights' Center in Minneapolis.

PLACE: *The family play room, neat except for a few "tattered" books.*
TIME: *Early morning.*
SOUND: *The theme music, a pensive mood music with a strong, underlying urgency, a subtle and anxious brooding.*

(MARY GOLDSTEIN *strolls out to the theme music. In her arms she carries a sleeping baby wrapped in pink blankets. She enters from stage left, crosses and exits stage right. She returns in a moment. Her nightrobe is housewifey but with enough of a personal twist to set off her strong-willed originality. That robe must be versatile, as it will become several "costumes" during the performance. She collects the tattered books, looks at them, sighs, stacks them neatly on a small table. She finally acknowledges the presence of an "audience.")*
MARY: Hello, my name is Mary Goldstein. Believe me, I'd never choose that name myself. Not that there's anything wrong with the name; it's just that it doesn't seem to go well with a schvartze, much less a Baptist person. But, hell, I didn't write this thing. Whattaya gonna do? I don't really care what name he gave me; what matters is that I'm a woman in a world currently dominated by men. You know, some men have a lot of nerve. Take the author of this spectacle for example. The only visible character in this place is a woman, and yet, the author is a man. I don't know what makes him think he is capable of creating believable womanhood on stage. I

suppose it's his male ego. But, personally, if I have to have me a man, I prefer one who has some nerve. All these words I'm speaking now were written by him. Some of you possibly thought I had been expressing myself, didn't you? Like I said, some men have a lot of nerve.(*Sighs heavily.*) I know you're not there, but you're real inside of me, and at least you listen and you understand...(*Pause.*)... because I believe you understand. (*As if snapping back to "reality."*) Okay, Mary, stop this dialogue with yourself. Now then, it is time to get down to the business at hand. Let's see; so far this morning I've done the laundry, started cleaning this lovely play room, got three beautiful kids washed, dressed, fed and off to school. I've got one baby nine months sleeping on a full stomach of titty milk. And now I've got to fry a few eggs for my darling husband. The rest of the day I will spend sewing, cleaning, shopping and cooking, in that order. (*Lapsing back into speaking to an "audience."*) And in the evening, after the children are in bed and the kitchen is cleaned, I'll write my poem for the day. That's the time when I feel like I'm glowing - almost like a brilliant, soft light. I even sleep better after I've written my poem. (*Fingering the neat stack of tattered books on the table.*) I may even get in 15 or 20 minutes reading time tonight, if these books survive today's onslaught. To think, I used to read four or five hours a day, and I took care of my books. But one day we'll have some new book shelves, or so my husband keeps promising. And speaking of Arnold, I suppose I'll have to give him a little snatch before I fall asleep. What's today? Friday, yeah, today is Friday, the time of the sacred rites of marriage bed. My rights don't seem to get much attention there lately. He snatches what he wants and goes. But I'm doing my duty - serving my function. It's been nine years, and now we so often seem like strangers to each other. Distant, hostile sometimes. I can't do anything right - sometimes I wonder if I'll even get to rest, a chance to sleep and bathe and read. Kind of fertilize myself, let my nails grow, see a good movie. I know he works hard, provides as best he can, meets all the payments on the mortgage, but why can't I get some understanding in turn? I mean, I'm a damn good mother! When my kids step out of this house, they're clean, well-fed, and they be smiling. Nobody out there sends home bad reports about my children. That must mean something, right? So what then if I break my husband's favorite cup or forget to put a tomato in his lunch basket? I don't do it on purpose. I try to do right; I try to take care of him the way he wants - but sometimes I mess up, and lately this seems to make him more and more aggravated. Sometimes I find myself tiptoeing around just to avoid his roar. Maybe, we're both tired. (*Sits in chair.*) We probably need a vacation off to ourselves. Since I've been such a good girl today, I'm going to suggest we go off together for a few days. At least I'll start suggesting it. Arnold doesn't like to be rushed into anything. I'll sort of slip it in while he's getting his breakfast. Then tonight while he's grunting and humping, I'll give him a little extra rhythm and mention the trip again. And then, tomorrow I'll serve him his favorite dish, pastrami and blackeye peas. And that should hook it all up. (*With quite conscious dramatic ostentation.*) And now, I'm going to prepare the bodies of three unborn chickens for my darling husband's breakfast. (*Off to door, exits via door to kitchen off. After a few moments of silence, a fierce argument explodes in the kitchen, its visualization created in the angry words.*)

ARNOLD: Dammit, Mary, you burned my eggs again! You know I can't eat burnt eggs.

MARY: I'll fry a couple more; no big problem. Calm down.

ARNOLD: Well, shit, Mary, eggs cost money.

MARY (*calmly*): I know the cost of an egg. I do all the shopping around here, remember? Be cool.

ARNOLD: I give ya da money, don't I? And you supposed to do da shopping by day way! And you supposed ta cook da food, not burn it. You need to cool it with them excuses you keep coming up with.

MARY: Well, what the hell do you want? You married a woman, not a damn computer.

ARNOLD: I married a dumb broad; that's what...

(*We hear a violent crashing of dishes and pots;* ARNOLD and MARY *yell at the same time.*)

ARNOLD: What in the hell is wrong wit' you, bitch? You crazy or something? Look at this damn mess! Who da hell you callin' a dummy, stupid bitch! CLEAN UP THE FUCKIN' MESS, BITCH! UM KICKIN' YO' ASS DIS MORNIN'!

MARY: Don't call me a broad! I do everything in this stinking house! Well, clean it up, dummy! Who the hell you calling a bitch, simple ass nigga? KISS MY SWEET BLACK ASS, BLACK BAS-TARD!!

(*We hear her screaming and in an instant see her burst from the kitchen, slam the door and quickly brace her body against the door. She grabs a child's baseball bat nearby as an afterthought. In the kitchen we hear ARNOLD stumble in the mess, fall, curse and rise. She laughs as much from fear as from humor. He pushes against the door a couple of times and yells.*)

ARNOLD: Open the fuckin' door. You're in for it now, bitch.

(*She pushes with all her strength, but his superior might is beginning to win out. In desperation she goes berserk; screams and yells as she ferociously beats about the door with the baseball bat.*)

MARY: You're the one in for it! I'll kill you! Come get me! I'll kill you! I'll kill you, man. I'll kill you! Open the door so I can kill you. (*She's silent for a moment. He says nothing for a moment.*)

ARNOLD: Mary...

(*She remains silent.*)

Mary...

MARY: WHAT?!

ARNOLD: Come down, baby.

MARY: LEAVE ME ALONE, DAMN-IT!

ARNOLD: Look, I'm gonna give you time to calm down. We'll talk about it when I get home from work, okay?

MARY: Okay.

(*He is heard walking away, opening and closing a back door. She registers complete relief from fear, starts laughing, softly at first, then loudly and hugely. She finally breathes a big sigh of relief, and says:*)

MARY: Whew! (*She drops the spatula, walks about the room thinking aloud to herself.*) Nine years, and now we've finally come to this. (*Frantically searching through the children's toy chest, she finds a replica of a Sioux headband and a tomahawk or whatever as creative imagination.*)

Give him to the squaws-
He is the enemy-
The enemy who comes to kill our children-
To destroy my sons with firewater and lies-
To defile my daughters with his long knife-
His tongue spits poison in my ears-
Let me cut it out-
Give him to the squaws-

We will cut off his scrotum
And make bags for Black Elk's medicine-
We will rip out his heart and liver;
Give him to the squaws-
We will peel his skin off slowly-
We will build a slow, sweet fire over which to roast him-
We will let the dogs tear the cooking flesh from his legs-
Give him to the squaws-
We are women
But we also know
What to do with the enemies of our people...

If my mother ever heard me say that poem, she'd try to commit me or send me to some psychiatrist. "Those are cruel things to say about your man; they're unwomanly, inhumane. What would you do without a man? A woman needs a good man," she'd say. "Get yourself a good man at all costs, and don't make a mistake like I did; get a good man." Well, I did just that.

(*She swirls about to a lovely dance tune, picks up a small purse and a hand bouquet of plastic flowers. After joyfully dancing a bit, she speaks.*)

Oh, Arnold, I had such a beauuuuuuuuutiful time at the senior prom tonight. This has been one night that I'll never forget. Arnold, we shouldn't wake up your brother and his wife. It's so late. They asked you to bring me by? To see us in our prom outfits? That's sweet. Oh, you have a key, your brother lets you have a key to his house?...Oh, just for tonight. (*Steps inside.*) Oh Arnold, you'd better wake them now we can get going. (*She walks around humming to herself, picking a bit of lint off her "dress," smoothing and brushing where appropriate. "ARNOLD" returns.*) They're not in? Why would they go out when they knew we were coming? Hey Arnold, why are you taking off your shoes and your jacket?...You want to rest for a minute? Oh, Arnold, couldn't we just rest at my house?...You don't want to wake my parents? But how will we wake them if we're only resting?...Oh Arnold, what are you doing?...Taking off my shoes?...I know you're taking off my shoes, but I want to know why...(*Suddenly whoops and wildly kicks out her legs.*) Oh Arnold, you're tickling me! Stop it! Arnold! (*Calms.*) See there, you know I'm ticklish on my feet and my knees and other places. Arnold, why are you on your knees in front of me?...You want to rub my tired little feet?...Oh how sweet, but don't tickle me you hear?...Oh Arnold, what are you doing? (*Suddenly whoops and "pushes" his hands off her knees.*) See there, that's unfair. I told you my knees and other places are ticklish. Oh Arnold, don't feel discouraged; you can still rub my feet if you want to...there. Isn't this nice and cozy...Oh Arnold, no baby...Oh Arnold, no baby...Oh Arnold, Arnold, Arnold...(*She "kicks" him solidly upside his head.*) Oh Arnold, I didn't mean to hurt you...I'm sorry...Honest...It was just the way you were licking my knees; it made me have a muscle spasm...Huh?...Did I like it? Oh, spasms are alright, I suppose; I...Oh, you mean did I like the licking? (*Giggles.*) Oh Arnold, No, I hated it. I mean the tickling. The licking is soothing...Well, we better be going now...Arnold, don't touch there; please don't touch me there...NO,NO, NO! (*Her whole body convulses backwards, away from* "ARNOLD.") Oh Arnold, your hands is all the way up to my other places...I told you I was ticklish there too...Oh Arnold, don't rub me like that...I can't stand it, your hands are so hot...Oh Arnold, no, no, baby, please, no... (*With one mighty heave of her whole body, she "throws" him off, shakes her head violently as if shaking off a spell and says firmly in a convincing show of mock anger but with a sense of victory, then softly:*) Arnold, we have to wait until we're married like we said...Oh, baby, I want you too...I know it don't make no difference, but we promised to wait...How long? We should wait at least until a wedding date has been set...You want to set a date now?...Oh Arnold, but this is so unexpected... You say six months from now?...Let's see; that would make the date June 23. OK. Is this what you really want, Arnold? Then I accept because what you want is what I want...Oh Arnold, you've made me so happy tonight...Oh Arnold, your fingers are so strong...Arnold, don't tear my dress...Oh Arnold, baby, baby, baby, yes, yes, baby...Oh Arnold...

The wedding day was sharp blue spring laughter, joy tears;
The time was new and the routine was secure.
It was the ritual of assurance;
That feeling of belonging,
I had a man,
Or rather, a man had me,
And we, his wife and his children,
We are what he calls his family

His family, mind you. I heard that one before. My father used to say the same thing. "When I get over, my family gets over." The only thing my father ever got over in his life was a cold. My daddy was a gambler. He would have gambled away damn near all of his money if my mama hadn't gotten to him first on payday. The horses, poker, coon can, sports, numbers, cockfights, anything where he could get odds. He'd even steal back money he gave mama. Once, when I was 13 years old, he gave me five dollars and I immediately went out and spent it on a book of poetry. I ran back home, filled up the bathtub and hopped in with my book. My father knocked on the bathroom door asking me where I put my five dollars. I said, "It's in the bathtub with me." He told me I was stupid for bathing with a five dollar bill, and he asked me to slip it under the door to him because he had to use it to play his latest hunch. I said, "Daddy, I can't slip it under the door because I'm reading it." He thought I was getting smart and he started pounding on the door. He kicked it open and stormed in. When he saw the book, he figured I had spent the money and in a fit he slapped me hard. When he hit me, I stood up and smashed the book in his face with all the force in my body, and I screamed and screamed and screamed! Gambling was Daddy's habit, but we all suffered, especially my mother. God knows how she managed to feed us, but she always treated us good, my six brothers and me, my mother's assistant. An assistant mother until I had my own children. I always swore I wouldn't be like my mother, the prime victim of a so-called modern family...

Some family!
We are the family but
I am the one who does all the family work.
He says I am the queen,
But I am the cog on which all else turns,
A workhorse,
A virtual slave,
I am the dizzy broad,
The "ole lady,"
The dumb cunt.
I am the black bitch
The saffire of burning nightmares-

But I am a woman,
a mother of poems and children-
I want to be free
To see
To self create.
Yet, all ways I am created by others,
Told to submit to the masculine mystique.
Look then at what has been created,
Enforced as reality:

(MARY's *motions indicate she is folding clothes as in a laundromat - talks to "another woman."*)

Yeah, girl, and you know she had nerve enough to tell me that I had better check myself. Like there's something wrong with me because my wigs only cost eight dollars. So, I talked about how flat her butt was. You know she don't like nobody saying she got a butt like a whitey. Naw, she don't want that. She want you to compliment her on her light complexion and her fine features. Want you to forget about them naps all matted down up under that yellow wig she wears. She ain't nothing but a poverty clerk and got nerve to say she can't relate to "minority housewives" like me because I only have a high school education. I was made to be some man's slave. She claim I'm physically dependent on one man. Dig how she say it: "A woman has the right to aggressively assert her sexual independence and preferences." Claimed she got her three men trying to hit on her for her body and her money. But, girl, let me tell you something. Me and her got the same gynecologist, and my cousin work for the gynecologist. You know my cousin, JoAnn, don't you? You know JoAnn is intelligent, and a nurse and all, and she don't tell no lies like most folks do. Yeah, well you shoulda heard what she told me about that woman. I can't tell you everything 'cause a gynecologist's files is s'posed ta be confidential, but between you and me, honey, I know she wish she had her one man 'cause the file say ain't nothing serious happening in the bush, if you know what I mean.

(MARY *in the park, sitting on a bench. We hear park sounds, distant traffic, as she speaks.*)

GET AWAY FROM THAT FENCE, YOU HEAR?
It was a complete madhouse.
Everything came out in the open today.

YAW STOP THROWING STONES!
Girl, I like to fainted when I found out.
Yeah, Carmella's husband was going with the gardener
Who was sleeping with Carmella's sister, Janice,
And Janice turned out to be a freak, girl,
'Cause when she was a child she got gang raped in the Girl
Scouts.
YAW TAKE TURNS ON THE SLIDE!
But Carmella's Daddy is a mess.
Remember the automobile accident when he went to the hospital?
Well, the cleaning woman caught him and a nurse in the bathroom;
They was doing a heavy number, honey. Oh Yeah.
Well the nurse turns out to be Carmella's aunt, her mother's
sister.
GET BACK. LEAVE THEM DOGS ALONE. THEY MIGHT BITE!
Carmella broke down and went to a psychiatrist.
Girl, let me tell you something.
The psychiatrist turned out to be a transvestite
Who had once assaulted Carmella's son,
The same son who got kicked out of school
For getting a black girl pregnant.
GET AWAY FROM THAT FENCE, YOU HEAR? DON'T LET
ME TELL YOU AGAIN!
Honey, I can't wait to see what them people gon' think of for
tomorrow's show.
Now if I have to, I swear umo lock them kids up in the basement
so I can hear my story in peace.
It's the only time I have to enjoy some relaxing entertainment.
UMO TEAR YOUR BUTT UP IF YOU HIT HER AGAIN! YOU
HEAR?
(*A sweet, gentle ballet music that was popular in America at the time
of American slavery* - MARY *hums and does a few graceful movements
as she finds and dons various items from the toy chest. Shortly, in long
gloves, sunbonnet and with a parasol,* MARY *pirouettes for a moment
and then begins a tasteful striptease in ballet form as she speaks. Her ballet is promenade about the space. She is a demure, seemingly shy young
virgin mistress of an antebellum American plantation, gracious, thor-*

*oughly polite, cultured, a lady of exquisite taste and charm, but as her real
intentions are revealed, so does her manner change.)*

Oh deah, where is that boy?
This glen is so dreadful looking this time in the afternoon.
Mosquitoes and other bugs,
This exasperating heat,
These gloomy shadows,
The shadows of the weeping trees, always bent over
Like sad darkies howling into empty cotton sacks.
But it's the perfect spot to safely practice.
Oh deah, it will be perfectly awful if I should fail to meet
Daddy on time.
Daddy gets so upset when I'm late
Because he rarely sees me these days.
He's opening up another 20,000 acres, 30 miles south.
Good rich black delta land,
He frightens me so; running here to purchase tools;
Running there to purchase lumber and livestock;
And running still again to the banks to borrow money
To purchase a new crop of Africans.
I do hope the boy will get here soon,
For I must not fail to soothe Daddy from his travels and inces-
sant work. (*Sets parasol down.*)
I DO THINK HE IS THE SLAVE AT TIMES. (*Begins removing
shoes.*)
But he scoffs at me,
Thinks it silly and childish of me to fret over him.
He tells me I should be thinking of finding myself a young man
of means.
Hah! Daddy would be so upset if he lost his sweet magnolia
blossom
To some young man.
That's what he affectionately calls me -
His sweet magnolia blossom. (*Begins removing dress.*)
Sometimes I play the mandolin for him
When he tires of hearing those darkies wail and moan.
He likes me to show him the new dresses I purchase in New York

and Europe;
But I just laugh
And I tease him because he always wants to know what kind of
perfume I wear. (*Removes all but bra and panties.*)
Father is so civilized when he's not working like a slave. (*Sees
"boy" approaching.*)
Oh, Boy! Yoo hoo! Over here! Yes, do hurry.
Don't just stand there! Take off your clothes.
You did scrub with soap and mint water like I told you, didn't
you?
Yes, well I hope you scrubbed thoroughly.
All the perfume in the world can't cover up darkie odor, you
know. (*Sees his erection.*)
Oh deah, look at that bast;
Come boy, show me how the black wenches do it;
Hurry before Daddy begins fretting...(*She continues speaking as
she puts on nightrobe.*)
Ancient rites of our fathers-
In all the lands
In all the times
Behind the masks have ruled the men: (*In a robot-like manner.*)
Good morning, Mr. Zocchi,
What, Mr. Zocchi?
You want it now, Mr. Zocchi?
But I'm really too tired, Mr. Zocchi.
I just had a rough period, Mr. Zocchi.
What, Mr. Zocchi?
You don't care, Mr. Zocchi?
Okay, Mr. Zocchi, don't get angry! Mr. Zocchi;
Come and get it, Mr. Zocchi
But please don't bite this time, Mr. Zocchi;
You see Mr. Peterson at 10, Mr. Zocchi.
Your coffee, Mr. Zocchi.
You'll have to come by 9:45, Mr. Zocchi.
Your wife called, Mr. Zocchi.
Here's your scotch, Mr. Zocchi.
The papers are on your desk, Mr. Zocchi.
Your son needs bail money, Mr. Zocchi.
Another scotch, Mr. Zocchi?

Your daughter has gonorrhea, Mr. Zocchi.
Another scotch, Mr. Zocchi?
The bank called, Mr. Zocchi.
The account is overdrawn, (Mr. Zocchi.)
They won't extend credit, (Mr. Zocchi.)
The pension fund has disappeared, Mr. Zocchi.
A double scotch, Mr. Zocchi.
You got a summons today, Mr. Zocchi.
We're being investigated, Mr. Zocchi.
A cut in salary, Mr. Zocchi?
My salary, Mr. Zocchi?
BULLSHIT, MR. ZOCCHI! (*Angrily pacing.*)
A modern homemaker
Or a corporate dishwasher-
Some petty power that sallies forth
From the lips of my vagina-
This ensures my rise in the company-
The company company company-
My place in history is located between my legs-
Leave the world to us men, they scream,
You have a good home-
Their world, the company,
Ancient ways of our fathers:
In all the lands
In all the times
Behind the masks have ruled the men:
A female infant is taught to be a "woman."
For the boy newborn
Bury his cord beneath the red pepper shrub
So that he may be fierce, brave, dangerous-
For the girl newborn
Bury her cord beneath the pawpaw tree
So that she may be gentle.
If the climate is a harsh enemy,
Better to have many warriors:
Surplus female infants must die.
Witness the burial of a live human being: (*Crouching dejectedly.*)
I am defiled-
I cannot enter the forest outside-

I am unclean-
My blood will call Death to every living plant-
My blood must be caught in a gourd,
Burned and the ashes in a secret cave-
I am dangerous-
I have to remain in this tiny hut but
Until my blood has finished leaking-
I cannot eat fresh food,
For I would blight the animals and the crops-
If I must walk about,
The old women tell me
To throw leaves in my path as a warning-
To men, pregnant women and babies
My leaking blood is a mysterious poison...
(As if binding her feet with yards of long, narrow white cloth.)
I will bind my feet,
Bend and crush the bones
So that I may walk soft, tiny steps
Far behind my husband.
The old women have given me these charms
So that my husband may feast on pleasure-
They have painted a rose on my buttocks,
Anointed my body with oils of sweet fruit
So that my husband will know he is entering a garden-
I will paint a blue mustache on my upper lip, bleach my skin,
Hotcomb my hair, cover my ankles and hands with bracelets
and rings,
Paint my body with red mud.
I will be too valuable for a young man to possess-
I will be too strong for an old man to hold-
Only a young, strong, rich chief will be able
TO OFFER REASONABLE CONSIDERATION TO MY
FAMILY FOR THE LOSS OF
SUCH A FINE DAUGHTER...
Through all the centuries
The impositions have remained.
I have tried to be a flower
To which warriors come to lick my sweet nectar.
But I am rotten meat in the sun

On which flies importantly strut about,
Leaving maggots
Black spots
And a sad, languid emptiness of spirit:
(MARY *in trancelike state as she stirs something on an imaginary*
stove.)
Good morning, heartache.
I almost forgot you were here...
I almost thought he was back
I would feel the heat from his body...
Rising firm
Slow hands rub heat
Into my soft wet body,
Brings back the dance of youth,
The sweet juices of memory...
There's something about his soft touches
He holds so much of me;
It feels so good.
His leg across my thigh–
I guess his leg wasn't really there last night,
But the smell was his lingering melody
Woven into the sheets,
But he's gone forever.
I'll have to take the sheets to the grocery store
So I can get me some more rice
And wash his shirts too,
Cause he might come back to get his shirts,
I could hide them
So he'd have to need me to find them
Maybe he'll be cooled off
Maybe he'll see how much he needs me
To need him;
Maybe he'll come back.
Maybe we could go away together,
A few days even,
Lie under the sun,
Smell the oatmeal burning...
Oh God, I done burned the oatmeal again...
Oh, my sisters, the hurts I must unburden,

The life I hold inside,
The dreams I cannot live, they say.
I am a woman,
a mother of poems and children.
I am not a cauldron of imposed categories:
Black, minority and working class.
I am not a white man-
I am not a white woman-
I am not a Black man-
I am-
I am a Black woman,
But ain't I just a woman?
Ain't I just am?

You know, sometimes I wonder about a decision, a big decision that might mean the end of this family. I've wondered what my children might think. I've wondered about the huge risk: I'm frightened, but I have to dream: I have to be free.

(*Striking the pose of a 12-year-old child writing, a pencil, a piece of paper.*)

Poem to my Mother Poet
I am a poet's son.
I live with my father's people.
My mother is too poor to feed me.
But she has made me rich-
Her vision ever revealing-
Her tears for me, for herself -
Her needs, hurts
Will one day be no mystery
To the black man yawning in me,
I am a poet's son.
My mother has made me rich
She has taken me to freedom
Your son, who loves you...

(*Flings aside pencil and paper. Struts about hiply in masculine stylization.*)

Yeah, why not take me some freedom,
Like they do,
Feel my own way,
Take my own chances,

Arrange everything around my own life,
They world ain't nothing special;
Any fool can master the master's ways;
I mean,
I could break loose and get down too:
(MARY *dons a yellow hardhat of construction worker, gestures frequently as if receiving a "pound" from a fellow worker - slapping palms. Behaves in a totally masculine manner. It is both a parody and self parody, done more in fun than gall.*)
Yo, sista, Shirley, whas to it, homes?
How da ole boy treatin' ya dose days?
Hole tight, pardna, don't break on me-
Um not crackin' on you and yo' old man.
Us sistas got to stick together.
You know where Um coming from.
I told ya the nigga was a dog six months ago.
And you know how dogs is.
A dog ain't shit,
And that's what every man is, a dog.
See, when you learn dat,
You'a know how to treat a dog.
Don't get me wrong, home.
My sexual preference is dogs, myself.
I love me some tasty dog meat,
But you got to know how to treat a dog.
I mean, we out here busting our asses
And the dog sitting at home lookin' at the goddamn tv.
You come in from a hard day's work
And the da dog wanna mess wit' you.
Wanna know why you ten minutes late-
Who you gave yo' money to-
Why don't you take him out-
Why don't you buy him a new dishwasher-
Well, shit!
I told my dog,
I said: "DOG, you better be glad you got some dishes to wash,
HOMES."
And I wish dat dog would come axing me to wash dishes.
You know me.

I'll put a dog in the street.
Find me another dog
Who know how to take care of a sista right, ya unnastan.
I mean, I don't be taking no shit from no dog
Ah got me another crib, das all.
Yeah, ah got me another crib
And I got dat bad boy laid out, chile.
Wall to wall carpet, color tv, a kingsize bed.
And, Look here,
That bed work go-o-o-od!
You know I got me a parade of dogs coming through dere.
You shoulda dug that fine puppy I had las' night!
I had da nigga whinin' and sniffin', ah swear to God!
He was fine
Broad shoulders,
muscular, but slim hard,
Just the way I like my dogs.
Tried to play hard to get at first.
Even pushed my hand off his thigh.
Come talkin' 'bout I caught him at a difficult time of the
month-
Said, he can't never concentrate around the first of the month-
So I digs da dog crackin' for the big gapper,
And ah mashes 20 dollas on da dog-
He squeals
And we gits it on.
I mean we gits down as low as you kin git.
When I got finish puttin' some of big mama on dat dog
HONEY, he give me my 20 dollas back and 20 mo'!
Dig dat! (*She angrily flings aside the hardhat as her parody has
catapulted her into a moment of realization and decision.*)
Shit, I don't wanna be no man!
I don't even wanna be like no man!
What's so big about being a man nowadays?
I am a woman
And I want to be free
The way I see
To self-create.
Listen, my brothers, lovers, fathers

And listen close:
Um not gon' be a foot rest
For no Black man. No more.
Um not gon' be yo' shock absorber no more;
You always shocked at our condition as a people,
But you keep blaming me! (*She stomps about, quite angry.*)
<u>They</u> cut you,
Not me,
Vent your rage at the enemy--
The master class has oppressed us all,
You, me
And what he calls <u>his</u> women.
We stand with you.
But you talk, talk, talk
About
Revolution, guerilla warfare, Black liberation,
Black Power, Black Capitalism, Black Communism,
Black Islam, Black Christ, Black History,
Black Culture, Black yuppies, Black conservatives,
But the sight of his red blood weakens you,
or so it seems,
But my blood is a different matter.
I am a creature of pain,
My pain, your pain, their pain.
Beat me!
Hide me behind veils-
Lock me in the house-
Tell me how dumb I am-
Tell me anything-
But let me tell you one thing:
Generations of black children
Will learn to despise you
For enslaving their mothers
You want to hang chastity belts on my loins
While the enemy hangs chains on your brains.
You scamper about the world of ideas;
Each year you return with a different one
For our liberation--
These are chains--

Break the chains--
(MARY *struts about angrily. Her anger gradually increases until the*
end of the piece.)
You like a ancient African warrior, right?
You said you supposed to wage war and hunt
While I layed at the hut nursing babies.
But it seem to me that we need more than a mattress
To build a new nation--
We hungry!
We got us a dispossess!
We all need shoes in case we got to walk out of here.
We got a turn-off notice;
The dog is in the basement holding off Con Edison!
Even the dog is doin' somethin'.
No, I ain't standing behind you no more-
You tell me to stand behind you
While you crawling in front of me.
This is my final notice:
I ain't gon' be yo' slave-
I ain't gon' be yo' children's slave
I done bought yo' food-
cooked yo' food-
washed yo' clothes-
cleaned yo' rug-
dusted yo' furniture-
swept yo' floors-
washed yo' windows-
taught yo' kids-
built yo' church-
read yo' books-
rubbed yo' back-
nursed you from sickness-
made you feel good-
took yo' abuse and ridicule
done everything I could to please you and yo' kids
And this family ain't done shit for me!
Well, I'm through!
This ain't no family!
This is a torture unit!

Yaw don't do nothin' but torture my spirit.
Umo create my own life outside of <u>your</u> family!
You can hire a maid.

(*She angrily begins to move toward the exit. The "baby" screams in sudden hunger at awakening. The crying sounds halt MARY who is initially startled and then torn. She tries to move toward the exit, away from the sound as if still determined to desert the family, but the sound of the baby crying shatters her will each time.*)

Your father will be here in a minute! (*Moves toward exit, but turns back.*) No, I can't let you keep me here. I won't. (*Moves toward exit, but turns back.*) You'll understand when you grow up! I want to live too! I need to live too. I've got to live too! (*Moves toward exit, but turns back and screams hysterically.*) SHUT UP SHUT UP SHUT UP SHUT UP SHUT UP SHUT UP SHUT UP SHUT UP SHUT UUUUUUUUUUP! (*Sobs uncontrollably for a moment and then hurries toward sound of baby crying. She hurries as if she intends to hurt the baby. She disappears offstage, and the baby shortly ceases crying. She enters cuddling a swaddled infant in her arms. The infant is sucking one of her breasts. She fusses over the blankets, coddles the infant, coos soft words to it. She crosses and takes a seat facing the audience.*) Well, like I told you, a man created this spectacle. What can you expect? Huh? But you listen closely to me: Man or no man, I am. I am a mother of children and poems; I will be free to create. I promise myself, my baby daughter here, and you too, that I am going to move beyond the male mystique that now rules this world and writes these very words I speak. (*She gives full attention to her baby, cooing softly and snuggling it. Lights fade slowly to black.*)

Daddy Says: A Play

by NTOZAKE SHANGE

Ntozake Shange is a playwright (*for colored girls who have considered suicide when the rainbow is enuf; Three Pieces*), poet (*nappy edges; A Daughter's Geography*) and novelist (*Sassafrass, Cypress & Indigo; Betsey Brown*).

Scene I

(*The scene opens with the two girls, LUCIE-MARIE and ANNIE-SHARON, practicing rope tricks and tie-down roping in their bedroom, which is decorated with rodeo and riding paraphernalia. There are lots of portraits of their mother in riding gear and rows of trophy belts that she won covering the walls. There is a large bed, a window and a saddle on a sawhorse. The doorway opens to a stairway which leads to the kitchen which is also a living room. It should be adequate but a little worn.*)

LUCIE-MARIE: Ain't that the way to do it?

ANNIE-SHARON: Well, I taught you, so you oughtta know whatchu doin' by now...

LUCIE-MARIE: Mama showed you everythin' you think you know/ & every single thin' you call yo'self teachin' me/ so there...

ANNIE-SHARON: You know I don' like discussin' Mama/ so cut it out, ya hear me. This bein' the day she died and all...

LUCIE-MARIE: By the time she was yo' age, she was awready a champion (*Pronounced "champeen."*). Whatchu call yo'self, since ya learnt how to walk, talk, crawl 'n' rope all single-handed like/ a new born heifer or somethin'?

ANNIE-SHARON: I call myself me, okay? 'Sides I am a champion.

LUCIE-MARIE: Naw ya ain't. Ya jus' won some first prizes/ bein' a champion means ya win everythin' there is to win/ more 'n' a few times/ likes season after season & year after year/ like Mama/ Twanda Rochelle Johnson/ that's my mama's name.

ANNIE-SHARON: Waz yo' mama's name.

233

LUCIE-MARIE: Yeah. You right abt Mama. (*Shifts mood.*) Ya know what Lincoln Maceo tol' me?

ANNIE-SHARON: Nope.

LUCIE-MARIE: He say that it gets up in there/ and ya getta baby.

ANNIE-SHARON: No lie.

LUCIE-SHARON: But if it's wiggly & squigly lookin'...like Mavis' li'l boy...

ANNIE-SHARON: Uh humhph. All cushy and curled up...

LUCIE-MARIE: Well, how could it get up anywhere?

ANNIE-SHARON: Mother Dear say it don't matter how/ it ain't s'posed to git nowhere/ sides where all it gonna go/ or are you fixin' to let me in on that?

LUCIE-MARIE: Up in here somewhere. (*Feeling her tummy.*)

ANNIE-SHARON: Girl, it cain't possibly get all up in there.

LUCIE-MARIE: Yeah it do. (*She gets up & they start to measure the lengths of rope against the inches from their pelvis' to their navels.*) See heah...Now look at that. (*Sees it's shorter.*)

ANNIE-SHARON: See, it'd have to be this big.

LUCIE-MARIE: That cain't be. Don't nobody want nothin' <u>that</u> big up in there!

ANNIE-SHARON: Well, I don' get how that's gonna happen. We jus' said whatever them li'l dicks is they still li'l ol' squigly wiggly things.

LUCIE-MARIE: Look like covered up snakes. (*Laughing.*)

ANNIE-SHARON: But they's all kinda snakes.

LUCIE-MARIE: Like Diamondbacks, right?

ANNIE-SHARON: Ya leave him outta this, heah. He don' talk to me 'bout stuff like this.

LUCIE-MARIE: Maybe ya oughtta ask him/ he might know how ya git it up in there.

ANNIE-SHARON: Mavis' boy/ what's that boy's name?

LUCIE-MARIE: Duke.

ANNIE-SHARON: He don' look like Duke to me. Looks mo' like a Sam to me.

LUCIE-MARIE: Don' say nothin' like that to Mavis. She think that li'l niggah is the Lord hisself crawlin' round in them ol' stink diapers.

ANNIE-SHARON: Daddy look like that.

LUCIE-MARIE: Like what?

ANNIE-SHARON: Ya know, all curled up & then all peein' in yo' face when it's stood up like when they pants' down.

LUCIE-MARIE: How cd you say somethin' like that/ ya know Daddy don' pee in his pants!

ANNIE-SHARON: Well, now he don't.

LUCIE-MARIE: I think he's all hot in his pants for that Cassie what barrel-races.

ANNIE-SHARON: Who her? That one over to the Madisonville Rodeo last month?

LUCIE-MARIE: Yeah, that the one.

ANNIE-SHARON: Humm. Ya think when Daddy gets hot in his pants/ it's like when I'm dancin' wit Diamondback and he squeezes me real hard and we git real close up on each other over at the Trailblazers/ & my drawers git all wet 'n' sticky?

LUCIE-MARIE: Naw. It ain't the same at all. 'Member when Mother Dear tol' us. It was all our own business & ours all by our own selfs/ if we got all hot 'n' bothered.

ANNIE-SHARON: Yeah.

LUCIE-MARIE: Well, Daddy's a boy/ a man/ ya know what I mean/ so it cain't be the same wit him as wit us/ cuz we girls.

ANNIE-SHARON: I ain't sho'.

LUCIE-MARIE: We cd ask him.

ANNIE-SHARON: Ya know he don' truck wit all that "personal" talk/ our butts be the onliest thing hot/ we come burnin' his ears/ talkin' bout boys 'n' kissin'/ mess like that.

LUCIE-MARIE: But Mama wda tol' us, huh? Whatchu think?

ANNIE-SHARON: Whatchu mean? Don' talk bout Mama. I don' wanna talk bout her. See you jus' cain't remember the way I do.

LUCIE-MARIE: But Annie-Sharon...

ANNIE-SHARON: I don' wanna talk bout her. (*Goes over to the wall where there are all kinds of prize winning buckles from rodeo races.*) Ya think she rides wit us when we race? (*Takes one belt down & wraps it around herself.*)

LUCIE-MARIE: Ya know Daddy don' like talk like that/ he say "let the dead rest" he say.

ANNIE-SHARON: I know what "he say"/ I don' know what make me think somethin' simpleminded like that.

LUCIE-MARIE: Tryin' to act like ya don' miss Mama & gittin' all riled up every which time I even call her name is what ya git talkin' all crazy & spooked.

ANNIE-SHARON: I jus' thought maybe/ if I could ride like Mama & make Daddy real proud/ maybe/ well/ maybe he might like us better.

LUCIE-MARIE: Not us/ you/ Daddy like me fine/ it's that Cassie woman what I'm worried 'bout...jus' cuz she races don't make her no match fo' Mama.

ANNIE-SHARON: Mama's dead/ cain't be no match for her now or no other time - jus' us's/ we the onliest ones...

LUCIE-MARIE: That's what I mean/ See, it's only Mama could tell us all we need to know/ so we could/ oh be beautiful/ you know like Linda Beauville or Tootsie Woo/ they Mama's do they hair up wit them perms 'n' stuff/ put that no chippin' polish on they nails/ fringes on they rodeo git-ups/ ya know make pies 'n' do for when they entertain/ that's what they Mama's do/ that's what our Mama wd be doin' too/.

ANNIE-SHARON: Well, we ain't got one. (*Throws belt across the room.*)

LUCIE-MARIE: You cain't do that/ Look whatchu did wit Mama's prize. (*Runs to pick up the belt.*)

ANNIE-SHARON: It ain't nothin' but a damned piece of raw hide wit some silver on it/ that ain't yo' Mama, fool/ that a symbol/ that's how she died/ that's how come she died/ broncbustin'/ everybody in the world knows cain't no woman in her right mind be no bronc-buster/ oh no/ but not your growed up Mama/ she gonna show the world what all she could do/ she the virgin mary in a cowboy hat/ cain't no wild thing buck/ she dead/ trampled for her living/ trampled to death like so much hog feed/ tryin' to prove she more powerful than a STALLIONNN/ that's yo' precious Mama/ who's gonna tell ya how to be a woman/ tell you whatchu need to know/ like she could grow nails on a cowgirl's hands/ all you need to know/ that's some dream ya got/.

LUCIE-MARIE: Don'tchu talk like that/ you take all them things back/ heifer. (*Lunges at her sister.*) Mama was wonderful/ don'tchu say no mo' mean things bout my mother.

ANNIE-SHARON: I ain't said nothin' but you ain't got one/ you ain't got no mother more 'n' I do/ she cared mo' bout them damn animals than us.

LUCIE-MARIE: STOP IT! I'm tellin' you/ She was a great bronc-buster...

ANNIE-SHARON: Daddy say bronc-bustin' ain't ladylike.

LUCIE-MARIE: What he know bout it? He a big ol' man.

ANNIE-SHARON: You think she knew somethin' bout it? Huh? (*Fighting over belt intensely.*)

LUCIE-MARIE: Don't say nothin' else bout Mommy/ Don't/ don't. (*Starts crying & shoving.*)

ANNIE-SHARON: Heah. That's whatchu got from "Mommy." (*Throws belt to LUCIE-MARIE.*)

LUCIE-MARIE: You don't know nothin'/ ya don' know how to act/ act like a hoodlum & don't hold nothin' dear. (*Puts belt around herself & goes over to the trophies & other belts on the wall.*) I remember when she won this heah one in Navasota/ at the All Women's Rodeo/ Come in at 14.3 barrel racing/ some night's she tied down that calf for second place/ after that Agnes Morales/ Look/ look, ain't this pretty?/ don't chu remember???

ANNIE-SHARON: YOU AIN'T GOT NO SENSE? YOU FULLY ACTUAL DUMB? Cain't figure out where babies come from or that yo' Mama was a steel doggin' damn fool/ dyin' on us...

LUCIE-MARIE: You hush up/ My mama rides wit me/ jus' like she did when she'd sing to me in the night in the trailer/ "you're jus' a cowgirl's baby/ ridin' the Sandman's prairie."

ANNIE-SHARON: Stop/ Stop/ I tol' you I don' wanna heah nothin' bout Mama/ Nothin'. (*Snatches belt as* TIE-DOWN BROWN *enters ominously.*) She dead/ I'm tellin' you/ (*Sees* TIE-DOWN.) Oh, Daddy...

TDB: What's that in yo' hands? (*Takes belt & slaps her.*) I tol' you to let what's past be past/ If I said it once I said it ten hundred times/ & today of all days.

ANNIE-SHARON: But Daddy, we was jus' lookin'.

TDB: Ya don' look wit your hands.

LUCIE-MARIE: Daddy, please, just this one time/ tell us somethin' bout Mama.

TDB: She died from bronco-bustin'/ tryin' to be more a man than a man/ that's all/ now put these things back/ & stop all this noise/ of all the damned days to ride.

LUCIE-MARIE: Daddy/ Please listen to me/ Daddy, did you love her? What was she like when she acted like a girl?/ Daddy/ not when she acted like a boy/ what was she like? Daddy, I've gotta know somethin' sides she died/ Daddy, did you think she was pretty?/ you usedta say I looked like her/ Do you think I'm pretty/ Daddy?/ please/ please tell me.

ANNIE-SHARON: Leave him alone Lucie/ Leave everybody alone/ ya heah.

TDB: Yeah/ listen to yo' sister/ What's in the past is in the past.

LUCIE-MARIE: But I look like her & I ain't in the past/ Daddy/ Please Daddy/ I wanna be just like her/ & oh I don' know...

ANNIE-SHARON: Lucie/ why are you talkin' all this mess? Cain't you see Daddy ain't up to this/ why you gonna put us through all this heah?

LUCIE-MARIE: You shut up/ I'm talkin' to my father.

ANNIE-SHARON: And he ain't mine too/ I ain't got no mama either/ but you gonna ruin my daddy's life talkin' 'bout how you gonna be jus' like her/ look what she did to Daddy/ he cain't hardly talk 'bout nothin' when somethin' brings her to mind/ you wanna take my Daddy 'way too/ you actual mo' dumb than I thought you was.

LUCIE-MARIE: I ain't dumb/ I jus' wanna heah some mo' 'bout Mommy/ I gotta right/ I'm her girl.

ANNIE-SHARON: And whatchu think I am, some kinda she-goat?

TDB: Lucie-Marie/ Annie-Sharon/ Hush all this quarrelin'/ Stop now. I guess/ I ain't been handlin' this like I oughtta. (*Takes two belts from the wall. Wraps one around each child.*) See, yo' mama & me/ Well/ we was jus' kids/ she was the prettiest li'l ol' thing/ look jus' like you.

LUCIE-MARIE: See/ I tol' ya/ I look jus' like her.

TDB: Most times in the summer/ when the sun wd getta settin'/ wild-like/ all red & orange wit magnolias & cypress reachin' up thru them clouds that be hangin' from the sky like cotton candy 'n' the grass smellin' ripe like/ times like that/ yo' mama 'n' me/ we'd jump on Masaya/ that's that mare Twanda set so much store by/ we'd climb up on Masaya/ & walk her thru them woods past the corral/ walk her real slow/ 'til we cd hear most everythin' there was to hear/ & then she/ Twanda wd sing/ to me/ some ol' somethin' she made up in her head/ jus' sing to me...then alla sudden she'd kick up, & off we went duckin' branches/ jumpin' fences/ damn fool gal/ 'most run us into the swamp/ Lawd, I'll never forget/ fearin' Masaya was fallin'/ I was fallin'/ Twanda was leanin' here & then thisaway/ & here come the mud up my pants legs & I cdn't tell if yo' mama was under the horse or down in   there smotherin' to death in the mud/ good jesus, that woman didn't have no kinda sense/ justa singin'/ & here we goin' right down offa this animal into the center of the earth/ humph/ that was somethin'/ I'm tellin' ya/ her cheekbones come way up like Cherokees/ real high & glowin' brown/ but - but, ain't no way to get 'round it...Both of ya favor her/ from time to time/ always on this day...

ANNIE-SHARON: How Daddy?

TDB: Right there by yo' eyes/ I reckon/ Annie/ but Lucie- Marie's carryin' her mother's mouth...yep/ y'all is Twanda's daughters/ that's for sho'/ Daddy's roughtough ridin' cutiepies/ right?

LUCIE-MARIE: Was she smart too/ Daddy?

ANNIE-SHARON: You know my mama wasn't dumb like you.

TDB: Smart as a whip 'fore she left school/ then she jus' set her mind on them horses & y'all...you know the rest.

LUCIE-MARIE: But Daddy, she was a champion/ Twanda Rochelle Johnson/ Southwestern Rodeo Association All Star/ three years in a row.

ANNIE-SHARON: And she wasn't but 28 when...

TDB: No more talk now/ y'all get yourselves ready/ Cassie's comin' over.

ANNIE-SHARON & LUCIE-MARIE: Cassie?

TDB: Yeah/ it'll be good to have a woman 'round heah.

LUCIE-MARIE: But I thought we were goin' to the rodeo at the Diamond-L/ & you don' never bring no woman 'round heah.

TDB: We is.

ANNIE-SHARON: She goin'?

TDB: She is.

(ANNIE-SHARON *and* LUCIE-MARIE *look at each other and then at their father. They finger their buckles and look back at each other and in unison say:*) Oh.

LUCIE-MARIE: She ridin' wit' us?

TDB: Yep.

ANNIE-SHARON: Like Mama?

TDB: Ain't nobody like yo' mama...but we gotta keep livin' is all.

(ANNIE-SHARON *goes over to the window.* TDB *exits.*)

LUCIE-MARIE: Nobody/ nobody ever gone be like Mama/ right Annie? Annie/ you hear me? Ain't no woman comin' in heah...this heah is our house...right Annie? Annie-Sharon/ you hear me?

(Lights.)

Scene II

(CASSIE *and* TDB *are coming up off the kitchen table. They are both giggling and fixing their pants.* TIE-DOWN *gets a couple of beers and a chaser of Jack Daniels.* CASSIE *sprawls across the chair nearest the table.)*

CASSIE: Now, Mistah Tie-down Brown/ that's just 'bout a good 'nough time as I've had myself lately/ I 'most ready to say we gotta do that on a mo' frequent basis/ but do ya think we could somehow or othah set a quilt or a towel even on that table/ all that rockin' on linoleum bothers my behind/ really it do. (CASSIE *rubs her backside.* TIE-DOWN *crosses over to her and gives her a swift whack on it.)*

TDB: I don' rightly see as how yo' tough-assed behind could be havin' no problems/ seein' as how ya spend most of yo' few sane moments ridin' wild horses/

CASSIE: Yeah, but I wasn't thinkin' you was one 'em/ damn fool.

TDB: Who you callin' fool?

CASSIE: Yo' sweet black ass/ that's who. 'Sides, I always had my eyes on you/ always/ even when me & Twanda was tight/ I jus' kept on thinkin'/ now I want me a man like that one/ one like that Tie-down Brown/ I feel/ well/ hell, I feel strange sometimes on accounta/ I'm bein' wit' you 'n' she bein' done passed/ well/ maybe I jus' done know 'xactly what to do wit' myself/ or wit' you/ ol' wild man/ come on, give me some mo' sugar.

TDB: What happened wit' Twanda couldn't nobody stop it/ not you or me/ & she wasn't the kinda gal what had a stinginess to her/ I bet my life if I was gonna take up wit' a woman/ she'd want it to be you/

CASSIE: Done be lyin' to me, ya hear me/ done be talkin' all out yo' senses cuz ya got a li'l bit & ya feelin' like a new man or some-thin'/ I honestly cain't remember no time when ya talked 'bout Twanda wit'out raisin' hell or gettin' them jaws so tight I thought I haveta call the vet/ to pry yo' mouth open.

TDB: Well/ it's the girls/ ya know they was talkin' to me this mornin' & sayin' they gotta right to know some mo' 'bout Twan-da/ & I guess/ I come to decide they right/ she half a whatever they is/ half a me & half a her/ it's just...damn, ya know some-times I jus' got this feelin' that I done understand 'em/ like I cain't talk to 'em/ less I carry a razor strap wit' me/ or make sho' I gotta hair brush stickin' out my back pocket/

CASSIE: One thing for sho', you done haveta beat no sense inta no chile/ ever/ I swear 'fo' God/ beatin' on a chile ain't never done nothin' but make 'em truly unruly/ yes, Jesus/ them what's 'bused & scorned gonna be partners wit' the devil his own self/ watch now/ see if I ain't tellin' you true.

TDB: I like that/ what you sayin'/ makes sense & reminds me how good you was feelin' to me/ jus' a li'l while back/ you got some sho' nough snappin' turtle...

CASSIE: Forget whatchu 'bout to say, niggah & tell me what you think 'bout the rodeo today.

TDB: Damn it, Cassie/ I done need to talk 'bout no rodeo now/ I need to be talkin' to yo' fine, sassy, liver-lipped self/

CASSIE: 'bout what?

TDB: 'bout us/ & 'bout them girls 'n' you/ cuz you the onliest woman I know who growed up wit'out a mama.

CASSIE: That's a lie/ I did have a mama/ she jus' drank a li'l much is all/ she wasn't no invalid or no moron or nothin'/ jus' she couldn't seem to hold things together sometimes/ but done you go 'round sayin' I didn't have no mama/

TDB: I didn't 'xactly mean that/ honey/ all what I was gettin' at is/ cuz of yo' situation & my situation/ you might could help me wit' Lucie-Marie & Annie-Sharon/ I'm jus' not doin' right/ some-thing I'm doin' jus' ain't right...

241

CASSIE: Well, there ain't no need to rush nothin'/ ya hear. I'ma be here/ I ain't goin' nowhere from you/ least not fo' long.

TDB: Lessen there's a rodeo comin' up in Oklahoma, right?

CASSIE: Yeah/ let's talk 'bout that/ I love me some rodeo talk/ & I love me some of this Tie-down Brown/ but you gonna haveta get some place softer...

TDB: Awright/ but I done tol'you ya gotta nice, soft behind up under them jeans.

CASSIE: We done had 'nough love talk/ now talk to me 'bout the rodeo/ I love me some cowboys/ oh Lawd, give me a blue black cowboy & I swear I'll give it up in the...

TDB: On the table.

CASSIE: The rodeo, niggah/ not yo' pleasure.

Scene III

(In the kitchen with a fireplace that also serves as a living room. Country & western music is on the radio. TDB and CASSIE are drinking beer and talking. He's cleaning up dishes and such.)

TDB: Yeah-you/ Amos sho' got his tail whipped by that bull.

CASSIE: #17/ that one was one mean-assed crittur.

TDB: Thought all them cowboys from Alvin was gonna get they asses dragged 'round this heah day.

CASSIE: All 'ceptin you.

TDB: That's right/ that ain't bad/ two first place & one second for a total of $233/ that ain't bad for a high school drop-out from the great state of Texas/ right/ whatchu say to that?

CASSIE: Well/ I didn't do so bad my damn self/ ya know.

TDB: Yeah/ but they's better ways for a gal to earn her money.

CASSIE: I don' do it for money.

TDB: How long that gonna last?

CASSIE: Look who's talkin'/ how long is it gonna last yo' black ass?

TDB: Ain't the same! I got two near full-growed girls/ I'm all settled down/ you got two colts & a stallion/what kinda family ya call that?

CASSIE: Stay outta my business/ boy/ I hadta finish school, & them horses is mine/ I bought 'em & paid for 'em wit' my own money, & right now that's plenty for me/ jus' wait 'til I qualify for the Regional/ Lawd/ I'ma be hot to trot/ first place/ calf-roping/ barrels/bronc-bustin'/steel-doggin'...

TDB: Whatchu sayin'?

CASSIE: Calf-roping/ barrels/bronc-bustin'/ steel-doggin'. I'ma do it all.

TDB: Good Jesus/ how do I do it?

CASSIE: Do what?

TDB: End up wit' gals what got they minds on foolishness.

CASSIE: Who you callin' foolish?

TDB: Look/looky-heah/ I don' mean to say nothin' 'bout you bein' simple-minded/ it's jus' you know how it was wit' Twanda/ like she could win & win/ but it wasn't never 'nough for her/ & she kept on 'til she damn near/ hell, she kep' on 'til she killt herself/now here you is talkin' 'bout steel-doggin'/ shit/ didn't you see them bulls tear inta these boys from Longview/ hell, they bigger 'n' I am/ what in the name of Christ is you gonna do humpin' one of them?/ ya wanna end up dead too?

CASSIE: No/ I don' think you was tryin' to tell me I'm some kinda fool/ but/ ya gotta understand/ I ain't never gointa college/ I ain't gonna be no vet or a doctor or a nurse even/ shit/ I probably couldn't even make it as a administrative assistants' assistant/ but I can ride/ & I wanna be the best I can/ I ain't got much left as a woman/you right/ I ain't got mucha family/ do you think that means I ain't 's'posed to want nothin' mo' out my life?

TDB: You bein' headstrong/willful/ jus' like she was/ that's how she left me wit' them two girls/

CASSIE: Who you gonna leave 'em wit'?

TDB: Don' talk like that/ you got no call to talk like that/ ya might mark me or somethin' (*Goes over to photograph of Twanda.*)

CASSIE: Jus' what is yo' problem, Tie-down? You don' wanna woman good as you/ smart as you/ brave as you? Whatchu gonna do wit' them girls, huh? Give 'em some make-up & mo' free time so they can get pregnant & drop outta school like Twanda had to?

TDB: That's what gals is s'poses to do/ have babies & keep a good house/ & you gettin' close to bein' outta your place/ my/ girls ain't none of yo' concern/ & as a matter of fact, fo' yo' information/ Twanda didn't like school no how/ she liked me...

CASSIE: And where did that git her?

TDB: Whatchu mean? You sayin' I'm the cause of Twanda's bein' pullt over a whole rodeo arena cuz she liked me & my kids/ she tried to git herself killt/ you crazy...

CASSIE: That ain't what I mean/ & you know it/ I mean ya didn't leave much else fo' her to do wit' her life/ nothin' but you & the kids/ & that jus' wasn't enough/at least at the rodeo she was important/ she had somethin' to be proud of/ somethin' she did on her own/ wit'out havin' to give yo' ass some credit/

TDB: Hey! You ain't got chick nor child! So you busy talkin' 'bout somethin' you got no knowledge of/ no knowledge.

CASSIE: Oh yeah? You know what yo' girls were busy doin' today over to the Diamond-L?

TDB: Sho' I know/ they was gettin' them trophies for ropin' & runnin' barrels.

CASSIE: That may be some of what all they did/ but that ain't all.

TDB: Would you talk sense & quit bein' so damned cute?

CASSIE: Whatchu gotta say 'bout horses' dicks?

TDB: Hell/I ain't got nothin' to say 'bout no damn horse dick.

CASSIE: I thought I heard 'em say somethin' like "Goddamn" & "Wow."

TDB: So what that s'posed to mean? If you was 10 or even 13/ wouldn't a big ol' horse dick make you say somethin', or you always been tight-mouthed & seen it all.

CASSIE: Oh Tie-down/ one of these days you gonna dig a hole so big all of yo' big head gonna fit in it/ cain't you see they growin' up on you/ man/ you actin' like they tottlin' colts, & I'm sayin' you got some wild-assed fillies on yo' hands/ if you ask me.

TDB: I ain't askin'.

(There's giggling and noise at the door/ some shuffling sounds. TDB and CASSIE look askance at the door. TDB peeks over the kitchen sink at the girls outside.)

ANNIE-SHARON: You got the key? *(Inebriated.)*

LUCIE-MARIE: Naw/ you got the key upside down.

ANNIE-SHARON: You sho' the key don' go thisaway?

LUCIE-MARIE: It ain't never gointa go in there upside down 'less you stand on yo' head & open the door wit' your teeth.

ANNIE-SHARON: Why I gotta open the door wit' my teeth jus' cuz I'ma be upside down?

LUCIE-MARIE: I don't know.

(TDB *opens door abruptly.*)

TDB: Well/ I done opened the door fo' both of y'all.

(*Girls tumble through the door on top of each other.*)

CASSIE: Tie-down, they drunk!

TDB: Ya know, I've jus' 'bout had it wit' you/ my girls ain't drunk/ I myself sat right in this heah kitchen & taught 'em how to drink/ they jus' been celebratin'/ shit.

ANNIE-SHARON: Oh/ Daddy, did you see what Diamond-back gave me? (*She pulls out a half gallon of malt liquor.*)

LUCIE-MARIE: He say it 'most like champagne.

CASSIE: You girls take those stink clothes off & git in the tub/ & git that mess off yo' faces...

ANNIE-SHARON: You ain't my mama/ I don' have to do diddlysquat you say...

TDB: Watch it girl.

LUCIE-MARIE: Oh Daddy, can we have one mo' li'l drink & a dance wit' you?/ let's do the Texas two-step or...

ANNIE-SHARON: I wanna "funkifize"/ I wanna "funkifize."

TDB: C'mon, we gonna do the cotton-eyed joe/

(*The girls turn on the record player and start dancing. They are terribly drunk. While the music is playing, they get very sloppy about their movement. As the music gets faster, ANNIE-SHARON runs out, apparently nauseous. TDB stops dancing and stops the music. LUCIE-MARIE keeps dancing, no matter there is no more music.*)

TDB: Annie/ whatsa matter witchu?

CASSIE: What in the hell you think?

TDB: Aw hell, she ain't sick/ why she's like her mama/ a hard-drinkin'/ hard-ridin' woman...

LUCIE-MARIE: Daddy/ why you say Mama don' ride wit' me? (*She twirls around and gets dizzy.*)

CASSIE: Heah/ chile sit down 'fore you fall on yo' face...

(ANNIE-SHARON *enters.*)

ANNIE-SHARON: Daddy, Daddy, I'm bleedin'...

TDB: Oh Lawd/ how come ya cain't race horses wit'out cuttin' yo'self all up?/ when you went 'round them barrels didn't you lift yo' leg so they wdn't crash that rim/ you gotta know by now/ that metal'll cut thru any kind of leather/

ANNIE-SHARON: I don't think it's that Daddy.

(CASSIE *is talking quietly to* LUCIE-MARIE, *soothing her.*)

TDB: Aw darlin', yo' time's come/ that's what it must be.

ANNIE-SHARON: Daddy, my time come two years ago.

TDB: Well, hell, whatchu tryin' to say? (*Pause.*) Annie-Sharon, you way outta line if you tellin' me what I think you tellin' me.

(ANNIE-SHARON *takes two steps back.*)

ANNIE-SHARON: Oh Daddy/ he/ well/ we, Diamond-back/ you know Diamondback/ right?/ well you know what a good friend he is, & he tol' me all kinds of things like/ well Daddy, he said nothin' would happen/ huh, uhm/ he said fine/ well I'd feel so good/ & it had to happen some time/ & we was so happy 'bout winnin'/ ya know Diamondback/ he the champion steel dogger/ junior division/ jus' like you was Daddy/ I liked it/ I mean/ I love Diamondback/ don'tchu Daddy?/ he's a great cowboy/ Daddy jus' like you was/ & wit' me & him together we cd both be champions/ right Daddy? (ANNIE-SHARON *gets more nervous as she speaks.* CASSIE *comes over to her and holds her.*) Daddy/ it's you know/ important to be special to somebody/ I jus' wanted to be special on my own/

TDB: Why is this happenin' to me? First Twanda jumps up & gets pregnant.

CASSIE: Oh that's what happened.

TDB: Damn it! This ain't no time to be funny.

CASSIE: What'd you expect? Ya git 'em all confused drinkin', dancin'/ downplayin' they talents/ like all it takes to be a woman is a fast dance, some lipstick & a man. Look at this chile/ it's awright Annie. You're gonna be okay/ whatchu did was real special/ I wantchu to go clean yo'self up/ & clear yo' head some...

ANNIE-SHARON: Why you bein' so nice to me?

CASSIE: I ain't got no reason not to be nice/ 'sides I was a girl way long 'fore I was a woman/ you jus' remindin' me of some things I'd wisht happened to me once/ & some things I wish had never happened.

ANNIE-SHARON: What thing ya wisht never happened?

CASSIE: We'll talk jus' me & you/ later awright/ now I jus' want you to relax yo'self/ git in the shower/ & rest. You've had a big ol' day/ winnin' all them prizes at the Diamond-L.

TDB: Yeah & some young ass fool is walkin' 'round wit' everything she done give away.

ANNIE-SHARON: You mad/ Daddy?

TDB: Jesus/ whatchu think? Wait one muthafuckin' minute/ Lucie-Marie/ Lucie-Marie/ what was you doin' while yo' sister was off/ off wit' Diamondback?

LUCIE-MARIE: Who/ me?/ (TDB *nods his head.*) Me & Lincoln Maceo went out to the Triple-R-Ranch to...ah...(*She looks all around.*) Annie-Sharon/ what should I say...?

(TDB *gets exasperated and moves toward* LUCIE-MARIE.)

TDB: Annie don' even know what's she's doin'/ she sho' cain't he'p you now/ cain't he'p herself none either.

CASSIE: Let the chile talk.

TDB: C'mon Lucie-Marie/ what were you & Lincoln Maceo doin' at the Triple R?

LUCIE-MARIE: We was breakin' horses with some of the guys from Bellville.

TDB: Growed men from Bellville?

LUCIE-MARIE: Yeah. Ya know the Saginaw brothers, Rufus Sanderson & Henry Watson/ them guys.

TDB: Lawd I need me a drink/ a beer/ Jesus. This un goes off rollin' in the hay somewhere & this un is jumpin' all on top of some wild-assed horses/ likedta break her fool neck/ Good Jesus/ what'd I do? I done right by you/ ain't I Lucie-Marie/ Annie-Sharon/ ain'tchu got clothes/ saddles/ horses/ them jeans wit' straight legs/ jeans wit' all puffed out legs/ alligator boots/ new ropin' gear/ real gold jewelry?/ not everythin'/ but I tried to do right by y'all/ take y'all out/ show ya a good time/ learnt yo' prayers/ ever since yo' mama died...oh hell.

CASSIE: My God/ boy/ cain't ya see/ if you cain't even talk 'bout Twanda passin'/ these girls gonna push & push 'til you see her in them/ a hard-drinkin'/ hard-ridin' woman/ 'cordin' to you.

TDB: That's not all she was/ Twanda was a whole lot more 'n' that.

LUCIE-MARIE: More 'n' me/ Daddy?

TDB: Mo' what than you?

LUCIE-MARIE: More woman than me.

TDB: Aw/ girl you still playin' wit' dolls.

CASSIE: You gonna be jus' as much a woman as yo' mama was, Lucie-Marie/ in time/ it don' all come at once/ is all.

TDB: Yeah/ I tol' ya how much ya favored.

ANNIE-SHARON: And me Daddy/ what about me?

TDB: What about yo' fast behind?

ANNIE-SHARON: Am I ever gonna be a lady? I mean...now?

TDB: I'ma haveta think on that/ after whatchu done gone & did to yo'self/ Lawd/ give some strength/ these gals is tearin' me up heah.

CASSIE: You a champion, right?

ANNIE-SHARON: Yes, M'am/ got first place twice runnin' barrels.

CASSIE: Seems to me you racin' to be a lady in the wrong arena these days/ keep hold to them horses/ Diamondback & all the other young bucks 'round heah can wait/ 'specially them gettin' grooves offa hard-drinkin', hard-ridin' gals/ they can wait.

ANNIE-SHARON: Wait/ Cassie?

TDB: Hell yes/ wait.

CASSIE: Go on 'n' say whatchu mean, Tie-down.

TDB: I mean, keep them legs closed.

LUCIE-MARIE: Daddy/ I cain't bronc-bust wit' my legs closed.

TDB: Cain't get pregnant neither.

CASSIE: Yes/ you can/ you don' know half of what comes outta yo' mouth.

TDB: Well how am I s'posed to talk to two girls 'bout/ this woman business/ all this mess...

CASSIE: It don' start out mess/ it don' get to be mess 'til some ol' young boy gits to messin' wit' it/ 'fore a girl gits to reachin' fo' woman before she can be one/ before it's meant/ go on to bed, now, girls.

TDB: Yeah/ get on outta heah/ we gonna talk fo' sho' tomorrow/ me & you/ both y'all.

(ANNIE-SHARON *and* LUCIE-MARIE *gather their things and kiss their father good night.*)

ANNIE-SHARON: Night, Daddy.

LUCIE-MARIE: Nighty night, Daddy.

(ANNIE-SHARON *and* LUCIE-MARIE *exit to the upstairs bedroom.* TDB *gets another beer. He's been drinking them all night.*)

TDB: Don't look at me like that Cassie/ this sure has been a helluva night.

CASSIE: Yeah.

TDB: I been tryin' to be a good father.

CASSIE: I do believe that's whatchu been tryin'.

TDB: Whatchu think I oughtta do now?

CASSIE: Let 'em be girls/ not all growed up before their time/ I remember I cain't tell ya how clearly/ I remember/ people scarin' me all the time/ like growin' up for a girl/ was a trep-e-da-tious thang/ I ain't foolin' neither/ why I thought fo' sho' that if some ol' boy looked at me crossedways/ I had musta sinned or somethin' the same as a sin/ yeah/ it takes a heap of courage to do what them girls gotta do/

TDB: Courage?

CASSIE: Uh huhmn. Makin' love for the first time/ breakin' wild horses...(*She goes to the stereo and puts on a slow drag.*)

TDB: Are you serious?

CASSIE: I'm all grown-up, Tie-down, I know what I'm doin'/ & I do it well/ cuz I carry my own protection/ ya see/ & that's one thing I'm goin' to pass on to those young rascals of yours/ men ain't the only ones 'round could be carryin' they own protection/ & still be good/ you know what I mean/ still be a real good ol' girl.

(*They begin to slow dance. Lights fade.*)

TDB: But don'tchu think I need to tear the hides off them gals?/ look at what they done/ disobey/ act a fool/ act a tramp/ disgracin' my name/ oh Jesus/ I gotta mind to go up there right now & beat the living daylights out them wenches/

CASSIE: Now Tie-down/ calm down.

TDB: Whatchu mean "calm down?"/ didn't you hear that heifer talkin' 'bout "I liked it?"

CASSIE: That ain't unusual/ most folks do like "it"/ & if ya don't mind/ I'd like a li'l mo' of "it"/ if ya can keep yo' pride from worryin' them girls to death.

TDB: You ain't got no mo' sense than they do/ shit/ if they was yours you wdn't be so damn easy on 'em/ "I liked it." (TIE-DOWN *breaks away from* CASSIE *to go upstairs.* CASSIE *stops him.*)

CASSIE: Niggah/ I ain't got all night/ & right this minute that kitchen table don't look half so bad as I was thinkin'/ c'mon/ I'll talk to them gals/ but right heah 'n' now/ you gotta woman on yo' hands/ Lawd you a sweet niggah/ my sweet black-eye pea/ we got time/ believe me we got plenty time/
(*Lights.*)

Scene IV

(*Girls are in their pajamas in their bedroom.* LUCIE-MARIE *is in the bed with a huge rag doll.*)

LUCIE-MARIE: My head hurts/ Annie/ does yours?
ANNIE-SHARON: No.
LUCIE-MARIE: Well, me & Lorinda gonna go to sleep/ now/ c'mon to bed/ please/ Annie/ I don' like sleepin' by myself/ that's a girl/ Lorinda/ say yo' prayers/ c'mon Annie/ come to bed/ please.
ANNIE-SHARON: In a second/ ya know there's somethin' I wanna tell/ Mama so bad/ somethin' only she could tell me 'bout/
LUCIE-MARIE: You the one said Mama couldn't tell ya nothin'.
ANNIE-SHARON: I was wrong/ I'm tryin' to get Mama to talk to me...(ANNIE-SHARON *is by the window.*) She's out there somewhere/ I think if she whispered sometimes/ every once in a while/ I might could understand/ I wouldn't be so lonely/ I'd always have somebody to talk to/
LUCIE-MARIE: I'm heah/ me & Lorinda.
ANNIE-SHARON: But you don' know 'bout nothin'/ I ain't got much confidence in Lorinda either.
LUCIE-MARIE: Cassie does...
ANNIE-SHARON: Cassie does what?
LUCIE-MARIE: Know 'bout things.
ANNIE-SHARON: Maybe. But she's not my mama.
LUCIE-MARIE: She ain't yo' mama now, leastways not yet...
ANNIE-SHARON: Naw. Lucie/ Mama is out there somewhere/always will be/ Mama are ya listenin' to me? I want ya to know me & I wantcha to hear me now/ I miss ya/ Mama/ I want

ya to be wit' me/ be my friend/ Mama/ Mama please/ please talk to me/ Mama/ I love you.

(ANNIE-SHARON *goes to the wall with the buckles. Gets a couple down. Takes a hat and a trophy. Piles them onto the bed and on herself. Pulls covers back.*)

ANNIE-SHARON: I'm gonna be jus' like you/ Mama/ I wanna do it so/ be like you/ but I get scared Mama/ I get scared/ I'm so much a li'l bit of you. (*She leans over to kiss* LUCIE-MARIE.) I'ma be as good as you Mama/ jus' you wait & see/ I can ride the hell out some horses/ & I'm learnin' how to kiss/no matter what all Daddy say. (*Lights.*)

The Past Is The Past

by RICHARD WESLEY

Richard Wesley was born in Newark, New Jersey, July 11, 1945. He is the author of eleven plays produced in New York between 1968 and 1978, including the *Black Terror* (1971), the *Sirens* (1974) and the *Mighty Gents* (1978). He has also authored the screenplays for the films *Uptown Saturday Night, Let's Do It Again, Fast Forward* and *Native Son*, as well as the television adaptation of Virginia Hamilton's novel, *The House of Dies Drear*, for PBS Wonderworks series in 1984. He is the former editor of *Black Theatre Magazine*, a teacher and lecturer, past winner of a Rockefeller Grant in playwrighting, as well as the prestigious Audelco Awards and the Drama Desk Award.

CHARACTERS:

EARL DAVIS - *Mid-40s. Well-dressed (generally casual wear). Probably a foreman on his job.*
EDDIE GREEN - *Age 26. College student. Grew up in an urban Black community.*

(*Lights up on* EARL DAVIS *playing pool at a solitary pool table. The only other object on stage is a jukebox in the background. Just after the lights go up, a* MAN'S VOICE *is heard as* DAVIS *plays.*)

MAN'S VOICE:
The years separate
Us
An abyss of time
Dimming our memories
Holding back our yearnings
To reach
Out
To one
Another
Time

How short a word
Yet signifying such
A long period in
Our lives
As we slowly drift
Away
From one another
To other places
Where, alone
We must wonder
If
Our lives
Will ever
Touch
Again.

(*Sounds of Billie Holiday come up.* EDDIE GREEN *enters from the darkness upstage and stands for a long time watching his father move cat-like about the table sinking shot after shot.* EDDIE *approaches the table.*)

EARL (*spying* EDDIE): Hey, what's happenin'?

EDDIE: You got it.

EARL: Naw, youngblood, it's all on you.

EDDIE (*chuckling*): Is that so?

EARL: There can be no doubt.

EDDIE: Okay, if you say so.

EARL: You new around here?

EDDIE: Yea.

EARL: Thought so. Didn't remember ever seein' you before. Though, I got to admit there sure is somethin' familiar-lookin' about you.

EDDIE: Yea?

EARL: You look a lot like someone I used to know. (*Looks at* EDDIE *more closely.*) What's your name?

EDDIE: Eddie. Eddie Green.

EARL: Green. Where you from?

EDDIE: Oh, I'm from outta state. I'm going to the community college here.

EARL: A college boy. Check that out. Watchu studyin' to be?

EDDIE: Ain't made up my mind, yet. Just takin' some general courses.

EARL: Oh. Well, whatever you do, work hard at it. Our folks need as many of you college boys as we can get. Don't mess it all up like I did.

EDDIE: You went to college?

EARL: Had a chance to, but I bullshitted around an' passed it up. Besides, World War II was on, an' I got drafted. Still don't know why in hell I went. Same day I went in, some white cop shot this colored soldier in New York, an' Harlem was in flames for three days. A good friend of mine got his leg blown off that day.

EDDIE: Wow, that was some tough shit.

EARL: Forget about it. The past is the past. Know what I mean? Yea, I coulda gone on to college but by the time I got out the war I had changed my mind about everything. Just didn't care no more. If you ever have to go fight in that Vietnam war, you'll see what I mean. That is, if you a super-sensitive cat like I used to be.

EDDIE: Maybe I am.

EARL: Naw, you kids today seem much harder than I can ever remember us bein'. Y'all got more, but you just seem unhappy. Know what I mean? Hey, you wanna play me a game?

EDDIE: I can't play that good.

EARL: Then whatchu doin' in here?

EDDIE: I came in to look for...I mean, I just came in to look around.

EARL: Don't you know anything about pool?

EDDIE: About the only thing I can play is "eight-ball."

EARL: Solid. We'll play that. Since I'm the oldest here, I'll break. Rack 'em, "house."

EDDIE (smiling): Oh wow, check my man out for bein' arbitrary an' shit. (EDDIE sets the balls up.)

EARL: I'll go light on you since you can't play.

EDDIE: That's okay, you don't have to give me no slack. You haven't before, have you?

EARL: Whatchu say?

EDDIE: Nothin'.

EARL: You know you a funny dude. You always talk to yourself?

EDDIE: I wasn't talkin' to myself.

EARL: Sure seemed like it.

EDDIE: Naw, I'm straightforward an' blunt. Never talk to myself. My mother says I'm just like my father.

EARL: Yea? (*The balls are set up and* EARL *breaks.*) Your father ain't around, huh?

EDDIE: Naw.

EARL: Didn't die, did he?

EDDIE: He split after I was born. Sent my mother some bucks for awhile, but even that stopped.

EARL: Yea, son, I know that story. Nine ball corner pocket. (*Shoots.*)

EDDIE: "Son?"

EARL: Six ball. Yea, I call all young men "son."

EDDIE: You got any kids?

EARL: Two by my wife. Three more here and there. Three ball.

EDDIE: Wow, man, you don't miss nothin', do ya? Hey, five kids. That's quite a brood.

EARL: That's right. I'm a nomad. Most colored men are. We got to be that way. Got no choice.

EDDIE: I don't know about that.

EARL: It's true. When you get out here in the real world with alla these hungry wolves snapping at your heels, you'll see I was tellin' you right. I'm a foreman at my plant, now. But before that I lived all over this country: Houston, New Orleans, Chicago, Philly, Detroit, Baltimore, all over. I've slopped hogs, built battleships, waited tables, poured cement, bell hopped, did just about everything I could to survive. Not to mention killin' men in the army. Now, on top of all that what you tryin' to do is find out what this life is all about an' what you gotta do to take your place in this world. I was born down South, but I left there because I knew at some point I was gonna haveta kill me a white man. Just knew it. There was no other way I was gonna take that shit. I was all of sixteen, then. I was on my own, tryin' to make it. Kep' in school to stay outta trouble, but I loved them streets, boy. My trouble was, I had no discipline. That's what messed me up in my young days. That's why a lotta black men is nomads. They got a lot of heart, lots 'n lots courage, but they not discipline, 'cause no one's taught it to them an' there's folks out there who wanna keep it that way. So, all we do is wander when we young, an' when we get old we ain't no good to nobody. We alone. Know what I mean?

EDDIE: But you got you a family.

EARL: Yea, they doin' alright. I'm one of the lucky ones, I guess. Got myself together before it was too late.

EDDIE: An' your other kids?

EARL: Five ball. They doin' okay. I s'pose. Got a daughter in Detroit. She's about 28 now, I guess. She had a fine-lookin' mama. Me an' her mama was goin' together off an' on for a long time. We was really tight. Good-lookin' woman. Light brown skin with hazel eyes. Not beautiful, just cute. You know? Teenage cute. Just breakin' into womanhood cute. An' had the biggest behind. We thought we was in love. Then she got pregnant. We started to fight a lot after that. I wasn't ready for the responsibility, an' neither was she. Plus, her mama was fillin' her head with a whole lotta shit. She went down South to have the baby, then moved on up to Detroit. (*Pause. EARL smiles.*) Just got a letter from that woman last week... Two ball.

EDDIE: Oh, y'all still tight?

EARL: No, just friends, now.

EDDIE: You ever see your daughter?

EARL: Coupla times, as she was growin' up. Went to her high school graduation an' to her weddin'. I think she an' her husband separated. She look just like her mama. Ain't never been a woman like her mama, though. Better believe it. Seven ball. (*Shoots and misses.*) Damn.

EDDIE: Now, it's my turn to run. Ten ball...(*Shoots.*)...twelve ball... (*Shoots.*)...fourteen.

EARL: Who you tryin' to be, Cicero Murphy or somebody?

EDDIE: No, just plain Eddie Green. You know, you ain't ever told me your name.

EARL: Earl Davis. (EDDIE *looks at* EARL *as though he recognizes him.*) Ring a bell?

EDDIE: Kind of. What about your other "outside" kids, man?

EARL: "Outside kids?" What's that about? My kids is my kids, man.

EDDIE: Yea, but three of your kids grew up without you.

EARL: I did what I could. You know? My other daughter in Baltimore, Alicia, I used to see her a lot. Really looked out for her 'cause her mama died in childbirth. I spoiled her, though. She got too used to gettin' everything she wanted. Little mama is somethin' else today. Grew up with her grandparents. Started livin' with them when I got restless an' started wantin' to get back out here in these

257

streets. Alicia's up in Newark somewhere. She got herself a good job, though. Least she ain't on welfare, or nothin' like that.

EDDIE (*somewhat bitterly*): An' the third child never saw you.

EARL: His mother was the first woman I ever really, really loved. She was somethin' else, man. Skin as black as night with eyes that could look right into your soul. She was <u>all</u> woman. It was like she could reach out an' touch you without ever raisin' her arms from her sides. A queen, man. Boy, did we ever have a thing goin' between us. She meant a lot to me, man. That's why it's hard for me to explain why I ever left her. You got to understand, Eddie. I just wasn't ready for any of them three children. Their mothers an' I, well, we was about tryin' to put somethin' in our lives that our parents wasn't able to put there. We was growin' up in days when every livin' minute was spent tryin' to survive, an' our parents was doin' the best they could with us, but they was "out there" an' we was left, man. So, we turned to each other. It was all we had. We just wasn't ready. That's why I try to be so close to my two younger kids, now. Maybe I can make things easier for them.

EDDIE: But that third kid never saw you. He might have needed you.

EARL: Yea, I s'pose he did. But in those days I had so little to give.

EDDIE: You had yourself.

EARL: For men, that just ain't enough. A man wants to give his children the world, if he can.

EDDIE: So you ran out.

EARL: You a young cat, man. You should learn to be quiet until you've learned a few things.

EDDIE: But that was a cold shot, man. A kid grows up without his father an' spends summa the time wonderin' if he'll ever see him, an' what should he do if he ever do see him.

EARL: Nothin' he can do, except try to understand.

EDDIE: I never saw my father.

EARL: You told me. I'll tell you somethin', too. I never saw mine, either. (EDDIE *looks surprised*.) It's true. Nigger passed through my life like a shadow. I spent my grown years tryin' to fill in the empty gaps in my life that he left. I tried to leave some of me in all my children, even if it didn't do no more than just pass on to them through they mamas.

EDDIE: I guess that's what the third woman did, huh?

EARL: Vessie? Yea, I guess so.

EDDIE: Hey man, look at me.

EARL: Yea.

EDDIE: I mean, really <u>look</u> at me.

EARL: I'm lookin'. Been lookin'. I knew who you was the minute you walked through that door. How'd you find me?

EDDIE: By accident. I was in a restaurant eatin' when I saw you come in. That picture mama got of you is twenty years old, but you ain't really changed that much.

EARL: Naw, runs in the family, I guess.

EDDIE: This sure ain't goin' down like I expected. I had imagined a whole lotta tears an' shit.

EARL (*laughing*): You seen too many movies, Eddie. (*Looks at* EDDIE.) Yea, there was no doubt when I saw you come in. You Vessie's spittin' image.

EDDIE: You know that's really funny 'cause moms always said I look just like you. Act like you, too.

EARL: So, what's happenin'?

EDDIE: Man, you actin' so cool about all this.

EARL (*perplexed*): Hey, man...what can I say?

EDDIE: Yea...I guess you right.

EARL: You lookin' mighty clean, man.

EDDIE: I got a part-time gig in a men's store. Sometimes I boost shit.

EARL: No kiddin'. An' your mama, how she doin'?

EDDIE: She doin' okay. Her an' this dude might get married.

EARL: Yea? What's he like?

EDDIE: Smooth-talkin' nigger from North Carolina. They may go down there to live. He's a lot like you in some ways.

EARL: No kiddin'?

EDDIE: That may be why I don't like him.

EARL: Yea. (*Pause.*) Why you come lookin' for me?

EDDIE: 'Cause I wanted to know who you was, an' I wanted you to see me.

EARL: Yea, you a fine-lookin' boy. Couldn't miss with me for a father.

EDDIE: I had another reason for wantin' to see you. Thirteen ball.

EARL: Uh-huh.

EDDIE: You gonna be a grandaddy, man. Eleven.

EARL: No kiddin'? Hey, that's really beautiful. Congratulations, Eddie. When's it due?

EDDIE: About six months.

EARL: Where's the mother at?

EDDIE: Back home.

EARL: You goin' through much hassle?

EDDIE: Some, but no more than the usual amount.

EARL: Probably be a boy.

EDDIE: I didn't want it at first. I told her to get an abortion.

EARL: Yea, that's what I told Vessie back when I found out she was carryin' you.

EDDIE: Wow, man, you sure know how to tighten somebody's jaws.

EARL: I'm sorry, son, but it was the truth. Vessie wanted to have you, though. She was determined about that. She cried an' everything, tellin' me if she had to raise you by herself she'd do it, but nobody was gonna rip her insides out. (*Looks at* EDDIE.) She did well raisin' you, boy.

EDDIE: Daddy...

EARL: Why you call me "Daddy?" You don't know me that well.

EDDIE: I want to.

EARL: Yea?

EDDIE: I <u>need</u> to.

EARL: The same way that kid of yours needs to. Your old lady didn't get that abortion, did she? (EDDIE *shakes his head.*) I didn't think so.

EDDIE: I'm here now 'cause there're some things I need to understand. I never had you there, man. When I truly needed you around. Someone to show me how to dribble a basketball, or tell me some stories, or just teach me <u>somethin'</u>. You wasn't <u>there</u>. All your other children had you, why not me?

EARL: I can't explain it, man. I was still a kid myself when you was born. A child leadin' a child; what kinda shit was that? I did the best I could with what I had. An' that's all you can do with your kid. Give him everything you feel you never got from me, or at least try to. That's all I can tell you.

EDDIE: But there's got to be more.

EARL: What else is there? Oh yea, the nights lyin' awake some-where wonderin' what your kids are growin' up to be like, won-derin' whether or not they're growin' up to hate you an' someday kill you, or the nights when you wonder why you don't care wheth-er they do or not. That's what it is, man.

EDDIE: There were nights when I wanted to kill you, but I want-ed more than anything just to be with you, my old man, the mys-tery cat in the picture my mother keeps hidden in her top dresser drawer. I wanted to hear you say you love me.

EARL: You're asking for the moon, son. You're from me but not of me.

EDDIE: Because you won't let me be.

EARL: Because I <u>can't</u> let you be.

EDDIE: Why not?

EARL: Because there's too much pain, that's why. Too many years an' tears I buried long ago. That's what you represent, boy.

EDDIE: I'm more than that. I'm your son.

EARL: A son I didn't want.

EDDIE: You were too young to understand.

EARL: I understood. (*Quietly.*) I...understood.

EDDIE: I love you, Daddy. That must mean <u>somethin'</u>. Hey, man, don't just shut me out. Don't pull this shit on me.

EARL: C'mon, Eddie. I'm not that important to you. I can't be.

EDDIE: Because you're my father an' because I don't wanna be standin' like this with my son twenty years from now.

EARL: My grandson. Wow. Will you name him after me?

EDDIE (*somewhat surprised by the reply*): Yea.

EARL: Tell him a little about me, an' bring him around so I can see him.

EDDIE: Why don't you come an' see him?

EARL: I don't know. We'll have to see.

EDDIE: Damn! Why you so cold, man?! Shit!

EARL: Eddie...

EDDIE: Forget it, man. I thought if I could get somethin' to-gether between you an' me maybe me an' my kid...Fuck it. I guess I'll just have to push on alone trippin' over shit like you did. It shouldn't have to be like that, man. It shouldn't have to.

EARL: But it is. Eddie, I've done all I can. I told you what I could. It's just too many years an' lost chances between us.

EDDIE: Then it's supposed to continue, huh? The same ol' bull-shit goin' down again. You puttin' me through the same changes you went through an' now you tellin' me to do the same with my kid.

EARL: It don't have to be that way. You can stop it right here. Maybe I can't love you. Hell, I don't even love myself, quiet as it's kept. But Vessie raised you strong. Strong enough to be able to break this cycle you talkin' about. I'm an old cat who's gonna die soon, so quit tryin' to relate to me an' deal with your son. He's the future, an' I'm the past. Forget me, son.

EDDIE: No.

EARL: Can I mean that much?

EDDIE: You're my father. (*They look at each other.*) Ain't nothin' more to say, huh? (EARL *does not answer.*) Look, I guess I got to make it.

EARL: We didn't finish the game.

EDDIE: Let's finish it tomorrow.

EARL: I may not be here.

EDDIE: Then I'll come day after tomorrow.

EARL: I may not be here then, either.

EDDIE: Then I'll keep comin' 'til I catch you.

EARL: You just like Vessie: persistent as hell.

(*Both laugh.*)

EDDIE: I'm gonna raise. Later.

EARL: Wait a minute. (EARL *moves to* EDDIE.) I'm glad I got to see you. I always been kinda scared I never would. (*The two men shake hands warmly. EDDIE might want to embrace his father, but EARL kind of keeps everything distant, yet displays a warmth that shows his aloofness diminishing. EDDIE turns to leave. With a slight trace of desperation in his voice...*) Eddie.

EDDIE: Yea?

Earl (*starts to say something, but decides against it*): I hope it's a boy. Tell your mother I said hello.

(EDDIE *smiles and goes out. Lights begin to dim on* EARL, *who fights back any emotion as he continues playing pool.* BLACKNESS.)

Pain In My Heart

by ROB PENNY

Rob Penny is a writer and an Associate Professor in the Department of Black Community Education Research and Development at the University of Pittsburgh. he is also the cofounder (along with August Wilson) and present coordinator of the Kuntu Writers Workshop, established in 1976. *Pain In My Heart* was part of two one-act plays by Rob Penny; the other one was entitled *Reachings*. *Pain In My Heart* was directed by Valerie Williams-Lawrence, produced by the Kuntu Repertory Theatre of DBCERD, University of Pittsburgh. The play opened April 16, 1987 and starred Victoria Bey as Millicent Morrison and Lee Kiburi as Abdullah Courtney with Kenneth Ellis as light and set designer.

CHARACTERS:

MILLICENT MORRISON
ABDULLAH COURTNEY

SCENE: *A rather comfortable convalescent room.* MILLICENT MORRISON, *dressed in a yellow robe, fingers the shower of yellow sunlight that punches its way into the room over the bed, walls, and chair.* I've Been Loving You Too Long, *a song by Otis Redding, eases into* MILLICENT's *head. A man enters. They slow drag. When the music ends, the man puts on his coat and exits without looking at her. Lights dim on* MILLICENT.

They come up. MILLICENT *now has on a red robe. She pantomimes talking to a man and a boy.*

MILLICENT: Okay, Matt. You will take good care of Omar, won't you? Oh, I know you will; I shouldn't have mentioned it. Nicaragua, huh. You all have a safe and progressive trip. (MILLICENT *waves after them. Pause.*) Been three years since I've been to Nicaragua. Well, Omar'll learn something. He's perceptive. Fifteen years old. My son's growing up fast. And Matt? What am I going to do with that man? Treats Omar like he's his own son. Matt's always around when I need him. He calls me a good woman. (*Smiles.*) I tell him, "Matt, I'm waiting for...for someone from my yesterdays." (MILLICENT *sits on the bed with a heavy sigh.*) I only come here...to rest. To kick off my shoes from my agency. And to doze off into my past away from the organization.

(*The lights change into her mood.*)

Oh, it's so alone in here. I am in the bell of Abdullah's horn. But there is no sound...no music...nothing. Only the spirit of him who soars...(*She cups both breasts.*)...that soars through his pride and joy. He used to say, "Look what the Lawd has given me." This one's pride, and this one's joy...

(*The light lowers. When they rise,* MILLICENT *has on a blue robe.*)

Blue is my color today. It was...I think...his favorite color too. (MILLICENT *stretches out on the bed.* ABDULLAH *enters the room. He removes his winter coat and scarf and hat. He caresses her ankles and toes.*)

ABDULLAH: Millicent.

MILLICENT (*awakes*): Abdullah?

ABDULLAH: Yes. How are you, baby?

MILLICENT (*fusses with her hair*): Abdullah...how did you find me?

ABDULLAH: Does it matter? I mean, I'm here.

MILLICENT: No.

ABDULLAH: If you really want to know how I found you...well, I called your father and...

MILLICENT: Oh, God. I don't want you to see me like this. Please go - no, don't go. (*Softer.*) Don't go, Abdullah. I lost contact with you for a while. What have you been up to, man?

ABDULLAH: Lots of good things, baby.

MILLICENT: You were always so sure of yourself.

ABDULLAH: No, not always, Millicent. Sometimes I was frontin'. You know I've been keeping up with you. Success story. Black Enterprise. M & M Advertising Agency. You've come a long way baby.

MILLICENT: No, not really. Not as far as you might think. And you? What about you?

ABDULLAH: Ah, look baby, I'm only in town for a few days.

MILLICENT: Oh?

ABDULLAH: For a political convention.

MILLICENT: I didn't know there was a black political...

ABDULLAH: Oh no, no, no, nothing like that. Well, what I was thinking...well...the doctor said you were leaving tomorrow...I thought I'd drop by your crib...spend a few days...with you...before I cut out...back to Detroit...

(*Pause.*)

MILLICENT: Abdullah...what happened? Me and you...?

ABDULLAH: Ah, we'll talk about it some other...

MILLICENT: Now, Abdullah. What happened? What...?

ABDULLAH (*reaching for his coat*): I got to postpone this, baby. Sorry.

MILLICENT: Tell me what happened, Abdullah.

ABDULLAH: I got...to go, baby. (*Takes a step away. Stops.*) You still have some pretty toes.

MILLICENT: Abdullah, you don't know: I never married.

ABDULLAH: I know, baby.

MILLICENT: You just left me with my soul in an envelope. Sealed without any forwarding address. I gave it to you and you took it all. You took it all, Abdullah.

ABDULLAH: I'll call you when you get home. Hear? Cool?

MILLICENT: Abdullah, give me some of it back.

ABDULLAH: Sure, baby. I will. I promise. Get some rest. Oh, Millicent, you always had the prettiest pride and joy I've ever seen. Bye, baby.

MILLICENT: Don't leave again, Abdullah.

ABDULLAH: Bye, baby.

MILLICENT: Bye-bye, Abdullah. Bye.

(*Music functions as transition. Lights dim and out. Lights come up on* MILLICENT's *living room. It is a bright, colorful decorated room. There are African artifacts, paintings by African-North-American artists, a shining black Steinway, photographs on the mantle above the fireplace...*MILLICENT *enters jingling keys. She has on a blue evening dress but not formal.*)

MILLICENT: Home. (*Tosses her purse on the couch.*) Lumber and bricks. (*She picks up a photograph.*) Omar, you are handsome. Honey, you're the only flower in my life. But you can't replace the roots of your birth, son. (*She returns the photograph and walks over to her bar and pours herself an icy drink.*) Singles bars. Oh, I know them well. Roosters sitting on weather vanes...flashing money and smiles...oh boy...and my cheeks spread on a barstool...my eyes open like a welcome mat...God, why do I put myself through such torture...when - when all I have to do is call Matt...and say...yes, yes, I'll be yours. (*Walks toward the piano.*) Oh, I feel as tight as a spool of thread...Lord knows I need to unravel...to remember to forget...(*She sits at the piano and plays. Off key, she stops.*) I still can't have fun. (*She rises and struts to the window, making a toast.*) To the stars. They can never touch my heart. And to those who have received the gift of forgetfulness. (*She downs the liquor in one gulp.*) I can't forget a damn thing. (*Takes off her shoes, raising them, she drops them.*) God bless you girl. You have a handsome son, an organization and a business. Yes indeed. God bless the woman that gots her own. (ABDULLAH *appears in suit with one arm behind his back.*)

ABDULLAH: Millicent Morrison, the movement's hardest worker.

MILLICENT: Ab...Abdullah Courtney?

ABDULLAH: It's me. Hi, baby.

MILLICENT: No. It's not you. A portrait in my mind. It's...

ABDULLAH: It's the blues, Millicent.

MILLICENT: What?

ABDULLAH: I said, it's the blues. Your blues always call me up. Blue. That's your favorite color, remember?

MILLICENT: No, that was your favorite...

ABDULLAH: Got it confused, baby. (*He holds a yellow rose before her.*) My favorite color. Ah Millicent, don't frown. I never liked a frown on your face.

MILLICENT: Oh, I'm sorry, Abdullah. (*Smelling the rose.*) Blue is my favorite color and yellow is yours. You remembered. Abdullah, are you really here this time?

ABDULLAH: Hey, baby, what is real? We wear our mask. But it's me...Abdullah Courtney. And as real as that BMW you just parked in your garage.

MILLICENT: But you're supposed to be in Detroit. A big-time politician, right? Three kids. And married to some white bitch, right?

ABDULLAH: Uh-uh, you sound bitter, baby.

MILLICENT: That's a polite way to put it.

ABDULLAH: You want me to leave - so you can get your head bad on a bottle of Scotch again tonight? Is that what you want?

MILLICENT: I didn't...exactly mean...for you to leave.

ABDULLAH: Millicent, what do you want, huh? You conjure me up when you hear that trumpet in your soul...

MILLICENT: What are you talking about, man?

ABDULLAH: You know, that Archie Shepp tune you used to play back in college. Look, I came all the way from Detroit to see you. Now I'm not sure whether or not you want me out of your memories or what?

MILLICENT: Yes, I - no, I - yes, no...

ABDULLAH: Make up your mind.

MILLICENT: Wait a minute. You got no right telling me what to do, Abdullah.

ABDULLAH: Boy, you always had fight in you. I was...attracted to that in you from the very beginning. You were a fighter. I could never fight as hard as you nor practice self-criticism the way you did.

MILLICENT: You weren't that bad at it.

ABDULLAH: Oh, boy, I faked it all, baby. 'Cause I had you in my arms.

MILLICENT: And I had my arms around you. You know I haven't released my grip in seventeen years. You believe me, don't you?

ABDULLAH: Millicent, I never asked that of you.

MILLICENT: You didn't have to. You can't plant a flower in my garden and not expect for it to give the seed life. Tears and time can't always erode...

ABDULLAH: Millicent...

MILLICENT: Some things you have to hear, Abdullah.

ABDULLAH: But Milli...

MILLICENT: Oh, you will stay awhile, won't you? Here, take off your coat. I'll change into something comfy and gentle. Something you'll like very...

ABDULLAH: Milli...

MILLICENT: You still like fried chicken? Of course, you do. Stay awhile this time. Go ahead, loosen up that tie. Rather, take it off. You can't talk to me all lynched up like that. Let's make tonight...like it used to be.

ABDULLAH: Like it used-to-be can never be.

MILLICENT: Abdullah, no philosophy tonight. We can... pretend...

ABDULLAH: Pretend? Millicent, baby, we're too old for that.

MILLICENT: I said, we can pretend. (*Pause.*) I do it sometimes, Abdullah. Sometimes when there are pauses in my stride.

ABDULLAH: But can we go back (*Snaps his fingers.*) just like that to our college days? The student sit-ins? Takeovers? Creating things by using political duress against white folk?

MILLICENT: Life was clearer then - than now, wasn't it?

ABDULLAH: Clearer? Us. Them. Black. White. Simplistic, maybe, but certainly not clearer. Racial narcissism. That's what I call it.

MILLICENT: Racial narcissism, huh. I see. But you messed that up, didn't you?

ABDULLAH: I did?

MILLICENT: Yes, you crossed over.

ABDULLAH: I simply did what...

MILLICENT: Simply nothing. You're dead from the neck up. A leopard without spots to proclaim. You're the 21st century Moses, leading our people out of the wilderness, while you kneel before the white woman, your burning bush.

ABDULLAH: Ain't we bitter.

MILLICENT: Yes, bitter. You gave up the daishiki for white pussy.

ABDULLAH: Wrong, baby. I never confused my politics with my pussy.

MILLICENT: But, Abdullah, you were the leader. Our leader. Our shining black example. Our role model.

ABDULLAH: I never felt that, Millicent (*Points to his heart.*) in here (*Stabs a finger in his temples.*) or up here.

MILLICENT: Oh, but you feel it now, huh? With your face between some white...?

ABDULLAH: Allah is my example. To submit to his Divine Will. To be the servant of Allah is my...

MILLICENT: So that's why you left me, me and my blackness... for God?

ABDULLAH: That's not a rational question, Millicent.

MILLICENT: Oh. (*Pause.*) Oh, I see. You left my wide hips for anorexian advertisements, is that it?

ABDULLAH: Millicent, please...

MILLICENT: Naw, you left me, brother, to hold up this heavy sky alone. To take back the night with only two hands. You left me out here with all your promises down my throat. You left me under the sheets alone. You took my charms and used my soul for ping-pong tit-for-tat until you perfected your game, and now you prey on the memories in my head.

ABDULLAH: Millicent, you got it all wrong.

MILLICENT: No, honey, you were wrong. You were wrong to do that to me. You were wrong then, and you are wrong now. God, where are all the good black men?

ABDULLAH: Millicent...what a pity.

MILLICENT: Well, don't pity me, brother. Pity yourself.

ABDULLAH: Millicent, look, there are no more race men. Except for the very old men who walk around in baggy pants and glance down at the ground of their broken past. We are the future for our people.

MILLICENT: We?

ABDULLAH: Us. The baby boomers. The black urban professionals. The entrepreneurs. The job-getters. The non-ideological writers and artists. Oh, you may call us the unblacks. But we're the future, baby. That's all to it. Face reality and...

MILLICENT: Shut up. Shut up, Abdullah. Just shut your lying mouth.

ABDULLAH: I'm not lying.

MILLICENT: I don't know what happened to you.

ABDULLAH: Only good things happened to me.

MILLICENT: As you see them. But somewhere along the way you...you got confused.

ABDULLAH: You never bent, did you?

Rob Penny

MILLICENT: Not that way, Abdullah. They said we were non-humans. Outside of history. Without a culture or a recorded past. They wanted us to be super human: to forgive and forget, to be color-blind by their whiteness, to deny our history and culture...

ABDULLAH: We got to, baby. We have no choice. Come on, let's drink and laugh and cut a fool. Anything. I don't want to argue with you about...

MILLICENT: Abdullah, when you said there were no race men...that...that hurt. But there are. There are still hardliners out there, fighting and struggling every day. And you - you better be right, brother, or I'll come...someone'll come looking for you, especially if you aren't right.

ABDULLAH: You can't keep beating a dead turkey.

MILLICENT: Dead turkey? I thought it was a dead horse.

ABDULLAH: I changed it, baby. Dead, dumb turkey: that's double dumb. Race is dumb. Take the Garveyites, they're almost like dodo birds today. Black students today want a degree that's going to pay off in green power. The black liberation movement has succumbed to getting a job, not creating jobs. Living in luxury. Not going back to a dead community.

MILLICENT: It's your fault - and mine.

ABDULLAH: Don't put it on me. Or yourself, Millicent. All I'm saying is break the cross mentality. 'Cause I'm not carrying that old rugged cross no more - for no one but me, Abdullah - and Allah.

MILLICENT: Oh, what about Mrs. Courtney?

ABDULLAH: You know what I mean.

MILLICENT: Of course, I do. Abdullah, were we that naive back then?

ABDULLAH: Naive's not hardly the word for it. On the serious side.

MILLICENT: Yes. On the black hand side.

ABDULLAH: See. See, that's what I'm talking about; you have to get that out of your head.

MILLICENT: What?

ABDULLAH: Black this. Black that. The song's too old to keep trying to revive in today's society. Okay, so the '60s were black. Black times. Rallies. Marches. Demands. Shoot-outs. And we - I was...I was caught up in it like a roach to honey.

MILLICENT: That's it, huh?

ABDULLAH: What? I don't follow you, Millicent.

MILLICENT: I couldn't see it then - because I was like a little bird, tightwalking on your fingers.

ABDULLAH: M & M.

MILLICENT: Oh, now it's...M & M.

ABDULLAH: That's what you were to me.

MILLICENT: I melted in your hands and in your mouth, right?

ABDULLAH: Down to the bone. Bet you still good. Probably better.

MILLICENT: I don't know, Abdullah. Haven't had much practice since you. (*The atmosphere intensifies.*) Are we...trying to set an atmosphere for...for something...funky?

ABDULLAH: There's nothing wrong with my saxophone, baby.

MILLICENT: Well, what makes you think I want someone who thinks of himself as a roach. Sure you don't prefer someone of a lighter complexion?

ABDULLAH: Tear out my heart with the juju of your mother-wit.

MILLICENT: No, I wouldn't hurt you - on a personal level. Abdullah, if I hurt you, I'll only be hurting myself.

ABDULLAH (*harshly*): Just drop the cross. (*Softer.*) I told you that a minute ago. Just drop it. How long do you think you can hang on to the crucifixion? The nails'll kill you sooner or later, you know that.

MILLICENT: Maybe they are loosening up right now.

ABDULLAH: Good.

MILLICENT: Abdullah...are you recruiting...for the crossover class?

ABDULLAH: You can't be serious with...?

MILLICENT: It's a valid question.

ABDULLAH: Yeah, why?

MILLICENT: Because men like you still think you can solve the racial problem in America with your penises.

ABDULLAH: Hey, baby, I need a drink on that one. (*Motions for a drink.*)

MILLICENT: Get your own drink. (*Changes her mind.*) No. Allow me. I'm the hostess. Ah, we black women know how to treat our men - even our used-to-be men.

ABDULLAH (*accepting the drink*): Thanks, baby.

MILLICENT: You're quite welcome, Mr. Courtney.

ABDULLAH: Toast?

MILLICENT: Just drink it, Abdullah.

ABDULLAH (*savors the liquor*): Good year. (*Pause.*) Go out dancing much? (*No reply.*) Remember when you joined the Pan-African Dance Troupe on campus? That was when we had our first real fight.

MILLICENT: You felt it was indecent for me to dance bare-breasted.

ABDULLAH: They were just too big to be flopping up and down on some stage.

MILLICENT: Sometimes, I guess, we were atavistic.

ABDULLAH: Not me. I was just caught up in the struggle like dry bushes in a raging fire. And the wind kept blowing in my face. Blinding me and pushing me into a red, black and green thing. But that wasn't what I wanted. All I wanted to be was a doctor. Nothing else. Not a nationalist. Not a revolutionary. Not a militant. Nothing else but a doctor. A hell of a doctor, too.

MILLICENT: You could've been both, Abdullah. A revolutionary nationalist and a doctor.

ABDULLAH: I couldn't. (*Pause.*) I couldn't.

MILLICENT: Oh, you poor man. The servant of Allah. All the poor man wanted to be was a doctor.

ABDULLAH: Don't make fun of me...

MILLICENT: Forgive me. But back then I thought all you wanted to do was hump on top of me and lead the people.

ABDULLAH: Cut blood, baby.

MILLICENT: No, you're the one who was always talking about cutting some blood if you caught a brother hitting on me. Remember? Or have you forgot that too?

ABDULLAH: Love'll make you...

MILLICENT: Oh, now it was love. Between my legs - you call that love?

ABDULLAH: The purest expression of love.

MILLICENT: Oh yeah, that's right. The purest expression of love is when a woman's in her natural prone position while you black men run your hands through our Angela Davis afros. Shit!

ABDULLAH: But you must admit we were dazzling lovers and movers.

MILLICENT: I couldn't've been that dazzling to you.

ABDULLAH: You were.

MILLICENT: Suddenly, I feel a growing distance between us, Abdullah.

ABDULLAH: Oh, I believe I can fix that. Feel like dancing?

MILLICENT: Dancing isn't exactly what I need.

ABDULLAH: Well, whatever it be, baby, I got it.

MILLICENT: Sure about that?

ABDULLAH: You never had any complaints in college.

MILLICENT: I was young...much younger then, Abdullah.

ABDULLAH: So was I. But we all carry our memories in our pockets every day of our lives.

MILLICENT: Guess you got something there. You filled my head with so many promises. So many lovely dreams. And visions. They tasted like strawberries rolling off your tongue. But they were lies. Lies. Cheap, nose-opening lies. It...it took a long time for me to stand up like a woman, Abdullah. When you left me...I - I folded like a boiled spaghetti. And you know, I'm still like that for you. Still. I can't even begin to explain to you the kind of internal shit... in here...that I went through because of...

ABDULLAH: Millicent. Millicent. Let's be civil. I come to visit you. I don't expect much while I'm here. But I'm here. And I don't think having a pisspoor attitude about yourself...

MILLICENT: A pisspoor attitude. Oh, a pisspoor attitude. Is that what I have?

ABDULLAH: Sounds that way to me.

MILLICENT: And what would you know about my attitude? The way you are now is the way you black men were back then.

ABDULLAH: That's emotionalism talking through...

MILLICENT: Well, mines might be emotionalism, brother, but yours ain't nothing but lies. Lies for promises. Now you think you can fix everything between us in ah - in - ah...(*Remembering.*)...with a drink and a dance. Yeah. (*Goes and puts record on the turntable.*)

Yeah. I could dance with you. Slow drag with you. (*Extends her hand to him.*) Just like old times. (*She slides her body into his arms.*) And feel you growing hard against me. And blowing in my ear. (*Pushes him away from her.*) But that don't get it no more, Abdullah. It takes more than a slick rap and a bank account to raise my window and pull down my blinds. No, I don't want to dance with you. Nor do I want to hear you talk trash to me.

ABDULLAH: I never talked trash to you.

MILLICENT: You did. I didn't know it then. You sprayed too much cologne on it. The boy from the Motor City. One of the first to receive a Marcus-Malcolm-Martin Scholarship. You filled my soul with so much nigger trash...

ABDULLAH: Look, if you feel like you've sold out to capitalism and the American Dream, don't blame it on me, on what you think I done to you in the past.

MILLICENT: I haven't sold out.

ABDULLAH: Me neither.

MILLICENT: I never thought we would ever reach a point where we couldn't see eye-to-eye on social and political issues.

ABDULLAH: Sorry about that, baby. But we do mature, you know. I could use another drink.

(MILLICENT, *apparently in deep thought, fixes* ABDULLAH *a drink.*)

MILLICENT: Abdullah.

ABDULLAH: Yes, baby.

MILLICENT: I don't know why you're here, but I'm not going to let you mess with my mind.

ABDULLAH: I'm here because you need me. You called me.

MILLICENT: I didn't call you.

ABDULLAH: You always call me when you're down in the dumps. When you're feeling sorry for yourself. When things haven't worked out the way you wanted them to. Or after you've paraded that fine brown body through the eyes of circus animals in singles bars. So you yank me out of your subconscious. Then pour all of your self-pity on me.

MILLICENT: That's what you think, Abdullah?

ABDULLAH: That's what I know, baby.

MILLICENT: I'm more of sound mind than you think you know, Abdullah.

ABDULLAH: Sure, baby. (*Takes the drink from her hand.*) Thanks.

MILLICENT: Oh, I admit I have some personal problems. But it's up to me to work them out. You see, I realize that I'm overworked at times. But the only reason I'm a workaholic is because I use my work as a means for passionate sublimation - which means you, Abdullah. Maybe, as you say my pisspoor attitude is a result of self-pity, but...

ABDULLAH: You got to practice self-criticism, don't you?

MILLICENT: I practice what I preach. So you came at the right times. My life's kind of at a standstill...

ABDULLAH: M & M, it's not my fault.

MILLICENT: Oh, yeah! Well, brother, you were here. Remember? You were here like no other brother. I was not a freebie. You touched my breasts, kissed my lips, and rubbed yourself all over my body and mind, didn't you?

ABDULLAH: I didn't rape you, Milli...

MILLICENT: What gives you black men the fucken right to...?

ABDULLAH: I didn't come here to be castrated...

MILLICENT: Wh-whatever happened to black love?

ABDULLAH: Human love took its place.

MILLICENT: Oh, I see. Human love. Something new on the planet, huh? Ah, Abdullah, am I not human?

ABDULLAH: Of course, you're human. You know that. What's your point?

MILLICENT: Well, if you have to ask me that, you missed my point. Tell me, honey, why didn't you, I mean, in God's name, why didn't you black men treat us like we were human beings then?

ABDULLAH: Hold it. I thought this was personal, not social.

MILLICENT: And I thought the social was the largest extension of the personal.

ABDULLAH: What?

MILLICENT: I said, I thought the social was the largest extension of the personal. And we would always live our lives as compliments to each other.

ABDULLAH: Dichotomies do exist, Millicent.

MILLICENT: Why, Abdullah, why didn't you go all the way like we planned? I mean, we spent nights burning the midnight oil together studying Black History and World History. Sekou Toure, Nkrumah, Fidel Castro, Amiri Baraka, Oliver Cox, Julius Nyerere, Amilcar Cabral, Ho, Malcolm X, Sojourner Truth, David Walker, Ida Wells Barnett, Harriet Tubman, Maulana Karenga...and the enumerations go on and on and...

ABDULLAH: Why! Why! You ask me why? Be-because there was no future in it. Not in any of it. (*Pause.*) Millicent...baby, does it...still matter?

MILLICENT: To me, it matters. Because I've kept you locked in my heart every waking day of my life for the past seventeen years. And every time I wanted to let go of you, the more I pulled you back into me. Yes, it matters. I want to tell you, right now, how much it matters. You see, I put clean sheets on my bed thinking of you. I shower with you. When I look into the mirror, combing hair, I turn into Billie Holiday with a gardenia stuck in my hair. Does it matter, you ask? What do you think? I'm a messed-up woman, a soul in limbo, unwilling to hate or love any man but you. Abdullah, what do you honestly think a woman is made out of, huh? What do you think we're made for? Neglect? The blues? Your cast-asides...?

ABDULLAH: I didn't realize it was that deep with you.

MILLICENT: You didn't realize...See, you never stopped to think that we have social histories. That when one of us suffers at your insensitivity, we all share in that personal history. That we don't want to be black men's victims some every ten years. So you can stand on the edge, away from us, and declare against us that you're a man.

ABDULLAH: Y'all beat us so bad, baby. What can we do? Be everyone's whipping boy?

MILLICENT: Abdullah, be black. Be terrible. That's what I want and that's all I have.

ABDULLAH: Naw, baby, you got more than poetics and ideology. Don't kid yourself. Blackness can never get anyone what you got. You got a thriving business. Boo-coo buxs. Fashionable clothes...from...where...Anne Klein? Or is it Sax Fifth Avenue? A gold card?

MILLICENT: My clothes are very inexpensive and not too fashionable. What about you. Look at you...

ABDULLAH: That's because I'm for self, baby. Freedom of choice. Yeah. I like Neiman Marcus. Perry Ellis. I read *Fortune*, *Business Week*, *Forbes Magazine*, and the *Wall Street Journal*.

MILLICENT: Proud of that shit, ain't you? Carry it around under your arms and on your back like leopard spots, huh?

ABDULLAH: No more than you do. Appearing in *Ebony* and *Black Enterprise*. That's cool. That's your thing. Look, you got this big ol' crib. You've achieved. You don't have to run around now, shouting "Black Power," "Power to the People," "Right On," or "Habari Gani," "Asalaam Aliekum," and submitting to black men with your arms folded across your breasts and your hair screaming "I'm black and I'm proud." You pass all that shit, baby.

MILLICENT: So, ah, who freed you niggers - Gloria Steinem, Bo Derick and Jane Fonda?

ABDULLAH: Naw, baby, we freed ourselves.

MILLICENT: From me - us, right?

ABDULLAH: Yes - no...no. We learned the "Man's" game, and now we're simply perfecting it.

MILLICENT: You sound so pathetic, I...

ABDULLAH: You can't walk on water, Millicent.

MILLICENT (*with disgust in her tone*): You are that which completes my existence...

ABDULLAH: Go on. Finish it.

MILLICENT: I don't have to. I don't even want to think about it.

ABDULLAH: That's it, baby. Let it rest. Let it be like a mountain on some forgotten island somewhere back in time. Give up on atavism. And dreams. History. The Revolutionary Nationalist is dead. The Dreamer is dead. We buried them on that island. The only thing that's left is old black and white film clips. You can just pop 'em into your VCR on cold nights when you feel nostalgic. (ABDULLAH *boldly stands before her, opening his arms.*) Millicent... (*She doesn't look at him.*)...Millicent...come into these arms.

MILLICENT: Abdullah, what do you want? My soul? My body? My mind?

ABDULLAH: You, Millicent. I want you. I want to wash off the dust of the past.

MILLICENT: You are that which completes my life and makes it perfect.

ABDULLAH: Come into these arms, baby.

MILLICENT: If I do...

ABDULLAH: Do it, baby.

MILLICENT: Will you...

ABDULLAH: Yes, baby.

MILLICENT: Be mine's...

ABDULLAH: Sho', baby.

MILLICENT: If I do...

ABDULLAH: You got to do it, baby.

MILLICENT: I give up on who I am...

ABDULLAH: About time, baby.

MILLICENT: I give up on our main nation...

ABDULLAH: Join the human nation.

MILLICENT: The Black Nation?

ABDULLAH: The human nation.

MILLICENT: Abdullah...

ABDULLAH: Come into these arms, baby. And get the answer to your blues. I want to tap your jellyroll until it row like okra.

MILLICENT: Abdullah, is this...this drive for capitalistic restoration the logical extension of the black liberation movement?

ABDULLAH: It's more logical than being in the underclass. Believe that.

MILLICENT: I always believed you. Believed in you, too. My mother still tells me that you aren't ever coming back to me. She says when a rooster done tasted another hen's pooter, he ain't hardly going to remember the taste of the first one.

ABDULLAH: Old folk tales, baby. To keep you quiet and dumb to the finer things in life. Columbus might've discovered America, but we got our Discover Cards now!

MILLICENT: Abdullah, I can't come into your arms because you don't know all about me.

ABDULLAH: Sure I do. What you got under them fine clothes you got on, the birthmark on your left breast. Nothing on you I don't know about.

MILLICENT: But I'm not just talking about surface. I want to be with you again and again. But I'm still growing.

ABDULLAH: Yeah, grow. Grow pass blackness. (*He looks around her crib.*) Betcha a dollar to a dime, you don't have one, not one stitch of African clothes in your closet. Not even one to lounge around in. I mean, I can dig the expensive artifacts you got scattered strategically around your crib. I mean, all that's fine - for show. Because we are the best show-boaters in the world. We can showboat our asses off to get ahead. I mean, we can front our asses off.

MILLICENT: I don't, Abdullah. I struggle for our people every day. I struggle for human rights like Malcolm said. You hear me. I do.

ABDULLAH: Look, I believe you. You don't have to try and convince me. Convince yourself.

MILLICENT: I'm convinced, brother.

ABDULLAH: See, I've learned what it takes to be somebody in this cold world. I've grabbed it in my fist and shook it until it was tamed, and now I can control it. What did we learn from studying all those revolutionary figures that can help us today?

MILLICENT: I've learned to keep struggling with my people. What did you learn? To fuck white women when you couldn't get some black leg?

ABDULLAH: Millicent, I told you I'm pass all that.

MILLICENT: Abdullah. Abdullah, doesn't it feel peculiar to your mind when you're doing it to her? Aren't you going against your sensibilities? Aesthetics? Doesn't it hurt? Give you the blueballs or something?

ABDULLAH: What can I say to that, Millicent, except that I manage. But I am for the people. All the people. Don't get me wrong now, I don't slight your people...

MILLICENT: Oh, back to my people, not your people anymore, huh?

ABDULLAH: To tell the truth, I just got into a habit of...let's say, phrasing it that way. It don't mean a thing...

MILLICENT: If it ain't got that swing. I know the tune, but it wasn't meant to be abused, Abdullah. And you know better. But, you'll abuse anything...honesty...trust...to get what you want.

ABDULLAH: I'm not evil, baby.

MILLICENT: Damn, but you're so close to it. Abdullah, you need to get your head relined. You swore up and down that you didn't do drugs, gays and white girls.

ABDULLAH: I still don't do gays and drugs.

MILLICENT: What about...?

ABDULLAH: Millicent...cross my heart...when we were in the movement, I didn't. And that's the honest to God truth.

MILLICENT: So Rosa Parks, George Jackson, Malcolm...all of their work...for...this - so you can make salats with some white broad. So we could become anything other than trying to be black? To go into business and become professionals without blackness? Without black values? Without identity, purpose and direction?

ABDULLAH: Millicent, we never took time to analyze our future.

MILLICENT: I did.

ABDULLAH: Well, I...like I said before, I was caught up in a maze and didn't even realize it. Did you smell flowers back then? Go to a Broadway show? Hop on a plane and fly to Europe? To Paris? Amsterdam? Or go to a movie? Remember, you wouldn't even wear the watch I bought you because it was manufactured by whites? But now you can feel better about yourself. Do things. Fly to Disneyland and not feel as though you're copping out on the brothers and sisters. Why? Because they're there too. With their hair stretched and jerri-curled back. With their li'l tan kids. And they can spell Mickey Mouse better than they can spell Mozambique, Kawaida, Kwanzaa or Marcus Garvey. You can lay up in this big ol' crib and drink Cuvee Dom Perignon...or snort a taste...if you're inclined to. That's real, baby. Freedom in the real world.

MILLICENT: I haven't changed as much as you think, Abdullah.

ABDULLAH: Ah hell, Millicent, you're a feminist just like my wife.

MILLICENT: I'm nothing like your wife, brother.

ABDULLAH: Millicent, get pass skin ideology. Then you'll see the truth . I mean, you're on top of it. How many women, especially black women, are in the position you're in? You tell men what to do.

MILLICENT: Employees.

ABDULLAH: Look at you. Still young. Got your shape. Pretty. Intelligent. You don't have to strut around the planet with an afro shouting to the world you be black. You're sophisticated. Talk the King's English. No buts, accept the truth.

MILLICENT: Your truth, huh?

ABDULLAH: It's the same truth in Alabama, Greensboro, Chicago, Mississippi. All I'm trying to do is to reach your rational mind...your common sense...I mean the last time I was here, you told me...

MILLICENT: The last time...? Abdullah...when were you in my house?

ABDULLAH: Not here...in your crib...when you were...in the hospital...resting...about two years ago...

MILLICENT: Oh yes, I remember. You sat on the bed beside me. You were playing with my toes.

ABDULLAH: I always loved your feet, didn't I?

MILLICENT: You sure did. Remember how much I loved the way you kissed me?

ABDULLAH: Slobs, we called them.

MILLICENT: Man, could you kiss.

ABDULLAH: Still can. Improved a lot, you know. My wife was just telling...

MILLICENT: Look, I don't want to hear what your...

ABDULLAH: Who do you resent...

MILLICENT: Forget you.

ABDULLAH: ...the most, me or...

MILLICENT: I couldn't care less than nothing about...

ABDULLAH: Who do you resent the most, me or my...?

MILLICENT: Nigger, if you don't get off my back...

ABDULLAH: Okay. Okay. I'm sorry.

MILLICENT: No, don't feel sorry. I don't want to hear anything a sorry man has to say to me ever again in life. And you're about the sorriest man I ever known.

ABDULLAH: 'Cause I don't worship the '60s?

MILLICENT: No. Because you fronted. Because you forgot. Because you're so damn pretentious. And because we struggled against racism and oppression together. And wrote poetry together. Because I loved you. I let you plug me. Because we were tall

281

together. Black consciousness. Meaningful. Unity. But you sold out, brother. You stole from the people and never returned their integrity. Now you got their spirit and gone in a new suit.

ABDULLAH: You have much more than I.

MILLICENT: Damn right about that. I've always had more than you. Maybe you don't know it, Abdullah, but race and economics are the only reason why you're where you are now. The same reasons why you niggers were elected during Black Reconstruction. As long as there're niggers out there like you to defend and develop the interests of capitalists...

ABDULLAH: "The white man, at best, is a very corny dude..." Remember that?

MILLICENT: I remember. You said the same thing. You said you hated...Oh, I got it. Not once did you say you hated the white woman. All the time you were lusting after her flat buns. All your stories and poems and plays reflected...where are they? I have them around here somewhere. Bet if I re-read them, the light...the truth...would shine through.

ABDULLAH: Millicent...

MILLICENT: Don't call me that. Call me naive. Vulnerable. But you have no right to call me anything else.

ABDULLAH: M & M...

MILLICENT: Definitely not that. Or baby. Abdullah, you have no right, you understand? No right!

ABDULLAH: I see you can't separate emotionalism from reality anymore.

MILLICENT: Bet you I've just about figured out which one you are.

ABDULLAH: Get ready for the 21st century, sister. Give up the ghost.

MILLICENT: Never known any ghosts. Ancestors or haints. If you can get next to that, my brother.

ABDULLAH: Nevertheless, there's but one reality. Civil rights drove it home. A great big, white Cadillac chauffeuring the Talented Tenth into the 21st century. No mystery about it. Today there's no religious or political organization or party or commercial on TV, for that matter, that doesn't have black and white together.

MILLICENT: Have you heard of the KKK or the Skin Heads? But that doesn't matter to you. The images you see on TV are indicative of the meaning you give to the struggle, right?

ABDULLAH: What you need to do...

MILLICENT: I know what I need to do better than you do.

ABDULLAH: Naw, I don't think so. What you need to do is to free your mind, your soul, so you can free your pussy.

MILLICENT: Just leave my pussy out of this.

ABDULLAH: Okay. Better to believe in the Easter Bunny again than to believe in the rise of black people as we did in the '60s. Join today's reality. Black culture has no success to offer you. Get real! (*Throws up his arms.*) And come off that black shit!

MILLICENT (*gathering up* ABDULLAH's *clothes*): Well, it's getting late and it...has been nice...you stopping by and all...for a chat. I enjoyed it. Appreciate it. Your kindness. Thank you, very much.

ABDULLAH: That's it? Just like that?

MILLICENT: Just like that.

ABDULLAH: I could stay overnight, you know.

MILLICENT: You black men never know when to stop begging, do you? No, don't attempt to answer that. I know you would like to stay overnight...for old times sake. I could lay my head on your chest. Intertwine my legs around yours. Cool out, sipping wine. Letting you love me until the morning bright sprinkles its golden strawberries on us.

ABDULLAH: You paint a beautiful picture in my head, baby. I love it.

MILLICENT: I bet you would, too. Love it to death, wouldn't you, honey?

ABDULLAH: Yep. Just like the old days. I could plant a yellow rose in your bushes spread right out here on top of your black Steinway.

MILLICENT: Ooooo, sounds kinky to me. But first, Abdullah, honey, Abdullah, my king, my black king, let me ask you one question: do you have two?

ABDULLAH: Huh? Two what?

MILLICENT: I said, do you have two? You don't think I'm going to let you dip the same one you dip into her into me, do you?

ABDULLAH: You always had a humorous funny bone in you.

MILLICENT: Yep. Glad you remembered. I've always been very particular about my politics and who I sleep with. Yep, very choosy.

ABDULLAH: Okay. Have it your way. But you lost. You lost.

MILLICENT: Yep. My loss. Someone's gain, I suppose. (ABDULLAH *prepares to leave.*) Abdullah. (*He stops.*) Never mind. (ABDULLAH *takes two more steps.*) Abdullah.

ABDULLAH: Yes, Millicent, what is it?

MILLICENT: Don't think you're a winner, 'cause you're not.

ABDULLAH: How's that?

MILLICENT: Because by law and a punishment to your wife, your children are labeled black. Their skin tone may not be dark, but they're black, Abdullah. Remember Jean Toomer and all the rest.

ABDULLAH: Be, ah, seeing you around.

MILLICENT: Yep.

ABDULLAH: A goodbye kiss?

MILLICENT: Nope.

ABDULLAH: Bye, baby.

MILLICENT: You got that right.

(ABDULLAH *exits.* MILLICENT *pours herself a drink, then dials the phone.*)

Hello, let me speak to Gene Cooper. (*Pause.*) Millicent Morrison. (*Wait.*) Gene. (*Pause.*) I'm fine. You? How's the family? (*Pause.*) Glad to hear that. Gene, look, I got another one for the party. He lives in Detroit. (*Pause.*) No. Tell Greg I want him to pick up the details from me in my office tomorrow - no later than 7:00 a.m. (*Pause.*) Yeah, I want Greg on this one. (*Pause.*) Yes, the usual. And I need to know just how responsive he is to the black community. Huh? (*Pause.*) No - yes, it's personal. This one's very important to me. I might have to handle this one myself. (*Pause.*) Yes, it's the way I want it. The way it's going to be. (*Pause.*) Omar? He's doing fine the last time I heard from him. He's one of the leaders in the Free South Africa Movement on the campus in Pittsburgh. (*Pause.*) Yeah, he better be cool. And not grow up like his father. I don't like repeaters. 'Cause I'll jump on a plane in a minute and get in his behind, wherever it may be. Look, Gene, gotta run. See you later. Bye-bye.

(MILLICENT *hangs up the phone, slides an album by Herbie Nichols on the turntable, and waterfalls more liquor over her ice cubes. She picks up the phone and carries it to the couch. Sprawling there, she dials the phone.)*

Hello, Matt? It's me, Millie. Say, it's still early yet. What if...listen first, man...what if I come by your place, pick you up, and show you a real good time...say...until the early morning bright. (*Pause.*) Yeah, I'm sure. (*Pause.*) More positive about this than ever before. Did you say red was your favorite color and you were crazy about Herbie Nichols and Bill Dixion. (*Pause.*) Well, I got your color and your music. (*Pause.*) No, don't fly over here. I have to fumigate this place...(*Interruption.*) No, man, it won't be that way anymore. I'm a changed person. Seriously. (*Pause.*) You're intrigued. I'm intrigued. (MILLICENT *listens to him. A warming smile opens her for the sweetness of intentions.*) Come on, stop it, Matt...Oooo, yes...hush yo' mouth...you black men lay me out...promise...stop it now...I'm going to hang up on you...Oooo, talk to me...well...hello...love it...Hallelujah...yes...oooo, I just love it that way...good Gordon Gin... (BLACKOUT.)

The Quest

by KALAMU YA SALAAM

Kalamu ya Salaam, born 24 March 1947, is a New Orleans native who is a professional writer and arts administrator. For thirteen years Mr. Salaam served as editor of The Black Collegian Magazine, a national publication. His journalism and creative writings have been widely published and anthologized. He has contributed linear notes for numerous jazz albums including the 1986 release from The Dirty Dozen Brass Band and the 1987 release from Alvin Red Tyler, both of whom are from New Orleans. Mr. Salaam currently serves as the Executive Director of the New Orleans Cultural Foundation, Inc. His books include: *The Blues Merchant* - poetry, *Hofu Ni Kwenu (My Fear Is For You)* - poetry, *Pamoja Tutashinda* - poetry, *Who Will Speak For Us: New Afrikan Folktales* - children's stories with Tayari kwa Salaam, *Ibura* - poetry, *Herufi: An Alphabet Reader* - children's literature with Tayari kwa Salaam, *Revolutionary Love* - poetry and social essays, *Iron Flowers: A Poetic Report On A Visit To Haiti* - poetry, and *Our Women Keep Our Skies From Falling* - essays on sexism.

CHARACTERS:

CLARENCE - *Late twenties. Wears tie but no coat. Is very intense.*
WOODY - *CLARENCE's younger brother. Dressed very casually and wearing a light windbreaker.*
MRS. WILLIAMS - *Mother of CLARENCE and WOODY. Is in her late forties.*
ODESSA - *Is married to CLARENCE. Late twenties. Wears hair in a short natural. Light-complexioned.*

SCENE: *The front room of a small, two-bedroom apartment in a modern complex. There are no windows. The walls are relatively bare. There is a painting of an African woman on the back wall. Green plants hanging in pots. A photograph of CLARENCE, ODESSA, and their two children on a small end-table. There is an inexpensive stereo system, a small library of books, including law books,* __Destruction of Black Civilization__*, Black poetry. An African artifact on the bookcase. A stack of about twenty to thirty albums on the floor by the stereo. It is 5:30, and there is*

Earl Klugh/Bob James on the box. WOODY *is sitting, facing the audience, and* CLARENCE *is in another room.*

CLARENCE: Hey man, why you always getting high, huh? What for? (*No answer.* WOODY *is still nodding slightly.* CLARENCE *enters.*) And then you come sliding 'round here.

WOODY: Aw, nigger. Leave me 'lone.

CLARENCE: How I'm going to leave you alone when you keep coming 'round me? I wasn't bothering you wherever you was at, doing whatever you was doing. But no, you to come 'round here, to mess with me...

WOODY: Fuck it, man. You want me to leave? You putting me out or something?

CLARENCE: Naw, man, it's just...

WOODY: Fuck it, man. It ain't no big thing, you know what I mean? I'm just high, see. Ain't nuthing wrong with being high, see. I live my way, and you do what you do, okay?

CLARENCE: Yeah. Yeah, okay lil' brother, but you got to grow up sometime. Sometime sooner or later, you gonna have to grow up, and then...

WOODY: And then what? I ain't gon' ever grow up like ya'll want me to grow up. Look at me, see. I can't even get through somebody jive school. I don't wear no glasses. I don't talk proper. I don't got no bigass IQ like my bigass IQ brother. I'm just yo...

CLARENCE: Woody, quit putting yourself down.

WOODY: I ain't putting me down. Ya'll putting me down. The man putting me down. Television putting me down. Sears, the telephone company. Yo' mamma...

CLARENCE: Aug Woody, man...we ain't...(*Knocking at door.*)... Damn! (CLARENCE *exits to answer door. Voices are heard offstage.*) Mamma! Hey, aug, how you doing...aug, Odessa ain't here...

MRS. WILLIAMS: Boy, quit stutterin'. Woody here?

CLARENCE: Yes, mamma. (*They enter.*) Mamma he's...

MRS. WILLIAMS: I can see for myself what he is. Son, stand up.

CLARENCE: Mamma, don't...

WOODY (*he looks up*): What you want mamma? What you want with me?

MRS. WILLIAMS: I want you to stand up and be a man, son. Stand up and take the responsibilities for your actions.

WOODY: Mamma, leave me 'lone.

MRS. WILLIAMS: You just like your pa, <u>triflin</u>...

WOODY: Yeah. Yeah. I know, I'm triflin. So, now leave me 'lone, huh.

CLARENCE: Mamma, come on, I mean, Woody, he don't hear you, mamma. He can't really hear a word you saying.

MRS. WILLIAMS: 'Cause he don't want to hear. He ain't never wanted to hear nothing nobody had to tell him.

WOODY (*jumps up screaming*): I hear you. I hear you all the god-damn time. I hear you. I hear you. I hear you, mamma. I hear you everywhere. Okay, all right? I hear you. I'm standing up now. I'm standing up, mamma. Mamma, I'm standing up listening to you...NOW MAKE A MAN OUT OF ME!

MRS. WILLIAMS: I hope they send you to jail. I hope that girl file charges on you.

CLARENCE: File charges...girl? What girl? Mamma, file charges for what?

WOODY: For making love! For sleeping with Ann! They got laws against that. Least wise god do. Don't he mamma? Don't your almighty white God laws against making love less you married? Don't he...

MRS. WILLIAMS: Woody, that girl pregnant with your baby, and you ain't...

WOODY: You don't know what I'm doing.

MRS. WILLIAMS: Nigger, I know you tried to make that po' girl get a abortion!

CLARENCE: Woody...

WOODY: So fucking what?

CLARENCE: Woody!

WOODY: Aug cool it, brer. Me and mamma talk like this all the time. She understand this language. You understand it too, even though you play like you don't.

CLARENCE: But an abortion, Woody?

WOODY: Yeah. They got enough niggers in the world already...

MRS. WILLIAMS: Sometimes I think they got too many!

WOODY: Who you talking about? Me or you?

MRS. WILLIAMS: You filthy...

CLARENCE: Mamma!

WOODY: Filthy nigger! Come on, mamma. Say it. Say filthy nigger! Come on, mamma. Fix yo' mouth up and say it.

MRS. WILLIAMS: Son, you ain't no good.

WOODY: Yeah, I know. You done told me that at least eighty million times.

MRS. WILLIAMS: The girl's mother called me. They concerned...

WOODY: Mamma, shut up.

CLARENCE: Woody be cool, huh? Look, come on y'all. Woody sit down. Mamma have a seat. Come on y'all. We can work this out. Let's sit down and discuss the problem and see if we can't come up with some solution.

WOODY: There ain't no solution. We all problems. All us. All of us ain't nothing but problems. I'm a problem, you a problem, and mamma -- mamma, she one big fucking problem. The whole world is a problem. In fact, a solution wouldn't be nothing but a problem. Just another problem. Solutions don't exist for niggers. Solutions are a myth. Everything that breathes is a problem. Problem!

CLARENCE: Come on, talk sense, man.

WOODY: Sense. Sense. Sense. What's the use of talking sense. How I'ma talk sense? What make sense to you don't mean nothing to me. What make sense to me don't mean nothing to mamma. And what sense to mamma don't make sense to me. Naw, man, you keep yo' damn sense, and I'll keep mine. Sense.

MRS. WILLIAMS: Son, you done loss your mind.

WOODY: Naw mamma, I ain't lost my mind. I done lost yo' mind!

MRS. WILLIAMS: You gon' know trouble son. You gon' live in sin. Hard times gon' be your bed and trouble gon' be a pillow for yo' head. The Lord gon' take care. The Lord he do take care. He take care of the good. He take care of the bad. And he gon' take care of you.

WOODY: What you trying to do, woman? You trying to put a curse on your own son head. Now is that what you trying to do? Is that what you think you doing? Well, let me tell you, if yo' old funky god so much as bend low to put a hand on me, I'm gon' scream on him. I'm gon' say take yo' jive ass hands off of me. I ain't yo' chile. (*He laughs.*) I ain't no damn christian!

MRS. WILLIAMS: You a sinner.

WOODY: No, I ain't mamma. I ain't no sinner. I'm just me. Just me. And, you know what else? I'm yo' child. You raised me...

MRS. WILLIAMS: No, Woody. That's my cross. I didn't raise you. The streets raised you. Them mannish boys what you stayed out with all night long, they raised you. No, Woody, Mamma Williams didn't raise you.

CLARENCE: The streets ain't raised Clarence. You raised Clarence.

MRS. WILLIAMS: Clarence was different.

WOODY: Clarence older than me. You raise him up. I come after him, and you ain't did nothing for me. Why, mamma?

MRS. WILLIAMS (*she sits slowly*): God only knows what make one man different from his brother. God only knows. I brung you both to church. I whips you both when you done wrong. I loved you both...

WOODYS: Naw, mamma. You didn't love me no mo' then you love daddy.

MRS. WILLIAMS: You wrong Woody. I love you. I love yo' pa. It just that a lot of colored mens don't know how to love back in return.

WOODY: You make it so hard to love. Y'all be wanting us to be something else. Something we ain't. And, y'all be hating what we is and loving what we ain't. How I'm love somebody if they keep throwing my love away?

CLARENCE: Hey, man...ain't nobody throwing you away. We here. We love you. We on your side.

WOODY: Naw, man. I'm on my side. Me. That's it. That's all on my side. Just me. Don't nobody else really give a damn.

CLARENCE: Woody, we care...

MRS. WILLIAMS: I can see ain't no sense in trying to help you, 'cause you want to be in the bad shape you in.

WOODY: I wants to be me. I wants to be respected for what I am, but I don't wants to be here, in this shape. I don't wants to live with all this. Roaches in the room, rats in the walls, niggers in the halls, cops in the streets. Naw. I don't want this!

CLARENCE: What do you want? Look Woody, how can we help you if you don't let us?

WOODY: You can't help me. And, I ain't got nothing to do with it. How you gon' help me when you can't even help yo'self?

CLARENCE: Woody, sit down and listen a minute.

WOODY: Man, you can't tell me nothing. Not nothing.

MRS. WILLIAMS: That's always been yo' problem boy. Couldn't nobody tell you nothing.

WOODY: Yeah, you right, mamma!

MRS. WILLIAMS: Boy, I ain't got but one thing to say to you, and that is you ought to be trying to do right by Ann and yo' baby she carrying.

CLARENCE: Woody, are you serious about Ann?

WOODY: Aug baby, you ain't no goddamn Andy Young. What you want to know for? What you think this like some middle east crisis shit, and you gon' come in and straighten all this mess out? Well, what if I am, what if I ain't? It don't mean nothing to you, not one way or the other.

CLARENCE: Yes it does, Woody. It makes a big difference to me, Woody.

(WOODY *jumps up. Looks at both of them. Turns away, and back to them. Briefly covers his ears. Stretches his hands above his head. Puts his hands in his pocket. Turns back to face them. His face says that he is no longer there.*)

MRS. WILLIAMS: Be what you want to be, but you ain't got to be dragging other peoples down with you.

CLARENCE: Woody. Woody, you my brother.

WOODY: Man, leave me 'lone!

CLARENCE: Woody, listen. Listen to me. Just listen a minute, damn it. There are some things that are too big for you to handle by yourself. Like, brer, whatever you want to do, whatever you want to be, well like that's all right. Ya' know. It's all right. All I'm saying is, is let me help you be what you want to be.

MRS. WILLIAMS: Clarence you talk to him. 'Cause I can't do nothing with him no more. I see he got trouble in his life, but I can't touch him. He too far down the road.

Son, I don't know how to reach you. I don't even know no more how to hardly call yo' name. It seem like you been gone from my house like someone done passed away. Son, I - I don't want to chastise you. I can't beat you no more. What can I do to make you see that I want to help you? Woody. Woody. Son. Son, please...

CLARENCE: Woody, mamma talking to you.

WOODY: I ain't got nothing more to say to you either.

CLARENCE: Woody, that's your mother you're talking to.

WOODY: Naw man, das yo' mamma! I ain't never had no mamma.

MRS. WILLIAMS: Woody, do you really feel that way?

WOODY: Do I really feel this way? Naw, I'm just saying it to pass the time of day. Do I really mean it! Did you really mean it when you called me trifling and no good and shiftless and all that? Did you really mean that?

MRS. WILLIAMS: Son, I was only trying to correct you...

WOODY: Correct me! (*Throws his hands up.*) Correct me!

CLARENCE: Woody, sit down.

WOODY: She was only trying to correct me! Mamma, that ain't no way to correct nobody. You trying to correct me that same way the white man trying to correct me. You and yo' goddamn white god. Yo' god ain't never had no time for me...

MRS. WILLIAMS: Son, don't curse the name of the Lord.

WOODY: You was trying to <u>kill</u> me!

MRS. WILLIAMS: Son, I wouldn't no more kill you then I would kill myself.

WOODY: You are killing yo'self. Yeah, you doing it. But, you don't know it see. I know what I'm doing with my life. But you don't about yourself, hooked on Jesus. All I do is drop some pills and smoke a lil' weed, but you - you mainlining Jesus all the way. The biggest goddamn drug in the community. You got this great big white gorilla riding your back who won't never let you get nowhere. And when you die you gon' cry in yo' grave when you find out the only afterlife you gon' have you don' already had. Yeah, you and yo' old preachers what don't never hit a lick of work. I used to hear um talking 'bout ya'll. But ya'll wouldn't never know no better. Yeah, mamma. I know yo' life, but you don't know it. It's all a hustle, a hustle mamma. Take the money and run. I know preachers that live my life and yours too.

MRS. WILLIAMS: Son, you must really think I'm stupid. You must think these old eyes ain't never seen all sides a life. I done seen it, son. I seen the wicked, and I seen the righteous. And every man got to count for his own life when the reckoning is done. Son, how you think you got here? How you think I fed you and your brother and your two sisters if I didn't know what my life was all about? Do you know what I had to do to get this far in life, to get this old? Do you know what I done seen? Do you know my life?

You got a brother and two sisters over twenty, Woody. And they didn't just pop up out no ground. I scrapped and scrimped and sacrificed to raise y'all. I gave you everything I could get my hands on. And I did it alone, without no man.

You all the time glorifying yo' pa, but did you ever live with a colored man? You hear me. Did you ever live with a colored man? Did you ever invest yo' life in a man? You ever gave a man everything you got, yo' young years, yo' heart, yo' hope? Ready to go where he go, do what he do? Believe everything he say? Huh, Woody? You ever trust a man?

Take any one of them so-called friends of yourn. You would love any them boys like I love yo' pa? Naw, I don't...nigger-men don't know how to love nothing good without 'busting it. Some a y'all tries, but most of y'all, y'all ain't nothing but a stone a woman break her heart on.

Woody, all I ever wanted from any of y'all was for y'all to try to lead a good life (WOODY *starts laughing.*), try to do right...

WOODY (*laughing hysterically*): Leads a good goddamn life. You bring me to this world, and your lord make me Black, and you ask me to lead a good life. Mamma, why did you have me? Why didn't you kill my ass when I was born, if you wanted me to lead a good life?

MRS. WILLIAMS: Son, I believe there was a chance...

WOODY: Why didn't you let me stay where I was? I was doing good there. Lead a good life? Shit.

MRS. WILLIAMS: Son, every man got his own life to lead.

WOODY: Not if he poor, he don't. Not if he Black, he don't. What kind of life I got to live? Huh, what kind? Except what them white folks letting me live?

MRS. WILLIAMS: The white folks don't control your heart?

WOODY: They control every goddamn thing else. Everything. When they finish with you on the street, on the job, in school, when they finish they just about got your heart too. And what they don't get, the niggers cop.

CLARENCE: Woody, there's more to life than niggers and white folks. You ain't got to be a nigger, and you can't be white, but you can be something else...

WOODY: I don't see nothing else, man. You show me something else.

CLARENCE: Woody, that's ghetto thinking...

WOODY: The world is a ghetto.

CLARENCE: Naw, Woody. No, it ain't. There's something more. We can reach for it, man. There's something else out there, man. I know it...

WOODY: How you know it, man. You a nigger, same as me. Got a lil' jive-ass law degree, work at city hall, but nigger, <u>you a nigger</u>, same as me. <u>Got a half-white wife</u>. <u>But you a nigger</u>. You got a credit card, <u>but you a nigger</u>.

When you get mad, you curse. You drink wine. Probably slip around on Odessa, messing with them secretaries and shit. And if you wasn't so square, you'd probably be smoking some dope. Me and you was raised here. Right on these streets. You ain't never been no wheres else. Me and you, <u>we is niggers</u>!

CLARENCE: You right, Woody. We're basically the same, except I had a couple of lucky breaks, and you didn't get um, but you can still climb up out of this. There is another side, Woody.

WOODY: If you represent the other side, I'm gon' keep my ass right here. Man, them lil' boogie niggers you hang with ain't shit. That's all they are, shit, shit with roll-on deodorant on it. Shit with a tie on. Shit with a college accent. Them niggers are punks.

CLARENCE: Look Woody, why don't you stay here for dinner and me and you'll have a talk...

WOODY: Have a long ass talk about nothing.

MRS. WILLIAMS: Like I said, I wash my hands of the matter.

WOODY: You mean you _re_wash your hands of the matter, 'cause you forgot about me a long time ago.

MRS. WILLIAMS: Yes, well, I guess that's that. This the bottom of the sack.

WOODY: Yeah, ain't nothing left. (WOODY *sits down, looks at Mamma, looks away, looks down. Silence.*)

CLARENCE: Mamma, why don't you come back next week and maybe we can work...

MRS. WILLIAMS: No, I know Woody. His mind is set. (*She and* CLARENCE *look at* WOODY. *He looks up, returning their stares without flinching.*) I guess that's all I come for. (*She gets up. Stands silently looking for a moment at* WOODY. *Starts to say something. Stops. Turns slowly. Turns back around.*) Before I leave, I did come for something else. (*She reaches into her large bag and takes out a book.*) I brung you something...(*Offers it to* WOODY. *He is not looking at her.*) It's for your birthday. Happy Birthday, Woody.

WOODY (*looking up*): It ain't my birthday, yet.

MRS. WILLIAMS: I know, but I reckoned that I wouldn't be seeing you tomorrow, so I was carrying it around for the last four or five days, and I decided I was going to give it to you the first chance I got.

WOODY (*without looking up*): Yeah, thanks. (*He does not accept the gift. She puts it on the table next to him.*)

MRS. WILLIAMS: It's a bible, son. Read it. Just read it once in a while. Oh, I know you ain't going to read it now, but maybe later on...you know. You read one or two pages. There's a lot of comfort in those pages.

WOODY: Yeah. Sho. Thanks, mamma.

MRS. WILLIAMS: Well, I guess I'll being leaving.

WOODY: Yeah.

MRS. WILLIAMS: God bless you, son.

WOODY: Yeah.

(*She turns slowly.*)

CLARENCE: I'll walk you to the door. Odessa got the car, else I'd bring you home.

MRS. WILLIAMS: It ain't dark yet. I can walk, Clarence. I'm old, but I ain't dead. One bus and I'm home.

CLARENCE: Mamma, wait. I'll call a cab. It's getting late. You know it ain't safe no more to be walking.

MRS. WILLIAMS: Everybody know me at home. I'll be all right. (*They walk to the door.*)

CLARENCE (*re-entering*): Wow! Man, you a trip. You know that, a trip!

WOODY: Fuck you too, big brother!

CLARENCE: Come on, Woody. You ain't got to fight everybody. You can't fight the whole world.

WOODY: Yeah. (*He gets up.*)

CLARENCE: Where you going, man?

WOODY (*looking around slowly*): I'm going to take a leak. If that's all right with you? Or maybe you don't want my piss in yo' toilet.

CLARENCE: Man, if you want to you can take a shit...(*He laughs.*)

WOODY: Yeah. (WOODY *exits.*)

ODESSA (*enters while* CLARENCE *is still standing smiling at* WOODY): Hey, baby. Clarence, what're you doing?

CLARENCE (*turning*): Hey. Nothing. I was talking to Woody. He's in the bathroom. I didn't hear you come in. Let me help you. (*He takes one of the bags of groceries from her.*)

ODESSA: Where's Aminia and Adimu? (*They both move toward the kitchen.*)

CLARENCE: They had Brownie meeting, remember?

ODESSA: I forgot.

WOODY (*has entered as they were exiting; he hollers after them*): Brownie meeting! Damn, man, why you want to send them kids through them kinds of changes. Lil' brown Brownies. I betcha it's integrated too.

ODESSA (*re-entering*): We send them because a lot of it's good for them. And we send them to gym at the Y and pretty soon, we'll give them music lessons. It's things neither one of us had when we were coming, remember? (*She goes up to him and kisses him.*) How you doing hard luck?

WOODY: I'm hanging in.

ODESSA: And yes, it's integrated. But I rather that then letting them play in the streets or sit in front of television looking at something weird. You know what I mean?

WOODY: Yeah, I guess so.

ODESSA: You know, it's important for them to learn how to work in an organization while they're young. It's all right to learn something as a child.

WOODY: Girl, you trying to pick a fight with me.

ODESSA: No. I'll let you slide today, Woody. Besides, you're their favorite uncle. (ODESSA *exits. She is going to change clothes.*)

WOODY: I'm their only uncle.

CLARENCE: Hey, man, why don't you sit down?

WOODY: I'm cool.

CLARENCE: I'm thirsty. How 'bout a beer, man?

WOODY: Yeah. Yeah. Why not.

CLARENCE: Cool us off. (*He exits. Quickly returns with two beers unopened. He hands one to* WOODY.) Here you go. (WOODY *pops the top and walks around drinking his beer.*) Woody, sit down, man, relax.

WOODY: Is it all right if I stand up if I feel like standing up?

CLARENCE: Yeah, man, but like why don't you relax a little. You look all tensed up. You know what I mean.

WOODY: Yeah.

CLARENCE: Relax, man.

WOODY: Yeah. (ODESSA *returns. She has on a sweatshirt and jeans, sneakers.*) Your husband done invited me to eat dinner.

ODESSA: That's good, 'cause it's his turn to cook anyway.

WOODY (*laughing*): Aw wow, check this shit. The woman making the nigger cook. Aw wow.

CLARENCE: Odessa don't make me cook. We share the work. What with her working, me working and just out of school and too, Odessa's taking night classes...

ODESSA: You don't have to explain anything to Woody.

CLARENCE: Yeah, I know, but I want him to understand...

WOODY: Nigger, you henpecked. Odessa got yo' shit in her back pocket.

ODESSA: You see, I told you. This is an unreconstructed negro male, macho as he want to be...

WOODY: And proud of it! (ODESSA *exits to the bathroom.* WOODY *is laughing.*)

CLARENCE: You didn't know I could cook, did you?

WOODY: How I'm suppose to know. You ain't never used to touch no pot at home. Janice and Robin and mamma did all the cooking.

CLARENCE: Times change.

WOODY: But being a man don't. I betcha deep down inside you resent that sharing shit. Sound like some women's lib shit to me.

CLARENCE: Regardless of what it sound like, it's working all right for us. It's the way we decided to live our life...

WOODY: ...All right. All right. Save the sermon. It's your life... (*He pulls a little envelope out of his pocket.*)...aug, you don't mine if I fly, do you?

CLARENCE: Fly?

WOODY: Yeah, you know, loosen up. (CLARENCE *gestures yes with an open hand.* WOODY *takes the pill out of the bank envelope, swallows it, and chases it with beer.*)

CLARENCE: Why do you do that shit, man?

WOODY: Why you don't do it?

CLARENCE: Seriously, man. I want to understand you. You know that stuff ain't good for your baby?

WOODY: What's good to you, got to be good for you brother. Besides, man you do it too. You take yo' aspirin when you get a headache. You got your compoze and your excedrin, and when you want something a lil' stronger, you tell the doctor to give you a prescription for a tranquilizer or some valium or something. You know what I mean? So, like when I get tight, I drop me a pill, too.

CLARENCE: It ain't the same.

WOODY: Naw, it ain't the same thing. 'Cause if it was the same thing then what I'm doing wouldn't be wrong. You jive mutha-fucka, why don't you just drink your beer and get high yo' way, and let me 'lone to get high mine!

CLARENCE: I ain't putting you down, man. I just asked you why you do it?

WOODY: 'Cause this life is a headache, and I need some relief. I need a break, sucker. This shit is a drag...

CLARENCE: What shit, Woody...

WOODY: Aug, man, wise up. You wasn't born rich. You know goddamn well what I'm talking about or have you forgotten?

CLARENCE: I ain't forgot nothing. I know that dope is a means of temporary escape for you and thousands of others...

WOODY: Can it, big brother. You don't want to know the truth about this system. You want me to believe that a nigger can make it. That a man can be a man. But ain't no way, Jose. This shit is rigged worse than a Louisiana election. (*Reaching into his pocket.*) Like you take this dope shit. What is alcohol? Alcohol is dope. What is cigarettes? Cigarettes is dope. What's the difference, between this shit I take and the shit that you suckers take? You want to know what the difference is? The difference is that yo' shit is legal and mine ain't. And what is legal. Legal ain't shit. Legal mean that the rich folks decided it was all right for everybody to have some. When the big boys decide that you niggers can have some, they make it legal. Meanwhile, for all that stuff what ain't legal it ain't nobody but the rich and poor motherfuckers who don't give a damn, and the greedy pimps and pushers what making money off of it what deals with it...I mean, it's all the same shit, man. Look at them damn judges. They catch me with a joint, they send my ass to the joint. Them same judges be dealing in coke and everything. Everything they can get. Aug, man, you know this shit ain't right. You know it. I know it. But see, I ain't in no position to do nuthing about it. So, for right now, I take it like I find it and leave like it is. Get what you can. Get what little pleasure you can. Get high when you can. Drink when you can. Eat when you can. Fuck when you can, and call it a day!

CLARENCE: Woody, that ain't...

ODESSA (*entering with a bundle of clothes*): I'm going put these clothes to wash. I'll be right back. (*She exits.*)

CLARENCE: Woody, that ain't all there is to life. Man, there was a time when we didn't have much choice, but now, man, now you can change to what you want to be. All you got to know is what you want to be.

WOODY (*starts to laugh quietly*): Hee, hee, hee. Yeah. Yeah, man. Brer, you always was square. Even though you was older than me, you always wasn't nothing but a jive dude. Remember how when you was twelve, and I wasn't nothing but ten, I usta could whip yo' ass? Hee, Hee, Hee, Hee. Jive! Man, when was the first time you cop some ass? Probably when you was in the Army, and you bought that from some hoe, ain't that right?

CLARENCE: What are you trying to prove, man?

WOODY: Hee, hee, hee. You all the time had yo' head up in them books, man. What for? It ain't gonna get you nowhere. Look where you at, brer. Nowhere, brer. You the same place I am. Right here in this funky-ass city.

CLARENCE: If you don't like the city, change the city, Woody. Change it!

WOODY: How? By voting. By putting nigger politician in office. By getting a Black mayor. Wow, big fucking deal. What difference do it make if it's a white boy or a half-white nigger kicking yo' ass? Yo' butt still hurt.

CLARENCE: You want to believe that can't nothing change, because then you don't have to do nothing. Long as it's hopeless, then, you ain't responsible for changing it.

WOODY: Aug man, save that city hall shit. You ain't at work, and I ain't asking for no advice on how to run my life.

CLARENCE: All right. Let's change the subject.

WOODY: Worse than a goddamn white boy. (*Quietly.*)

CLARENCE: What?

WOODY: I said you worse than a goddamn white boy! Nigger, you believe in that white shit harder than they do. You just trying to be white. Hee, hee, hee. Nigger trying to be white.

CLARENCE: I ain't trying to be white.

WOODY: Aug nigger, if you ain't trying to be white, you crazy! I mean 'cause they ain't no other excuse for acting the way you acting man, damn. Ain't no nigger in his right mind would be doing what you doing unless he was trying to get away from being a nigger. And, if you ain't a nigger, you white. It's as simple as that!

CLARENCE: Woody, you don't understand the world.

WOODY: I understand niggers. Sheeiittt. Hee, hee, hee. You the one don't understand. You trying to fight it see. You trying to play the game. You trying to make something outta yo'self...

CLARENCE: And what's wrong with being something? What's wrong with having a goal in your life? What's wrong with trying to achieve something?

WOODY: The only thing wrong with it brer is you ain't never gon' get it.

CLARENCE: You don't know that. You don't know that, man. What you know about getting anything? What you know about what I'm trying to do? Huh? What you know about trying to be a man, huh?

WOODY: I know you white. I know you trying to be white. A white nigger, brer. A white nigger...

CLARENCE: Woody, shut up.

WOODY: My brother, da white man! Hee, hee, hee.

CLARENCE: Woody...

WOODY: Reared by an old negro mammy that scrubbed white folks floors to buy his nigger books. Married to a half-white, high fallutin saddity-ass, nigger bitch dat works as a secretary (*Standing on the end table, left of the sofa, waving the beer can.*) downtown with the white folks and she done gave him two little chocolate brownies. Get yo' tickets. Get yo' tickets and come see my brother, da' white man. Hee, hee, hee.

CLARENCE: You leave Odessa and the kids out of this, man.

WOODY: Color by technicolor, by panacolor, by no color - all white. Hurry, hurry, hurry, come see my brother, da' white man!

CLARENCE: Man, you should talk about being white the way you be running around with them white bitches.

WOODY: And that's just what they bees too, my white bitches! They give me everything I want, when I want. And, you see, when I need something, I just take it from the white man's bitches. I ain't got to go through no changes to get it, see. All I got to do is say, "Bitch, come here." And, I got it. I can get anything the white man got. All I got to do is ask one of my white hoes for it!

CLARENCE: You think you can find your manhood up in between some white woman's legs?

WOODY: <u>Naw</u>, <u>man</u>. (*Grabbing his genitals.*) I <u>put</u> my manhood up between them bitches legs. Hee, hee, hee.

CLARENCE: And that's just where it stays, man. You loss your manhood behind a piece of white pussy! (ODESSA *enters silently, stands still and listens.*)

WOODY: Yeah. You ought to try the real white pussy instead of (*He sees* ODESSA, *but* CLARENCE *does not.*) that half-white wife of yours.

CLARENCE: I ain't never wanted no white girl, Woody. I coulda' had one by now if I wanted one, but that ain't what I want in life. Odessa is just as Black as you or me, maybe more so 'cause her head is on straight. She ain't got no fucked up ideas about who she is or who she ain't and what she want out of life. Ya' know what I mean? She was lucky, man. Luckier than me or you. She never grew up hating herself 'cause she was Black, and her parents didn't raise her to be white...I feel sorry for you. You know, there's more to women than sex. You ain't no Black man. Black men love women, Woody. You hate um. You hate mamma. You hate them white girls you hang out with. You hate all those girls you used to bring 'round to the house and then talk about the next day and you pro...

WOODY: Naw, man, it ain't...

CLARENCE: Don't tell me what it ain't. I know you, brer. You the one trying to be white!

WOODY: Aug, wow, this here is too much!

CLARENCE: Yeah, Woody. I'm just starting to figure you out.

WOODY: Aug man, you sick. You been reading too many books.

CLARENCE: Yeah, you just like the white man. You going to try and misuse everybody for your own ends. You got your white women, plus you want to have some Black girls on the side. That's why you messing with that girl, Ann, ain't it?

WOODY: You shut up about that, man! 'Cause you don't know nothing about that. You don't even know what's going on with Ann, man. You don't know what's going on with nothing. You out of it, man. You out of it. What you know, brer? You don't know nothing. Nothing at all, man. You don't know nothing about what I'm doing. They don't write about me in them books, man. And you don't be out there on them streets, brer. You don't know what's going on. You don't know, man. You don't know.

CLARENCE: I know little brother. I can look at you and tell what's going on. I can look at what the streets have done to you and tell you what's out there, baby.

WOODY: Man, leave me 'lone.

CLARENCE: What you talking about. Leave you 'lone. I live here. You come around here, man. You came looking for me? What for? What for?

WOODY: You don't know nothing, man. You don't know.

CLARENCE: And you don't know either! That's it, isn't it, Woody? You thought you knew, and when you found out you didn't know, it scared you to death, huh?

WOODY: What you know? You don't know nothing, man. I know you don't know.

CLARENCES: Well, then why you come around here all the time, huh? Why, Woody?

WOODY: Leave me 'lone. (*He sits down. His leg is shaking.*)

(ODESSA *crosses to* CLARENCE *and touches him. They look at each other briefly.* ODESSA *moves over to* WOODY. *Touches him on the shoulder.*)

ODESSA: Hey, let's eat. (*He draws away from her.*)

CLARENCE: Come on, man, I'm cooking. Let's eat.

WOODY: Naw. (*Shaking his head.*) Naw, man, you don't know. You don't know. You don't know me. You don't know what I'm going through.

CLARENCE: Let's talk about it over some food.

ODESSA: Come on, let's eat.

WOODY: Don't tell me what to do!

ODESSA: Woody, can't nobody tell you what to do. You your own man, Woody. You tell yourself what to do. Come on, eat. If you don't feel like eating, then don't, that's all right too. Okay? You decide, Woody. Okay? Woody, is that okay?

WOODY: Yeah. Yeah.

ODESSA: Clarence, it's getting late. What you gon' fix? I got a class at seven...

CLARENCE: Yeah. Um, a sandwich, and some lettuce, tomato, and cucumber.

ODESSA: Didn't you put the rice on when you came in? We got beans in the crock pot.

CLARENCE: Hey Woody, which one you want? Sandwiches and salad or beans and rice?

WOODY: I eat whatever the cook fix. Fuck it. I eat anything.

CLARENCE: Hey, man. It's me, your brother. Come on. (WOODY *puts his head down.* CLARENCE *crosses to* WOODY. ODESSA *watches.* CLARENCE *sees the bible, picks it up.*) Come on man, sit up. Here man. Here's the present mamma gave you.

WOODY (*looking up at* CLARENCE): What I want with a damn bible, Clarence? Huh man? What I need with a damn bible? Why it's always got to be like that with me? Huh man? Why me? What the fuck am I that my mamma gives me a bible for my birthday? I don't need no bible, man. Did mamma give you a bible for your birthday, huh?

CLARENCE: No.

WOODY: What she give you, man?

CLARENCE: She gave the kids some clothes.

WOODY: Well then, why she want to go and give me a bible? She coulda' gave me some clothes. I like clothes. Why she couldn't give me some clothes? I don't need no bible.

CLARENCE: Look man. You know how mamma is. Look, just take it for right now. When you leave, you can - you can throw it away if you don't want it. (CLARENCE *holds the bible in front of* WOODY's *face.*)

WOODY: I don't want it. (*He knocks the bible out of* CLARENCE's *hand with an upward motion. The bible flies up in the air. Some money falls out the bible.*)

CLARENCE: Woody, look! (*Pointing to the money.*)

WOODY (*looks at the money, gets up and kneels down beside the bible*): Money. Goddamn money. I don't...Clarence, why mamma want to give me money? Clarence, I don't need money. That ain't what I'm after. Man, I aug – man, damn. Damn! (*He picks the bible up, throws it down.*) Man, I don't need...aug, shit!

CLARENCE: Woody, come on man. Get up.

WOODY: Damn, man. Damn her! I don't care. (*He throws the bible across the room.*) Damn her!

CLARENCE: Woody...

WOODY: Damn her! I don't care. I don't need her. I don't need nobody. She ain't got to love me. It's all right. I'ma man, see. I can take care of myself. I don't need nobody else. See. I'ma man. Ain't nobody got to care about me, see.

CLARENCE: Come on, Woody. (*Going over to him, trying to help him up.*)

WOODY (*shaking off CLARENCE's help*): Yeah. Yeah. I'ma man. (*Standing up.*) I got everything under control. I'm going, man. I'm going somewhere.

CLARENCE: Woody, stay here and eat. Come on, man.

WOODY: Naw, man. I'm all right. I'm cool, see. I ate already. I'm okay. I can take care of myself. Don't worry about me, man. I'm all right. I'm all right.

CLARENCE: <u>Woody, sit down</u>.

WOODY: Naw, man, I'm going.

ODESSA: Woody, you welcomed to stay here. You can sleep on the sofa; it pulls out. We got food.

WOODY: I got a place to stay.

ODESSA: Woody, you don't need to be by yourself right now. Woody, you ought to be around people who care about you. What's out there in those streets, Woody? You know and I know, ain't nothing what love you out there.

CLARENCE: Woody, Ann ain't out there. We ain't out there...

WOODY: I'm out there.

CLARENCE: Woody, hey man, come in from out the cold. Cut it loose before it kills you...

ODESSA: What about if...

WOODY: What time it is?

CLARENCE (looking at his watch): It's a quarter after six.

WOODY: Well, look here, I got to go. See, I got to be somewhere at 6:30, and I'm, you know, I'm just now remembering it. It's important, ya know. I got to be there. I got to. I got, ya know, I got business to take care of. I got to go. (*Wipes his eye.*)

CLARENCE: Hey man, you okay?

WOODY: Yeah. Yeah. I'm cool.

CLARENCE: Well, look stay here and eat, and I'll drive you where you got to go. (*Looking at* ODESSA.) We'll eat. I'll drop you off, bring Odessa to class, pick up the kids, and...

WOODY: Naw, that's all right, I can take care of myself. I'm all right. I just got to go. That's all. I got something to do.

ODESSA: Woody, please.

WOODY: I got to do something. (*Reaches into his pocket for the bank envelope. Pulls it out. ODESSA walks over to him. Covers* WOODY's *hand as he is about to put the pill in his mouth.*)

ODESSA: <u>Woody</u>.

(*He jerks his hand away. Drops the pill. Doesn't bother to look for it. Searches for another one. The envelope is empty. He crumples it up and throws it down.*)

WOODY (*screaming*): Shiiiiitttttt! Leave me 'lone. Leave me 'lone or I'm gon' hurt cha. I swear, leave me the fuck alone or I'm gon' hurt somebody. Somebody gon' die. Leave me 'lone. Leave me 'lone!

ODESSA (*she grabs his arm*): Woody, you gon' hurt yourself. (*He pushes her, and* ODESSA *falls to the couch.*)

CLARENCE: Goddamn it, Woody! (CLARENCE *lunges at* WOODY, *grabbing him around the waist.*)

WOODY: Fuck it! Fuck it. Leave me 'lone. (*He screams out.* CLARENCE *lets him loose and turns to see* ODESSA.)

CLARENCE: Odessa, you okay? Odessa. (WOODY *has reached inside his shirt and pulled out his gun. He is pointing it at the back of* CLARENCE's *head.* CLARENCE *does not see the gun.*)

ODESSA (*urgently, but quietly*): Clarence, Woody's got a gun. (WOODY *walks toward* CLARENCE, *the gun outstretched in* CLARENCE's *face.*)

CLARENCE: Woo...

WOODY: Shut up! Don't say nothing. I want to talk to you. I want to tell you something.

CLARENCE: Woody, put the gun down.

WOODY (*shouting*): Clarence, shut the fuck up, and let me talk. Let <u>me</u> talk. Listen to me. Shut up. Listen to me!

CLARENCE: I'm listening, Woody.

WOODY: Daddy ran away. Joe went on junk. Spider, he stabbed William Charles. Crip shot Soldier. Red joined the army. Smokey workin' in a parking lot. Clarence you know what I'm talking about? I used to be mad at you. I was mad 'cause you was getting out. It ain't fair, Clarence. It ain't fair for you to get out and for me to stay. What you got, I ain't got. I was smarter'n than you. I was stronger.

CLARENCE: Woody, I ain't...

WOODY: Shut up! (*Nobody moves.*) So maybe I ought to...aug fuck. (WOODY *starts to point the gun at his own head, slowly. WOODY is looking straight at CLARENCE the whole time. He doesn't see ODESSA who has slowly risen to her feet.*)

CLARENCE: Woody, don't. (ODESSA *makes her move toward* WOODY, *grabbing the gun and pointing it toward the ceiling. CLARENCE hesitates as ODESSA and WOODY struggle to control the gun. When the gun goes off, CLARENCE grabs WOODY in a bear hug. ODESSA throws her weight on WOODY. All of them fall to the floor. The gun flies loose. CLARENCE is on top of WOODY. WOODY throws CLARENCE off. ODESSA lunges for the gun, grabs it. WOODY is reaching for the gun, but his outstretched hands search futilely. CLARENCE grabs him again. ODESSA points the gun at WOODY.*)

WOODY (*screaming*): Shoot bitch! (*He tries to lunge at her. CLARENCE is holding him.*)

ODESSA (ODESSA *is up on one knee.*): Freeze Woody. (WOODY *tries to lunge at her again, almost breaking free from CLARENCE. ODESSA shoots one shot over his head.*) FREEZE!

CLARENCE: Odessa. (ODESSA *stands up slowly and backs a few steps away from* WOODY, *but keeps the pistol aimed at* WOODY.)

ODESSA: Woody, just stay cool. Clarence, move away. (CLARENCE *slowly lets* WOODY *loose and reluctantly moves away.*) Clarence, call the hospital and tell them to bring some restraints. This shit is crazy. This just the way the party ended. Niggers shooting niggers, while the man downtown gets clean away. This shit is crazy. We starting to turn on ourselves. I mean this is madness. America has got to go. We got to put a stop to this shit before it kills us. Clarence, make that call! (CLARENCE *is moving toward the telephone.*) You see what the man doing to us...

CLARENCE: Operator. I need the number for Mercy Hospital. Thank you. Odessa, look, let's just talk this...

ODESSA (*shaking her head, momentarily covering her mouth with her free hand, finally running her hand through her hair; she keeps the gun aimed at* WOODY; *shakes her head again*): Clarence, this is crazy. He's sick. He needs help.

CLARENCE: I know.

ODESSA: Are we sick, or are we sick? We flipping out everyday. Woody's going to end up on the front page of somebody's newspaper for some kind of weird move he's going to make. You can see it. He's going to blow up. Him and a whole bunch of other brothers. Look, I know what Woody is feeling. I know what's inside of him clawing to come out. But - but, Clarence, some of us ain't going to make it. Some of us gon' die, gon' go crazy, gon' jump off a bridge or something, or go on dope. Some of us gon' die. You ever see somebody die?

CLARENCE: No.

ODESSA: I have. When I was in the party, I saw it happen. That day, I happened to have had to make a stop, so I was late getting back. I watched it from across the street. I saw a brother die, and there was nothing I could do. He was shot, and he was bleeding. He was dying. I was watching him. He knew he was dying. I knew he was dying.

CLARENCE: What happened...

ODESSA: Like I said, he died. That taught me something. When the deal goes down, sometimes the only thing you can do is save yourself. It ain't always possible to save your brother.

CLARENCE: No, long as Woody's breathing, there's hope.

ODESSA: Clarence, we can't reach Woody. There's more tearing him down faster than we can build him back up. Clarence, you can't always save somebody. Sometimes, we can't reach none of the Woody's. Sometimes we can. When we can help, we should, and we do. Clarence, you do what you can do, but then sometimes you can't do no more, you understand? And, meanwhile, we got to keep living. And you ain't got to feel guilty 'cause you living and he's dying. Clarence, hey baby, let's live. Let's make a commitment that we're going to hang tough, that we're going to fight back...

(WOODY *jumps up screaming.*)

CLARENCE: Odessa, don't.

(WOODY *runs for the door.* ODESSA *spins tracking him in the pistol's sight.*)

CLARENCE: Odessa, don't shoot. (*He rushes toward her, pushing her arms away.* WOODY *runs out.* CLARENCE *looks at* ODESSA. *Her arms are at her side. She is still holding the pistol.* ODESSA *returns* CLARENCE's *gaze. They look at each other. After five seconds,* CLARENCE *looks toward the door through which* WOODY *has just run. He half runs to the door - offstage - and returns shortly.*) He's gone. (ODESSA *hands the gun to* CLARENCE. *He doesn't know what to do with it. He puts it down on the couch.* ODESSA *picks it up, empties it, puts the bullets in her pocket. Clears the gun. Points it to the floor, pulls the trigger twice.* CLARENCE *watches her do this and then turns toward the door through which* WOODY *had exited.*)

CLARENCE: We hated each other as kids. All the time we were growing up, we were fighting each other. One trying to be on top the other. I'm sorry about that now. I really am.

ODESSA: Don't blame yourself. It's not your fault.

CLARENCE: Well, whose fault is it that Black people don't love each other enough?

ODESSA: It's the system, ya' know. It's not your fault. It's not my fault. We've got to recognize that we don't make niggers. They system makes niggers. Our children, Amina and Adimu, our girls aren't niggers. I didn't give birth to niggers. Our job is to teach them stronger than the system tries to teach them. Our job is to make them strong enough to deal with all the bullshit that you got to deal with, that Woody got to deal with, that I got to deal with, that every Black person in America got to deal with.

CLARENCE: Yeah. But what about the Woodys.

ODESSA: Clarence, I told you, Woody's too far gone. I mean bloods are blowing themselves away everyday in a thousand different ways. Some of it's suicide, some of it's homicide, some of it's disease, some is junk...Clarence, I don't know...

CLARENCE: Woody's my brother.

ODESSA: Clarence, that Black man I watched die was my brother. You hear me? I watched my brother die, and right then and there, I learned not to waste tears over what I couldn't deal with. I believe in loving the living and helping those we can reach...

CLARENCE: And what about people who need it and never get it. People like my daddy. Didn't nobody love him. Not me, not Woody - really Woody didn't even know him since he split right after Woody was born. Woody don't even know what he looked like...

ODESSA: Our girls know what you look like, and that's important. Give them all that love you got for Woody. They need it, and more than need it, they can make use of it. You can make them strong. It's not too late for them. But, Woody...

CLARENCE: So, you telling me to forget my brother?

ODESSA: What you want me to say? You want me to lie to you? You want me to tell you I think you can save Woody? Clarence, this is America. They kill niggers here, everyday, all kinds of ways. Right from the time we born, they kill us here, and this the only life we got. I know how cold this all sound, but baby, it's really about love. For real, ya' know? I love Woody, but I'm real about it. The system got him.

CLARENCE: The system! The system! What goddamn system? I don't...

ODESSA: The one you and I work in everyday. The moral majority. Them crazy white men in Washington. The Ford Motor Company and Love Canal. You working down at City Hall. Me working at IBM. My brother on the police force. Your brother running wild out there in them streets. Niggers riding 'round in big cars, clean clothes and no job. You know damn well what system...

CLARENCE: But we can change it...

ODESSA: Overthrow it...

CLARENCE: Change it. You tried overthrowing it. You picked up the gun, what difference did it make?

ODESSA: You got your black-ass mayor, what difference did it make? (*They stare at each other.*) Let's not fight. I'm tired of fighting...

CLARENCE: Just a minute ago you were talking about overthrowing the system, now you're tired of fighting...

ODESSA: I'm tired of fighting niggers! Don't you understand? I'm not quitting, but I'm tired fighting each other. I don't know... (CLARENCE *looks at her. Exits, comes back quickly, putting his coat on.*) Clarence where are you going?

CLARENCE: I'm going to find Woody. I'm going find him before he hurts himself, or hurts somebody else. I've got to find him and talk to him. He's my brother.

ODESSA: How are you going to find Woody out there? He could be anywhere.

CLARENCE: I'll find him.

ODESSA: And then what?

CLARENCE: And then I'll - I'll bring him here. I'll bring him home.

ODESSA: Clarence, the children - I don't want that man around our children. I mean that. I can take care of myself. You can defend yourself, but the kids, Clarence, it's crazy.

CLARENCE: Odessa, you understand, I got to find him. He's my brother. I got to find my brother. (*He starts to exit.*)

ODESSA: You're supposed to pick up the kids and drop me off at class. What are we supposed to do?

CLARENCE: Odessa. Baby, look, you take the car.

ODESSA: What about the kids?

CLARENCE: Odessa, don't you understand? I got to find my brother.

ODESSA: Okay. Okay. Do what you gotta do. (*Shaking her head, talking more to herself than to* CLARENCE.) This shit is crazy. I'll get the kids. I'll miss class. I'll sit here and wait, and if you find him, you can bring him here. You go do what you got to do. Goddamn it. Go find Woody. We'll do what we can.

CLARENCE: Hey...(*He kisses her.*) Thanks. I mean...

ODESSA: No. Just go on and hurry back and all that shit. (*She looks away as* CLARENCE *exits. Looks at the gun on the sofa. Picks it up.*) This shit ain't real. The shit you got to go through to live in this place. There's got to be something better than this. (*She walks toward the bedroom carrying the gun. Lights fade fast.*)

THE END.

ABOUT THE EDITOR

Woodie King, Jr. is the Director of New Federal Theatre at Henry Street Settlement in New York City. He is the producer of over 50 plays. He was the co-producer of Amiri Baraka's *Slaveship* and the motion pictures *Right On!, Black Theatre Movement, The Long Night, Torture of Mothers* and *Death of a Prophet.* He has written articles and stories for *Black World, Liberator, Variety Magazine, Tulane Drama Review,* Association for the Study of Negro Life and History, *Black Theatre Magazine,* etc. He has been published in many anthologies, including Langston Hughes' *Best Short Stories By Negro Writers* and Sonia Sanchez's *We A Bad People.* Other books by Woodie King are *A Black Quartet, Black Drama Anthology* (with Ron Milner), *Poets And Prophets* (with Earl Anthony), *Blackspirits, Black Short Story Anthology, Forerunners* and *Black Theatre - Present Condition.*

ALSO AVAILABLE FROM THIRD WORLD PRESS

Nonfiction

The Destruction Of Black
Civilization: Great Issues
Of A Race From 4500 B.C.
To 200 A.D.
by Dr. Chancellor Williams $16.95

The Cultural Unity Of
Black Africa
by Cheikh Anta Diop $14.95

Home Is A Dirty Street
by Useni Eugene Perkins $9.95

From Plan To Planet
Life Studies: The Need
For Afrikan Minds And
Institutions
by Haki R. Madhubuti $7.95

Enemies: The Clash Of Races
by Haki R. Madhubuti $12.95

Kwanzaa: A Progressive And
Uplifting African-American
Holiday
by Institute of Positive Education
Intro. by Haki R. Madhubuti $2.50

Harvesting New Generations:
The Positive Development Of
Black Youth
by Useni Eugene Perkins $12.95

Explosion Of Chicago
Black Street Gangs
by Useni Eugene Perkins $6.95

The Psychopathic Racial
Personality And Other Essays
by Dr. Bobby E. Wright $5.95

Black Women, Feminism And Black
Liberation: Which Way?
by Vivian V. Gordon $5.95

Black Rituals
by Sterling Plumpp $8.95

The Redemption Of Africa
And Black Religion
by St. Clair Drake $6.95

How I Wrote Jubilee
by Margaret Walker $1.50

A Lonely Place Against The Sky
by Dorothy Palmer Smith $7.95

Fiction

Mostly Womenfolk And A Man
Or Two: A Collection
by Mignon Holland Anderson $5.95

Sortilege (Black Mystery)
by Abdias do Nascimento $2.95

Poetry

To Disembark
by Gwendolyn Brooks $6.95

I've Been A Woman
by Sonia Sanchez $7.95

My One Good Nerve		
by Ruby Dee	$8.95	

Geechies	
by Gregory Millard	$6.95

Earthquakes And Sunrise Missions	
by Haki R. Madhubuti	$8.95

Killing Memory: Seeking Ancestors	
by Haki R. Madhubuti	$8.00

Say That The River Turns:	
The Impact Of Gwendolyn Brooks	
(Anthology)	
Ed.by Haki R. Madhubuti	$8.95

Octavia And Other Poems	
by Naomi Long Madgett	$8.00

A Move Further South	
by Ruth Garnett	$7.95

Manish	
by Alfred Woods	$8.00

Children's Books

The Day They Stole	
The Letter J	
by Jabari Mahiri	$3.95

The Tiger Who Wore	
White Gloves	
by Gwendolyn Brooks	$5.00

A Sound Investment	
by Sonia Sanchez	$2.95

I Look At Me	
by Mari Evans	$2.50

Black Books Bulletin

A limited number of back issues of this unique journal are available at $3.00 each:

Vol. 1, Fall '71	Interview with Hoyt W. Fuller
Vol. 1, No. 3	Interview with Lerone Bennett, Jr.
Vol. 5, No. 3	Science & Struggle
Vol. 5, No. 4	Blacks & Jews
Vol. 7, No. 3	The South

*Order from **Third World Press***
7524 S. Cottage Grove Ave.
Chicago, IL 60619

Shipping: Add $1.50 for first book and .25 for each additional book.